I glanced at the first page of *Searching for Spenser* and from that moment on, I did not want to put the book down. Our electricity went out early one morning while I was reading, so I went and found a flashlight, which imperfectly lit the pages as I continued to read.

The book is compelling because Margaret Kramar is a gifted story teller, drawing us into her life. I grew to love the author because of her honesty, bravery and transparency. She does not give us a sugar-coated story, written by a perfect person with perfect answers. She gives us a real story about a person whose life did not go the way she planned.

There were many times that tears came to my eyes and lumps rose in my throat, but over all this book is a tribute to a beautiful and loving world. This book is a masterpiece. I loved it.

~ Dianne Lawson, *Extraordinary Relationships through Astrology*

This is a deeply moving, humbling, beautiful and true account of the short journey of a very special little boy. Any parent dealing with a special needs child-and what child isn't special needs at some point-will run the gamut of emotions in reading this book. I sobbed, laughed out loud, prayed, was amazed, and sometimes angry. Because of this book, I was grateful for being able to have the opportunity to learn what purity of soul really means. Through *Searching for Spenser*, this little boy will continue to touch the hearts of others for years to come.

~ Diane Rose

Kramar doesn't hold back in sharing her life with the reader. She takes us by the hand and we walk through her days as mother, wife, friend and advocate. It is a journey fraught with difficult decisions, frustrating outcomes, intense sorrow and yet, a powerful love that weaves through the story driving her on to never stop caring and fighting for her son, Spenser. As a parent of a young child who went through long periods of medical treatment and lost her life to childhood cancer, I recommend this book to parents, caregivers and all others who wish to gain an understanding of advocating for a loved one.

~ Bill Sowers

SEARCHING
FOR
SPENSER

SEARCHING
FOR
SPENSER

Margaret Kramar

Anamcara Press LLC

Published in 2018 by Anamcara Press LLC
Author © 2018 by Margaret Kramar, margaret.kramar.com
Cover image by Nina Niebuhr, Shutterstock, Another Journey: "Misty Flowers."
Cover & Book design by Maureen Carroll
Garamond, Myriad Pro, Lane-Narrow, Medusa Gothic, and Verdana.
Printed in the United States of America.

Parenting can be a struggle, especially parenting a child with Sotos syndrome. In her heartrending memoir, Kramar skillfully describes championing her disabled child through his short life. Written in starkly honest prose, Searching for Spenser examines the experience of loving and losing a child.

ANAMCARA PRESS LLC
P.O. Box 442072, Lawrence, KS 66044
https://anamcara-press.com

Ordering Information:
Quantity sales. Special discounts are available on quantity purchases by corporations, associations, and others. For details, contact the publisher at the address above.
Orders by U.S. trade bookstores and wholesalers. Please contact Ingram Distribution.

Publisher's Cataloging-in-Publication data
Kramar, Margaret, Author
Searching for Spenser / Margaret Kramar

ISBN-13: Searching For Spenser, 978-1-941237-18-2 (Paperback)
ISBN-13: Searching For Spenser, 978-1-941237-21-2 (Hardcover)

BIOGRAPHY & AUTOBIOGRAPHY / People with Disabilities.
FAMILY & RELATIONSHIPS / Death, Grief, Bereavement / Children with Special Needs.]

For Spenser

To die will be an awfully big adventure.
~ James M. Barrie, *Peter Pan.*

Then I, the weak one, the simpleton,
Resting in a little corner of life,
Saw a vision, and through me many saw the vision,
Not knowing it was through me.
Thus a tree sprang
From me, a mustard seed.

~ Edgar Lee Masters, *Spoon River Anthology*

Contents

Foreword

The first time I encountered Margaret Kramar was in a graduate class I was teaching at the University of Kansas. She introduced me to herself as a writer and a mother, and we were immediately drawn to one another. Adults juggling multiple responsibilities as they pursue their education excite me as much as they mirror my own experience. I was elated to see another mother for whom multitasking had become a decided strength. My children were sandwiched in-between earning degrees, writing books, and teaching, and I was more than familiar with the twists and turns of motherhood. She told me she had returned for another degree because she wanted to write a story about her son Spenser, the child she had lost. Grief is a hard process to manage, the loss of a child nearly impossible. Little did I know that we were rehearsing my own experience of a few years later.

I trusted Margaret as a veteran journalist and had confidence in her ability to resist the emotional rollercoaster that necessarily accompanies a book about death and dying. Dealing with deadlines and drawing the reader in were common practice for her, but the story she was telling did not come from outside sources. Rather, she was making a private experience public.

Margaret followed that difficult path of putting words to paper, of confronting that version of herself that remained after Spenser died, her struggle to reconnect with family and community. Loss takes different forms, causing self-doubt and anger. At times, she become a stranger to those to whom she felt the closest. But Margaret also experienced the joy of tending to the land, watching the cycle of nature replenish itself as it would her.

The beauty of *Searching for Spenser: A Mother's Journey Through Grief* is its brutal honesty and its risk taking. There's nothing made up about it. Reconstructions of memory can have perilous consequences, but Margaret allows us to live with and through the experience with her. Finding the route to composing a book about losing a child is no small task, and Margaret's entry into that world was enabled by those who knew she had to write it as much as we needed to read it. Finding friendship and support in a writing community helped to clear the path, even as she confronted the uncertainty of committing to a new life partner.

Her guide was always Spenser, the explorer, risk taker, actor. He was "the" adult in situations more often than the real adults were. I never met him but came to know him well in these pages. Telling us Spenser's story and her search to understand the gift of his short life, Margaret allows us meet someone whose terminal illness made him wise beyond his years.

As an author, Margaret's greatest risk was writing a story that was part of her without knowing where it might lead. The difficulty was not only in the writing but more importantly in letting the book go once finished. Having relived the experience, there is that obligation to keep it for yourself. We are grateful that Margaret persisted. That she made the choice to "fashion a life that honors the child."

What Margaret learned she has imparted to us, and certainly to me: that the end of a life is an opportunity to begin another, and that it is rarely one of your choosing. That it requires engaging in critical acts of self-discovery and remaking. Laying of the soul bare exposes deep layers of truth, but not without the fear that one is violating certain loyalties.

Searching for Spenser is a faithful reflection of too common an experience; mothers endure the pain of childbirth, loving a child deeply who is taken away too soon. But Margaret does not need our sympathy. This book is a reminder that living with a most difficult and pain-

ful thing gives us choices. Making the right one makes all the difference. Margaret Kramar has written this story for all the right reasons.
And no matter who you are, you will find yourself in these pages.

~ *Maryemma Graham, University of Kansas Distinguished Professor &*
Founder/Director, Project on the History of Black Writing.

The Memory Bank

There's nothing suspenseful about this story. I'm telling you right up front that he died when he was ten. I've learned some things since giving birth to Spenser, a child with a developmental disability. Quite a few, actually.

Voices. Words. Sometimes in the pauses of long distance telephone conversations, words of other speakers, distant and disembodied, seep through. Words not intended for me. Words bridging time zones, geographic regions, territories of the heart. Likewise in subways, department stores or theatres as the lights dim, more words. We are always blanketed by the soft, reassuring drone of words, too muffled to be understood, that tell us we are not alone. It is the chorus, the low constant buzzing, that connects us.

I bring to mind Spenser's words, the sound of his voice, but can only hear a few conversations distinctly. The soprano of his voice is becoming garbled, far off. He did make cooing sounds as a baby. Sometimes he yelled "No" when forced to do his spelling words. His constant congestion caused his vocal tone to be nasal and mangled his words. In his usual school outfit of a turtle-neck pullover and blue jeans, he would make emphatic declarations, but I don't remember what they were, because I was too busy, grabbing for the phone or the cookbook.

I sift through my memory bank for visual images of Spenser, framed with longing, as I slide my thumb over his photograph, my face reflected in the glass. My baby. My boy. His blonde hair is as fine as corn silk. His almond eyes are set slightly apart, on either side of the flat bridge of his tiny nose, diagnostic characteristics of Sotos syndrome, his disability.

Spenser, where have you gone? He doesn't answer, but his smiling expression in his portrait on the desk never changes, whether the glass reflects the east light of dawn or the long afternoon rays of the sun, which extend and then recede like the tide through the seasons. I pretend that the elementary school photo was taken only months ago, that I can hear him playing downstairs, that he never died.

But he is suspended in mid-sentence, says nothing. I study the details of his face, his eyebrows darker than I remembered, a small crater of dimple that indents his cheek, which he inherited from me.

In a newsletter, a bereaved mother suggested cataloguing memories on notecards, four by six inches, which she stored neatly in a compact box. I don't want to write on notecards because my recipe boxes are a disaster, overflowing with partially alphabetized clippings. This manuscript is my memory box. In it I reconstruct Spenser from the memories of family, teachers and friends. I record his whispers, carried by the wind. I might glimpse him, darting past the twining clematis in a brightly-colored cap on a summer afternoon. He can't have gone that far.

CHAPTER 1

Star Wars

On January 30, 1991, Spenser was born on a Wednesday under a full moon when all kinds of terrors were being unleashed in the Persian Gulf.

I lay on my side in a hospital bed between silver chrome bars; my white hospital gown tied loosely several places in the back. With my swollen stomach, breasts engorged with milk and eyes tightly shut, I breathed in furtive rhythm, like a hibernating animal. I could hear voices speaking around me, and feel hands being placed on my body.

"We have to check to see how much you've dilated. An eight." A short woman with peppery hair appeared far away at the end of my legs. The pain of the contractions dwarfed the discomfort of her inserted fingers.

"Margaret, we'll be in the waiting room." My mother and sister stood with their coats on. My mother doesn't want to be around when things get visceral, so they left, but I couldn't have related to them, because I was spiraling into a deep vortex.

The monotone sound of the television broadcasted news correspondents who incessantly chattered about the imminent invasion of Kuwait. In their trench coats they clutched their microphones, visibly aroused by the prospect of war. With lurid grins, they recited facts for the camera that did not mask their gleeful anticipation of the slaughter.

"Turn it off, turn it off!" I yelled at the television.

I was powerless to stop this war, even though when pregnant a month before I had lugged this unborn baby around the state capitol in my womb through a sea of voices during an anti-war march. But it was no use, because the country was whipped up in patriotic fervor. The majority exulted in the bright lights of Star Wars. The men in charge who announced official statements were not unlike a small boy who secretly crushes insects on the driveway, titillated by the agony of death. The country was suiting up for a war utilizing the latest macho technology, and the dying wails of the innocent be damned.

My husband Stan, a frightened onlooker, shut off the television, but his yellow paper gown and spectacles were fading away. As the drug Pitocin intensified the contractions, I just let go, and my soul floated out to the hill overlooking Lake Pierre, where I had ridden my horse past fields of purple scurf pea, white daisies and bright orange butterfly milkweed. As the grasses bowed away from the wind, his hoofs hit the ground and drummed on our shadows. I entreated the baby, "Please come to us. You'll have a wonderful life, and a big brother."

The peppery-haired nurse came back.

"This is why they call it labor. It's the most strenuous physical thing you've ever done." She spoke in a loud voice, as though I were deaf.

This wasn't the most physically taxing thing I had ever done. When I was twelve years old, our junior lifesaving instructor led us out to the end of a very long dock flanked by the lapping whitecaps of the lake, and told us to jump in and swim back to shore. After I plunged in with a scissor kick, the chilly water surged through my body like electricity, and all I could see was dirty green water. My arms and legs wiggled like a frilly paramecium, while the waves tossed me from side to side.

"I don't know if I can do this," I said as I gasped for breath.

The instructor, his wet hair flattened around his tan face, squinted at me.

"Are you chicken?" he yelled.

So there was no choice. It was preferable to drown than admit fear. I slapped my aching arms and legs on top of the rocking waves, where they thrust and kicked like pistons in an engine. When my feet finally touched sand, I staggered under my weight.

"I have to measure to see how far you've dilated," the peppery-haired nurse said. With great effort, I flopped my massive body onto my back, as though I were a beached whale. From between the frame of my spread legs, the sharp glint in her eyes signaled that she didn't like what she saw.

"Everything's proceeding very nicely. You're a good girl," she said as she pulled down my gown.

"The doctor! Where's the doctor?" she shouted as she charged into the hall.

Distant voices told me that I was fully dilated, but it was too late for any pain medication.

"Push, push," the nurses cheered from the sidelines. I pushed. With my hands clasped around my knees I strained at the height of every contraction, but nothing happened. I had no urge to push and the baby did not descend.

The doctor, a small man with neatly-trimmed dark hair, surveyed the situation. A profusion of chest hair sprouted from the V at the top of his green scrubs. Once I was transferred to the darkened delivery room, he scurried around, pacing from one apparatus to another. Evidently he had been delayed by his other surgery, and now he had walked into a mess. His hand, gloved in squeaky plastic, entered my vagina and felt the baby's head. Again I pushed against the same resistance.

Next the doctor directed a nurse to roll a machine with a big box toward me. He pried open my vagina and attached a suction cup. They probably use this when they evacuate the contents of the uterus, or perform abortions. The machine rattled for a few futile moments, like a jackhammer on a distant construction site. Nothing happened.

The doctor increased his pace, traversing quickly from one point near the gurney to another. He inserted steel cold forceps and yanked hard, turning me inside out. I howled.

Then the doctor stopped. He was sitting on a rolling stool at the end of the table, with his head and shoulders encircled by the white glare of the surgery lamp. He propped his arm on my leg, and his head dropped onto my thigh.

"I'm going to have to cut you open," he said in a low voice.

He and the nurse moved away from my view, into the shadows outside the surgery lamp.

"Will she have a spinal block or general anesthesia?" the nurse asked.

"General," the doctor said in defeat, and crossed to get another instrument.

As the waves of contractions kept rolling inside my body, I was pushed on a creaky gurney through doors that opened and shut.

The human figures at the periphery of my vision talked quietly around me as the intravenous injection dripped into my vein. The fluid in a plastic bag swung from the metal contraption overhead. After pushing for hours, I longed for the peaceful darkness the anesthesia would bring.

When I regained consciousness, I found myself on a gurney in a darkened enclosure with sheets as walls. As a dark-haired nurse felt my pulse, and asked small, simple questions, I resisted consciousness, craving to slip back into the oblivion because I was bottomed out, and lacked even the excitement about the baby who had just been born.

From this curtained enclosure, the gurney rolled me down the hospital hallway, emitting long squeaks. I didn't know where they were taking me because nobody told me anything, but I assumed it was to see the baby. The elevator dinged, thrust open its doors, and buzzed again after a descent. Other people passed by, a moving kaleidoscope of white jackets, stethoscopes, and light green scrubs. We rolled past proud parents and relatives making little motions through the window at the healthy newborns on display. Why weren't we stopping here?

The gurney paused before the automatic doors of the neonatal intensive care unit.

We shouldn't be in here. Something was not right. When I was wheeled beside the isolette containing my baby, I saw a tiny, thin figure, whose eyes were sealed shut and cheeks bruised from the forceps, who shuddered slightly as though from grief and pain.

Is that the baby?

I would always feel guilty about my first impression, but with his little wizened face and slightly slanted eyes, he was peculiar. There was something foreign about him, unnatural, that suggested that he couldn't be my child.

I was finally rolled into a deathly still wing of the maternity ward. Although I could hear noisy throngs of relatives with flowers and balloons moving down the hallways of the ward, my room was quiet. A photograph of the modern sculpture in the hospital courtyard titled "The Tear" adorned my door.

"Why is that picture next to my name?" I asked the nurse who passed on rounds.

"That's for mothers who are sad because of miscarriage or stillbirth. It serves as a warning for the staff who enter the room."

I didn't want that thing on my door, or to be labeled a tragedy case. I expected a healthy baby, and flowers from smiling people offering congratulations. The jarring image of that thin wasted body with the agonized face haunted me.

The birth certificate would read 2:39 p.m. Stan drifted in and out of my room. He was shocked by the turn of events, but ineffectual, a shade who spoke a few garbled words I couldn't comprehend. When he asked me a question, even though I intended to answer and could formulate a response in my mind, the drugs prevented me from articulating the words, so the conversation between us pooled up and died in the long pauses.

"The baby looks like a drowned rat, doesn't he?" I said to Stan, when I was conscious enough to realize he was sitting in the corner, a still life, dressed in his suit and tie.

"He didn't look right. I guess it was the big head," Stan answered.

"What, what are they saying about him?"

"He had an Apgar score of two on a scale of ten. I don't think he cried right away either. The doctors and nurses were talking to each other in a subdued tone," Stan said.

"Well, where, after he was born, you were in the delivery room, what did you do?"

"I felt sick to my stomach so I went to the parking garage," Stan said.

The afternoon passed that way. No nurse brought a fat baby swaddled in a blanket, wearing a pastel knit cap. No medical personnel came to talk to me.

The end of January is anti-climactic, a letdown, something to be survived. Despite the illumination of the fluorescent lights in the hallway, I peered through the window panes at infinite blackness. I slept through low talking outside in the hallway, the sound of people passing, some shuffling, some with sharply clicking heels. Nobody else besides Stan came into the room because I was barricaded by the tear.

I sat up in my hospital bed. The anesthesia was lifting, so the television screen clicked into focus. The camera pictured a Marine, dressed in fatigues, one of the first casualties of Desert Storm. He drew out his words and gazed off to the side as though in a trance.

"The bullet entered my leg and I started bleeding, but that's not what got to me. What really got to me was knowing that," he continued, "was knowing that I'd been hit."

Two weeks, a month ago, I could not have comprehended the Marine's words, but now they resonated with me because I, too, had been hit. I had been safe within our English Tudor cottage, with the snow softly falling around the blue "It's a Boy" sign displayed on the lawn when our older son was born. We told Brendan, our perfect, typically developing child, that he should expect a baby brother. Anesthetized within our comfortable suburban existence, we considered ourselves immune against misfortune. Those tragedies reported on the news, with police sirens blaring and floodlights piercing the darkness, were for other people, in other neighborhoods. The Marine had probably been buoyed up with all the optimistic military propaganda he had been fed until he wrenched in pain as the bullet flayed his flesh. The gauzy worldview which shielded our eyes as we floated through our days had been rent, ripped apart with a jagged slash. We had both been hit.

When I woke up the next morning, I could hear the sounds of the hospital coming to life. An orderly wheeled in a breakfast tray. I lifted the silver cover and the steam from the scrambled eggs caressed my face. My head had cleared and I was hungry. As I was sipping my orange juice, I heard the very welcome, friendly voice of my sister.

"Hi," she said as she smiled, carrying helium balloons that bounced against each other which she set next to the window. She swept into that room bringing the best of what was happening in the outside world with her. She has saved my life countless times.

"Girl, you were out there. Tell me what happened yesterday," I said to her.

"Well, when you were in the hospital room while Mom and I were there, you were excited, you were happy. Stan was in there pacing because he didn't know what to do. He has never known. Then we left after they gave you an epidural because, I don't know, we thought—how gross is this?" she said.

"Sit down. Pull up that chair. So then what happened?"

"We spent hours and hours in the waiting room and couldn't figure out why nobody told us anything. Oh girl, get this. We were watching the soap opera, *The Guiding Light*. There was a guy in there watching it with us and in response to the scene, he shook his head and said, 'Cold. That's really cold.'"

We both started laughing at how well his words matched the televised situation. "So he shook his head and said 'Cold, that's really cold?'" I repeated.

"Yes, just like that time on *The Young and the Restless* when Phillip Chancellor died, and when Jill came into his room there was only a stripped hospital bed. Remember that? Even Oprah Winfrey talked about that once on her television show," my sister said.

"So then what?"

"I finally found out from the nurse who said it looks like they're going to do a C-section. We didn't see you until you were in recovery. You were out of it. Stan said, 'There's something wrong with the baby. He has gashes from the suction and did not respond.'"

"Gashes? He said there were gashes?"

"Then they rolled Spenser by in the hallway. He was really quiet, but I didn't see any gashes, I mean, like visible stitches. They weren't telling anybody anything. When I got to your room, I saw that they put one of those things, that picture of the tear sculpture on your door. Now that thing is morbid, isn't it?"

"Yeah, I guess they're trying to be tactful, especially around women who really freak out." I braced my hands on either side of myself, and pulled myself up straighter in the bed. My lower abdominal region, lacerated and bandaged from the C-section, felt like a leaden weight.

"So what about Stan's parents? What have they been doing?" I asked her.

"Well, we all did go out to dinner. Remember, you were depressed because nobody would tell you anything about the baby, so you told us to please go out with them because you didn't want them here. When we were by the elevator, Stan's father said that he couldn't understand why they let babies like that live."

"Oh, great." I made another effort to sit up straighter. "So how was Stan doing?"

"Stan was real depressed, but for the most part everyone eventually did have a good time. Oh, I also talked to one of the nurses, you know,

Libby from the church, who said they were all so sorry about Margaret's baby. Oh yeah, and then Mom said, 'If Dr. Glendenning would have been on call, none of this would have happened.'"

We again erupted into laughter at my mother's blind faith that any obstetrician could have prevented the congenital challenges that faced this baby. At some point, whether at conception or during the pregnancy, a darkness descended on my womb that nobody could have predicted.

CHAPTER 2

Marriage

Like my mother said, Dr. Glendenning, who delivered Brendan three years earlier, was experienced, skilled, dependable, everything an obstetrician should be. A kind of "Father Knows Best"obstetrician, after the television show that aired in the 1950s when women didn't need to worry their silly little heads about anything because the all-knowing male, portrayed by the actor Robert Young, would take care of them. Not that Dr. Glendenning was a male chauvinist. No, he was terrific in every way.

As for Stan, let's just say that he and I were raised in families that had differing attitudes in regard to the role of women. Stan's father, the unquestioned patriarch, threw a fit when Stan's mother applied for her own credit card. Stan's two older married brothers, following the mold, had wives who raised children, end of sentence. His parents and I were also on opposite ends of the political spectrum. When we were newly-married, they mailed newspaper and magazine clippings espousing right-wing views, especially in regard to abortion. In response, I sent them a newspaper cartoon that featured a drawing of an acorn. The caption read, "What is this? If you're a Right-to-Lifer, it's a tree."

In my family, I was the oldest child, a girl in the 1950s when girls were not worth as much as boys. In the backyard as a small, babbling child, my father was not listening as he pushed me on the swing, but one day on a windy street corner, when I deciphered the words on a sign, I came into his view.

"Margaret, that's right, that's what those words mean. You read that?" His hands were in his pants pockets. The breeze nudged his tie. I strutted across the street, queen for the day, the object of his total attention. I subsequently became the vessel for his unrealized ambition of becoming a college history professor instead of a physician. Accomplishments, good grades, honors, won my daddy's heart.

After college, I racked up the accomplishments, but it was after graduate school at a conference awards dinner that the ground beneath me shifted. For the occasion, I dressed in a black suit that resembled a tuxedo. There was no one sitting to my right or left whom I knew very well. The applause swelled as the winner of the award approached the microphone, haloed by a spotlight. Her husband, seated in front of me, clapped the loudest. I considered my framed diplomas, hanging on the wall, and the accumulating accolades, tallied on my resume, stashed in a drawer. After the dinner, in my hotel room, I stepped out of my heels, and sat on the bed facing a blank television screen. I was approaching my late twenties, and did not want to be alone forever.

So why was I single if I wanted to be coupled, and why did I marry Stan, who turned out to be a somewhat disastrous choice? Several years before, cross-legged on the floor by the light of a candle, I shuffled my tarot cards and laid them out in a spread. Although I was on the precipice of my professional career without any job offers, that was not why I was reading the cards. I sought predictions about love.

The final outcome card jumped out at me, the Nine of Swords. A woman sat upright in bed under a colorful quilt, her face buried in her hands. It is a terrible card, one of the worst in the deck, because it foretells suffering, desolation, loss and deep emotional despair. During my twenties, it all came true, as one failed relationship after another resulted in heartbreak. The girl who appeared in my mirror was attractive and intelligent enough. This same girl received rave reviews for a leading glamorous role in a local theatrical production, with the aplomb extending to strangers who stopped me in the street.

"Weren't you in *Vanities?*" asked the bundled-up man at the pedestrian light in driving snow, or the waitress in the restaurant, or the clerk who sold me a baking pan. What they didn't know is that this leading lady returned to an empty apartment after the theatre was dark, and that as she drifted off to sleep she reassured herself that she felt the pulse of a true blue heart coursing through her veins.

"Someday, someone will realize that I'm a great find. Somebody will love me, somebody will love me," I chanted like a mantra. I really believed it. It had to be true.

So I dated widely. Predictably, some of those love affairs became serious, and we danced through the evening as though the music would never stop, but it always did. Usually the reasons were beyond my control. One prospective husband ultimately decided that his wife should be Jewish. Another fell in love with somebody else. The third wasn't ready to commit. They were all dashing, and eminently eligible, and told me that they loved me, but I always ended up in the back bedroom of my basement apartment, sitting on the floor in the grey, filtered light with my arms wrapped around my knees, sobbing my heart out.

Also in my late twenties, I landed a job as a civil rights investigator for a state agency that investigates discrimination complaints. I dressed in suits and heels, had secretaries who screened my calls and did my typing, and traveled through the state on a mission of justice and equality. Some of the men I encountered, such as attorneys for the Complainant or Respondent had potential, but because we investigated sexual harassment, being on the prowl for romantic entanglements was, at best, viewed as unethical, and at worst, illegal. More importantly, I never came across a man who was worth the risk. The interesting challenges I encountered made the day fly by, but at night I faced the same four walls. So, I spent the evenings being cast in one play and then another, constantly either in rehearsal or in production.

Yet underneath the veneer of my professional successes, I struggled with the blackness of abject loneliness and despair. Nobody loved me, and perhaps nobody ever would. I grew to hate going out, but got dressed up, put on my makeup, frequented bars, and started inane conversations with strangers. I signed up for various classes and activities, but if I didn't see anyone even remotely interesting during the first meeting, I would abandon the venture. Online dating sites were still in the future, and the anonymous person behind the newspaper personal ad who enjoyed moonlight walks and candlelight dinners could be a serial killer. Adrift yet determined, I enrolled in law school, which could take my career to new heights and would place me back in a pool of eligible young men.

Actually, the law school party where I met Spenser's father was an act of rebellion. I had been dating Robbie, whose younger brother had been killed in an automobile accident. His parents had received the call, gone to the emergency room, and identified the body of his brother only a few months earlier.

Early one morning in his maroon bathrobe, Robbie sat motionless at his desk, contemplating his brother's picture which rested in his right hand. I sat up in bed, enveloped by the warmth of the blanket and detergent aroma of the clean sheets. The glare of the desk lamp fell on the pages of an opened law book, and Robbie held the picture aloft over the black-and-white print. He said nothing, but continued gazing at the picture. Maybe through this behavior Robbie was signaling to me the depth of his grief, or maybe he longed for his brother and could care less whether I was in the room. I knew nothing of dead children—would not understand until years later when Spenser died, so could not bring the silence to full circle. I only stood in the wings, a helpless bystander.

A few days later in the law school library, Robbie told me he was going home to Milwaukee because his parents were on the verge of a divorce. I didn't receive a letter from him during the Christmas holidays, nor did he contact me during January. I spent most of my college years pining over a boy who didn't write because he didn't love me. I was not going to let that happen again.

So, at a law school party on Valentine's Day, immersed in the noisy hubbub of law students conversing in groups while sipping their beers, I scanned the crowd and threaded my way to someone I recognized, Carter Canby, a red-headed friend whose affect could lean toward the grandiose.

"Well, hello, Margaret, are you enjoying yourself?" Carter gestured to his right. "Do you know Stan Gardner?" Stan emerged from the sea of bodies and stood opposite me.

Why had I never seen him before in the classroom, or among the throngs of students circulating throughout the hallways? He had an interesting face, and eyes that were almost pretty. Clad in a plaid shirt, he clutched a beer can in one hand and cigarette in the other. Something about his countenance, in stark relief from the shadowy backdrop of the others assembled, hinted at unforeseen possibilities. I switched on my animated persona and bragged about being a leading actress.

"I was Joanne in *Vanities* at Warehouse Stage on the Levee just a few years ago. It was sold out for the entire run and got rave reviews."

"Warehouse Stage on the Levee. Yes, I've been to several performances." He shifted his weight to the other foot.

"Where are you from?" I needed an anchor.

"Springfield."

"Springfield. Now where is that?" I asked. There was something about his eyes, and he increasingly impressed me as vaguely attractive and somewhat charming.

"Central Missouri. My parents have a ranch that I grew up on. Well, my father works as a physician, but they have cattle and horses."

"You live out in the country, on a farm, or a ranch?" The pitch of my voice rose higher. In kindergarten, I drew a Crayola portrait of all the farm animals, with the horse and cow in the back row, the goat, sheep and pig in the middle and the chickens and ducks in the front row. These were not plain white chickens I colored in, but black, brown, gold and speckled chickens. I wanted to live on a farm.

I wrote my phone number down on a scrap of paper, whether or not he asked for it. I hoped that he would call, and within a few days, he did. I don't remember what we talked about, just that he was interesting and intelligent enough that I wanted to hear more. After the first night we spent together, Stan left the bed early in the morning to go watch television. I wondered whether he ever washed those sheets. But still he intrigued me, and offered hope. He resurrected my dream of a life in the country, the promise of new growth laden under sodden grief.

After more phone calls and a few dates, he called with a proposition.

"Margaret, I've decided that you and I should live together to see if our relationship has any future," he said.

I stood my ground. "I don't want to live together. The woman gets to clean, cook and do the laundry. The man gets all those services, the sex, and a free ride. No, if you want to live together, we should just get married. If you're serious about it, you need to come over to my house and ask my father."

By the end of the conversation, we had agreed to get married. I put the phone back on the receiver. With no sun coming through the skylight, the room was a muted grey. This was not the romantic proposal I had expected, but time was running out. I was thirty years old, and there had been way too much romantic carnage during the past ten years. In my antiseptic apartment, the rug was always vacuumed, the wooden surfaces were always dusted, and the only disarray was a little stack of unpaid bills. I needed more chaos.

Later that afternoon, Stan sat on the couch, across from my father in his armchair, forcing lame jokes and laughter. Stan's recent haircut was too short. The black Labrador retriever and coonhound, who had always dominated the household, sighed in their respective chairs. My father only wanted what was best for his little girl. He knew of my previous romantic breakups, had heard the screaming and crying. Stan was a decent prospect—he was a law student, and came from a good family. I wasn't passionately in love with Stan when I got engaged to him, but could not imagine never playing the part of wife and mother. We would still have a happy ending, even if I had to manufacture it.

The spring before the July wedding was a protracted song. As we watched a production of *Oklahoma* in Kansas City, our spirits soared during the finale as the actors behind the footlights erupted into the eponymous theme song with "We know we belong to the land, and the land we belong to is grand." Later as we strolled with our black Labrador retriever though the neighborhood on a summer evening, we started singing together "People Will Say We're in Love," in exaggerated operatic voices. A woman came out on her porch.

"We're sorry, we didn't mean to be that loud," we said.

"No, it sounds great," she answered. With the end of our singing, she retreated back into her house, a suburban split-level with a wide expanse of lawn.

Over my lunch hours, I shopped downtown for the wedding invitation stationery, choosing for the front piece—inscribed in pale blue—the language of the traditional vows: "From this day forward, for better, for worse, for richer, for poorer, in sickness and in health, to love and to cherish, till death do us part."

Stan had mentioned, sometime during the preparations, something about a prenuptial agreement, but I had put it out of my mind. During a phone call, he brought up the subject again.

"I'm working on the contract of our prenuptial agreement," he said.

I sat down on the bed and twisted the phone cord around my fingers.

"Why should we need that thing?" I asked.

"Because my father has considerable property and assets tied up in Southbow Farm," Stan said. His voice had an angry edge.

"But those are his assets, not yours. You don't have them yet."

"Yes, but if this marriage should not work out, I wouldn't want those assets to leave the family."

"Don't you trust me? What makes you think I'm such a gold digger that I would try to get my hands on any of that, even if we did get divorced? No, I think it's insulting. I don't want to sign it." I hung up the telephone.

A few nights later during a drive, Stan gripped the steering wheel. Every time I turned to him, I viewed the outline of his resolute profile.

"The wedding is getting closer, and one last detail that needs to happen is that you need to sign that prenuptial agreement," he said. We sped by huge green street signs that indicated the exits of the interstate.

"No, to me it indicates an absolute lack of trust. You apparently don't know me. I would never grasp for what was not rightfully mine. Money isn't that important to me, anyway," I said.

"So, you're not going to sign it?" He pressed his foot down on the accelerator.

"No, that's a horrible way to start a marriage, that you don't trust me, that there are legal contracts between us," I answered.

"Then you're not getting out of this car. You're not getting out of this car until you agree to sign it," he said, accelerating further.

I watched the illuminated green signs of the McBride exit speed by, and then the Fairview exit. We were heading the wrong direction, out into the country away from the city, at a high speed.

"What, are you crazy, what are you doing?" His eyes were fixed on the road. We kept hurtling down the interstate away from the city. "I have to get back home so I can go to work tomorrow. I can't tolerate this," I protested. He was holding me hostage, and I was frightened.

"Then agree to sign the prenuptial contract," he stated calmly.

"Okay, I'll sign it," I screamed. The car slowed down, and he circled back at the next exit.

After this display of domestic violence, I should have called off the engagement, but I had already sent out the invitations and nearly completed the preparations. I could not face the humiliation of cancelling the wedding. At thirty years old with my biological clock ticking, how long would it take to meet someone else, spend time dating, and hope against hope that the new relationship would be successful? Rather than start again at the beginning, I resolved to pour my energies into this one. Maybe something like this would never happen again.

CHAPTER 3

After the Wedding

After the wedding, Stan and I rented the upstairs apartment of an old house across from the law school. It had four small rooms: a bedroom, a bathroom, a kitchen, and the living room, which had formerly been the sleeping porch. When the trees crowded around all the windows, and gyrated slowly in the wind, it was like camping in our own treehouse. I painted discarded ice cream parlor chairs a candy apple green, and found dotted Swiss curtains to match.

We talked late into the night. Stan cleaned the apartment and had a meal cooked by the time I got home. We boogied to the music of *The Rocky Horror Picture Show* or watched nature shows that he had prerecorded during the day. Coming home to him was so wonderful. I had shed the lonely ache of worrying whether the phone would ring, or what I would be doing Saturday night.

"You know, now that we're married, maybe we should have a baby," Stan said one Saturday morning in our treehouse room. He was barefoot, and dug his toes into the shag carpeting.

"What, now? But you still have two years of law school. Shouldn't we wait?"

He considered this, as the trees swayed beyond the window. The television murmured a steady drone.

"Like how many kids do you think we should have?" I asked.

"At least three or four," he answered.

"I don't know about four. Three, at least."

In the meantime we adopted a cat, a small black kitten from the humane society we named Samantha. Once home in her unfamiliar surroundings, she hid under heavy furniture. Stan studied Samantha, his languorous grey eyes pools of sympathy. When I returned a few hours later, she was nestled inside a makeshift box that he had created, purring.

For the most part, the summer days stretched on, with the indolent sun creating latticework on our double bed, but sometimes our discourse ignited into arguments. We mistakenly believed that the tempestuous passions of our youth were behind us, and tended to bring out the worst in each other due to selfishness, impatience and the unrealistic expectation that one's spouse could be bent to one's will because we were conjoined.

I came home one evening to find a plate from my pottery set cracked, with a thin line etched into the plain surface. I had carted these particular plates, laden with memories of living on my own, from one apartment to another for at least five years.

"How did this plate get cracked? Did you put it in the oven?"

Stan stood by the edge of the stove. "Because it seemed to be ovenware, I thought it could withstand the heat," he said.

"No, you've cracked it. It's ruined," I said, my eyes clouding with tears and my voice rising.

Stan paused, then challenged me. "If you say one more word about that plate, I'm going to smash it on the counter."

We squared off. He stood by the edge of the stove and I stood in front of the sink. I searched his face, and decided to test him.

"Did you put this plate in the oven?" I asked in staccato, emphasizing each word.

Stan seized the plate with both hands, raised it over his head and shattered it on the corner of the stove. Huge shards of pottery spun across the counter and came to rest on the floor. I was horrified, feeling as though I was entering unchartered, dangerous territory, because my parents had never treated each other this way.

I wrote faithfully to his parents, long newsy letters containing descriptive adjectives relaying a humorous incident, balanced against the challenges of dealing with Stan's temper. I beseeched them for insight into how they managed their son. The letters came back with more news about Springfield, but nothing about how to handle Stan. In the interstices of our polite exchanges, they avoided both this unpleasantness and inquiries about their heart's desire—news of a grandchild. During a visit, Stan's father broached the subject at the dining room table, the same dining room table where Stan and I would linger for hours after a meal. Because I was now a civil rights investigator and he an attorney, we analyzed each other's cases, dissecting them for hours, examining every piece of evidence. As a respite from our frequent arguing, we relished the camaraderie we experienced when poised over our empty plates. Not everything about the marriage was negative.

"Well, Margaret, what are you going to do about children?" Stan's father asked me. His hand rested by his glass of water.

"I already have one child, and that is Stan. Why should I have another? I'm waiting for Stan to grow up."

Stan's father slowly shook his head.

Yet the years passed, and I had read that age thirty-five was a watershed for female fertility. If we were going to do this thing, we had better do it now. After all, we both had stable jobs and had been married five years, but other than a few dubious babysitting episodes, I really didn't know anything about babies. So I stood on the cliff and peered into the void, which summoned the pleasures of growing up in a small house brimming over with laughter and love. Because I wanted to replicate the positive foundation my parents had given me, I slid toward this daydream of myself as a mother. Years later, I would pronounce that Brendan and Spenser were the best things that ever happened to me.

It was March, and the days, cool and rainy, transformed into even cooler nights. The darkness had fallen outside the windows. Stan had gone to a law school party, but I wanted to stay home. I paced through the empty house, wondering whether I was even biologically able to have a child. We had decided to give it a try this very weekend.

At the dining room table under the chandelier in our new house, the house we had bought with bedrooms for children, I shuffled my tarot cards, the Eden Gray edition with the keys on the back. After they flapped in my fingers, I held the cards to my heart, and also to my head, wondering whether I could, or would, have a child.

"This crosses me, this covers me," I said after cutting the deck three times to the left. "This is the foundation of the matter, this is just passing away." I laid out a few more cards. "This will happen in the future." I put down the sixth card, and the Empress appeared, right side up, her youthful face framed by long, flowing hair. The meaning of the card is marriage, and fertility to would-be parents. I emitted a short gasp.

The tarot deck contains seventy-eight cards. It doesn't take a statistician to determine that the chance of drawing one particular card is one in seventy-eight. But what are the odds of drawing one specific card in the sixth position of a ten-card layout?

Brendan was conceived the next day, a Saturday morning, the first time I had ever tried to get pregnant. Later in the afternoon when I took a walk through the neighborhood, I wondered if the cells of an embryo were multiplying inside my body.

"Let's do it one more time, to increase our chances," I said to Stan on Sunday night.

"No, let's wait to see if this took," he answered.

Two weeks later, my menstrual period, regular as clockwork, had not come. Over my lunch break, I called the clinic, fearing that the pregnancy was not certain, but intuiting that I was genuinely, for the first time, positively pregnant.

The nurse confirmed what I already suspected. It took.

I nearly sprinted to Stan's office a few blocks away, and climbed the stairs to his office with the glass window overlooking the main avenue.

"I'm pregnant," I said to him, panting to get enough air.

He beamed, momentarily speechless. No shadows played in the corners of that office infused with sunlight. This is how it should be, exactly how it should be in the happy marriage script. A few months later the clinic confirmed it was a boy.

CHAPTER 4

Brendan

Even though I was pregnant, I couldn't keep away from the theatre. Acting out roles, the camaraderie of cast parties, the excitement and pizzazz of opening night were a part of my DNA. When cast as the character Popeye in a production of *The Miss Firecracker Contest*, I was not very pregnant, but enough to be over the crushing nausea and tidal fatigue of the first trimester, which was not fun. I would flop down on the bed after work, and would not have moved if there were a bomb planted under it. Stan would stand over me, still dressed in his suit and tie.

"You can't come home and collapse like this. How will you ever cope when we have the baby?" I squinted at his outline, silhouetted against a shaft of evening light coming in from the window. Stan might have been anxious, but his panic stemmed from the unknown obligations of parenthood, rather than any genuine concern about my health.

For example, on the sunny March morning when we delivered my urine to the lab for a pregnancy test, Stan banged on the front door of the building with both fists because it was eight in the morning and the door was supposed to be unlocked.

"I'm really sorry about my husband's behavior," I later said to the receptionist at the desk.

She shot me a deadpan glance. "No, I'm sorry for you, because you have to live with him."

Stan was fighting demons I could not imagine, because after the initial first trimester discomfort, I glowed, enraptured with the thought of having a child. He, on the other hand, was a mess.

"We need to drive to the emergency room because I think I'm having a heart attack," Stan said to me one evening when he picked me up from the office. I was puzzled, because seated behind the wheel in his suit and tie, he did not look like he was having any symptoms, and had no previous history of cardiovascular disease. Nevertheless, I reclined in a chair with my protruding belly while Stan was wheeled away in a gurney. He was released after a brief interval and an electrocardiogram. The doctors determined he was not having a heart attack.

I auditioned for the production because I did not anticipate that the pregnancy would create any obstacle. The show ran in June and the baby was due in December. One afternoon in rehearsal, as I memorized my lines while the director coached other actors, something thumped in the deep recesses of my body, a sensation I had never experienced before. So this is how mothers form bonds with an unborn child, this is when it starts. The boy we would name Brendan was announcing himself.

On stage I wore a hideous loose-fitting polyester dress of blue and white brocade, parted my hair in the middle, and pressed it down with barrettes. The character Popeye is economically disadvantaged, developmentally delayed, and probably a touch crazy as well. To her credit, Popeye has some unique insights, but out of costume, nobody would want to trade places with this character, because no one would elect to be disabled.

During my last prenatal visit, Dr. Glendenning stood with his back to me as I sat on the examining table, tapping his pencil against the chart. Brendan's head had not moved downward into the birth canal.

"To be safe we'd better schedule a C-section. Do you want to be admitted on December eighteenth or nineteenth?"

"The eighteenth," I answered, so that his birthday could be an even number. Even though he would not be delivered naturally, I was confident that nothing would go wrong. Women did not die in childbirth anymore, and my experienced obstetrician and medical technology would avert any mishaps. Expecting Brendan, as the days hastened toward the winter solstice, was akin to waiting for Santa Claus, who this Christmas would bring the most magnificent, wondrous gift of all.

I projected this phantom child into our kitchen as a toddler, the boy graduating from high school, the college senior, even though I could not discern his facial features. Onto this ephemeral character, I envisioned a future of unfathomable potential. His accomplishments would expand our boundaries, take us on unrevealed journeys, and deeply enrich our lives. As things played out with the actual Brendan, at times his petulant behavior would peeve us, but he never exhibited any challenges that couldn't be resolved by a time-out. What I never predicted was that he would be anything less than the perfect child: attractive, intelligent, and successful in every way.

A soft snow had fallen earlier on the morning we went to the hospital, a week before Christmas. Everything, from the snow twinkling under the moonlight, to the carols playing on the radio, was magical. I stepped out of the shower, holding onto the railing while balancing my lopsided weight. I also applied makeup, so I wouldn't look strung out. With a planned C-section, I might not even muss my hair.

After I was prepped for delivery, I wobbled down the hall pushing an IV frame. In the delivery room, the nurses assisted me onto the gurney and rolled me over on my side. The sharp sting of the needle pricked my back with the insertion of the epidural anesthetic. A huge curtain blocked my view of the lower half of my body. Stan donned a yellow paper gown, and a mask, and then vanished from my sight. While under the influence of the anesthetic, voices murmured that did not form words or sentences. While I floated, I felt occasional tugs, originating in my womb, but mainly, it was as though the lower half of my body were no longer attached to me, but at the other end of the room.

Then the room started to spin slowly, and quickly gained momentum, like water that forms a whirlpool when it is sucked down the drain. The room spun faster and faster and then stopped.

"Waaa, waaa, waaa." Brendan was born. His soul had entered his body, right before birth, when the funnel had reached its finale. This soul, from who knows where, manifested at that moment within Brendan. Women either in the throes of labor, or unconscious, cannot detect when the soul enters the body, but those who view the threshold during a spinal epidural might catch a glimpse.

The nurses, clothed in sterile gowns and plastic gloves, wiped Brendan.

"Waaa, waaa." He squalled like an insistent foghorn.

"Whoa," a nurse exclaimed as she jumped back. I could see out of the corner of my eye that Brendan had swatted at her with his arm. Next, a nurse presented the naked Brendan, holding him horizontally, with one hand grasping his head and neck and the other his pelvis. He did not open his eyes.

Back in the maternity ward, I could have all the chocolate milk I could possibly drink. I had a wonderful little boy, and visitors were bringing flowers and Christmas ornaments as gifts.

The next morning a nurse deposited a huge plastic sack crammed with pamphlets about caring for a newborn at the side of my bed.

"Have you read all of that material yet? Especially that part of what you have to do to bond with your baby?" Stan quizzed me when he arrived from the office.

"No," I replied. Of course I had not read all of that material. Besides, everything was going to be just fine. I had no idea whether I had "bonded" with Brendan or not, and quite frankly, wasn't worried about it.

"Well, okay, you blew it then," he said, only half joking.

In the middle of the next night, I woke from a deep sleep to the cries of Brendan coming closer. The clock on the wall registered 1:37 a.m. I struggled to pull myself up despite the surgical incision by grasping the bar that hung over the bed. The shaft of light from the hallway illuminated the darkened room, as Brendan was wheeled head first in his isolette. With the light shining on his face, I could distinguish each of his features. Looking back at me was a face remarkably like mine. With his neck craned back so that he could see me, his wide open eyes communicated to me, through the long hallways of many years, "I have found you again."

When we were discharged, Brendan laid in my lap as we were wheeled past the information desk. He folded one arm on top of the other, just like a little man. I figured I had pretty much done it all: graduated from college and earned a graduate degree, had a career and travelled to England, but nothing surpassed the deep and enduring happiness of being a mother to this baby.

Christmas came a week later with another soft snowfall. With the house lit by candlelight due to a temporary power outage, we reclined in its glow deep into the evening. Even surrounded by darkness, with Brendan in my arms, I foresaw a future that promised nothing but happiness.

On maternity leave, I was content to let my life revolve around Brendan, nothing but Brendan. Early in the morning, he stared ahead with his blue eyes, in his room papered with pastel rabbits. I carried him all over the house, while inhaling his sweet smell. At night I gave him a bath, and rocked and sang to him until he fell asleep. All through the winter, there was nothing more important than Brendan, until the crab apple tree in the front yard burst into a shower of pink blossoms, and I wondered whether I could pull off performing in the upcoming production of *Stepping Out*.

Somebody would have to watch Brendan while I was at rehearsals. I called my mother from the telephone in the kitchen.

"Are you out of your mind? No, Margaret, you have a baby to take care of. You certainly can't be in any play." She was absolute in her decision, but I knew that my friend Megan's mother babysat her babies through several shows. Also, when I was Frenchy in *Grease*, another actress had a young baby at home, and nobody questioned why she wasn't home with him.

So that left Stan. I approached him when he was watching the television evening news with his bare feet crossed. "I would really like to try out for this play. I don't know if I'll get cast, or whether I even want to do the show, but at least would like to try out." I stood facing him wearing my lime green sweats with the three embroidered bears, my maternity leave uniform.

"I don't want you to." He tightened his grip on the arm rests of his chair.

"Auditions. I just want to go to auditions, to test the waters. Why not?" My voice rose as the conversation became a stand-off.

"I just don't want you to. I'd be left with all the work. What's more, if you're serious about going, I'll get in that car right now and drive away."

Brendan was crying upstairs. I put him to my breast with an eye on the digital clock: fifteen minutes to get to auditions. When I pulled my nipple out of his mouth, his face screwed up, and he wailed at the rude interruption.

An engine fired up, and from the upstairs window I could see that the driveway below was now empty. Stan had carried out his threat, and this was not the first time he had pulled this stunt.

On the way to Colorado a few years earlier—because he was angry by the time we reached an A&W root beer restaurant in the middle of Kansas—Stan drove away, leaving me without saying a word. I sat clutching my drink, tamping down my increasing panic so I could think logically. Should I call my mother? My brother? Who might be willing to drive all the way out here? He returned after about ten minutes. Once we arrived in Colorado, we went to our ski lesson to be told we were too late. Once again, Stan walked away. Other skiers, strangers, trudged by me, their boots crunching in the snow. I was abandoned— lost on the mountain— in Vail, and Stan had the keys and the maps.

Now stranded with the child, I was again in the same predicament, overpowered by a bully. If I acquiesced to his behavior today, would he be more likely to employ these tactics when we encountered future disagreements?

I laid Brendan in his crib while contemplating the consequences of my leaving him to go to auditions. He was not able to crawl out, could not even stand. It was unlikely that someone would break into the house, which probably was not going to burn down. Besides, I knew that Brendan would be left alone for only a few minutes. Stan would drive around just long enough to make me late and then come home to roost in front of his television for the evening.

I grabbed my keys and a light jacket. Risking Brendan's safety was a desperate choice, but if I lost this battle, I would lose them all.

When I arrived in the darkened theatre, the director did not acknowledge my arrival. His back was turned away from me, toward the actresses on stage wearing sleek, lacy outfits. My engorged breasts leaked on the pads of the nursing bra, a huge, elaborate contraption. My waist ballooned out from the delivery, so I could never pour myself into one of those tight-fitting bodices. I was a huge cow with a swaying udder. As the evening progressed, the director did not even ask me to read. There was no role in this production for me. By attending auditions, I banished any lingering doubts.

When I got home, Stan was again in his usual chair in front of the television. His face was drained of color.

"I can't believe that you really drove off and left him," he said.

"Well, I did," I replied.

I sprinted upstairs to find Brendan asleep in his crib. Although he was safe, I knew I might not be as lucky next time. Brendan was in a precarious situation, along with all the other children whose parents are driven to suboptimal choices due to poverty, mental illness, addictions, or unstable relationships. Yet he was also privileged, living with educated parents who read to him every night and provided him with all the amenities of the middle class, a lifestyle created by two professional incomes. Nearly every day I calibrated my marriage with the precision of a mathematician, weighing the consequences of Stan's occasional immature episodes against the losses I would incur if he were no longer in the equation. With all things considered, I kept coming to the same conclusion: the three of us were better off together.

As the months passed, Brendan progressed through the developmental milestones on schedule. He rolled over, sat up, stood up and began walking. Stan became a doting father. He bundled up Brendan in his green quilted jumpsuit on Saturday mornings to attend a class for fathers and newborns. He took him grocery shopping, and photographed Brendan in his crib as he waved his rattle and brushed it across his cheek. I celebrated the positive, while rationalizing away the less than perfect aspects of our marriage. Nobody can have it all. Stan did not want any more children, probably because one child was all his nerves could handle, but by the time Brendan was a toddler, I convinced him that Brendan should have a sibling.

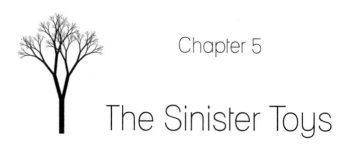

Chapter 5

The Sinister Toys

In the days immediately following giving birth to Spenser, the doctors and nurses avoided my hospital room, because when the baby isn't normal, things get messy. When helium balloons and congratulatory bouquets are replaced by a grim medical diagnosis, nobody knows what to say. New mothers especially, with their post-partum hormones compounding the situation, might cry, or even become hysterical. Time for an exit.

To make matters worse, Brendan's pediatrician had left the helm to serve in Desert Storm, so nobody seemed to be in charge. When Brendan was born, Dr. Copeland, tall and confident, would pop into the room every day to say the baby was doing well. One day he reported that he temporarily placed Brendan under some lights to fight jaundice. Nothing serious, nothing to worry about.

Spenser's birth was considerably more complicated. I couldn't deny that Spenser was different. With his long narrow face and prominent forehead, he resembled E.T., the extraterrestrial of movie fame, who was very tentative about being on this earth. When the doctors did report to me, I didn't want to hear what they had to say about him. I shut out their worried murmurings describing the baby's head, hands and feet as being asymmetrically large that might indicate a rare syndrome, possibly Marfan's or Sotos syndrome.

I flicked off the television remote, silencing the daytime dramas with their manicured living room sets and actresses with perfectly coiffed hairstyles, acutely aware that I had produced a child who did not measure up to their standards of perfection. Finally, tired of moping in the bed, I shoved away my food tray with the grey plastic dome beaded with moisture and decided to go see the baby. I swung my feet around to the floor, slowly shifted my weight, and shuffled ahead, doubled over by the tight incision.

After donning a crinkly yellow gown, I pushed the button that opened the automatic doors of the neonatal unit. Immobile infants sequestered in their tiny catacombs with monitors that flashed and beeped lined the perimeter of the unit. I found Spenser, who lay motionless on his side. I arched over him and peered into his face, but his sorrowful countenance of down-slanting eyes and bruised cheeks from the forceps delivery sealed me out. Spenser's pediatrician joked with his colleagues as he approached, but his hearty laugh stopped at the sight of my child. When we were in high school choir together, this pediatrician had been a scrawny kid with a beautiful tenor voice. Now that he had become a doctor, his frame had filled out and his hair no longer spiked up in unruly tufts.

He regarded Spenser as though he were peeping into a coffin of the deceased.

"Scott, Scott," I implored, "just tell me that he's eventually going to be all right."

He bowed his head toward the little extraterrestrial. "I can't promise you that because I don't know, Margaret," was his reply. Then he swiveled and walked away.

I rushed back to the hospital room, and surveyed through tears the new baby toys lining the counters and window sills. Now the blue, green and pink pastels of the crocheted blanket bled together in jeering hues. The corpulent teddy bear stared blankly through his wire glasses, joining the conspiracy formed by the spotted giraffe and fluffy lion. Only a macabre choo-choo train engine, with an insolent cap perched upon his head, dared to break the silence with a mocking music box rendition of "Happy Days Are Here Again."

This is not what I had bargained for. I wanted another baby like Brendan—healthy, robust and solidly squared off like a bean bag. At his December birth everyone came to visit with flowers, Christmas tree ornament gifts and laughing exclamations. Now my sole visitor, other than immediate family, was the official delegate from the church, a plump, short middle-aged woman whose petrified smile hid her confusion as to whether to offer congratulations or condolences. I wanted to throw out all the baby paraphernalia and run down the hallway, screaming until my lungs burst.

A few hours later, the phone rang. I maneuvered toward it, supporting my weight with the overhead bar.

"Hello?" I waited for the voice on the other end.

"Hi, it's Kim from the office." Kim sounded encouraging. "We heard you had the baby and were all wondering how everything was going."

My mind raced around searching for my next sentence. How much should I say? That he might not be normal? That he might be retarded? That we might be spending the rest of our lives caring for a custodial vegetable?

"Actually it was kind of a rough birth." I jerked the coiled telephone cord.

"So, who does he look like?" I couldn't blame Kim for asking all the usual questions. The hard part was figuring out how to deliver bad news to an innocent ambassador of good will.

"We really can't tell yet." I endeavored to hear some hopeful tidings from Kim's cheery voice that she was unable to provide, because she didn't know anything about the gravity of Spenser's condition.

"Isn't he in the room with you?"

"This baby is in the neonatal intensive care unit."

"Oh," Kim hesitated, "probably something minor, like jaundice?"

"Yeah, just for a few days. Nothing serious." I did not have the stamina for the truth. "A nurse is waiting on me. It was nice of you to call."

After clicking the receiver back in place, I thought about the special education students at my school who careened down the halls with choppy, robotic gaits, their emotionless faces staring straight ahead. With their crisp button-down shirts, pleated wool skirts and sturdy Oxford shoes, it was apparent that their parents tried to dress them well, but they missed out on all the subtle social cues. For example, we never wore solid squared off Oxfords, but the more fashionable black and white "bubbles" with pointed toes. Boys never wore belts with their tight-fitting Levis. Nobody conversed with or attempted to befriend these special ed kids, because they might let out a loud laugh, flap their hands, drool, or shout out your name in exuberance so that every kid in the whole school would instantly know that you were as weird as they were. They were the worst of the worst, the most outcast pariahs. My parents had taught me to always be nice, but other students subjected these kids to the cruelest of taunts, the most horrible dirty tricks. Now my baby, for whom I had lovingly shopped for the soft blue sleeper, my baby, so helpless and innocent, faced a similar future.

Day after day the woman from the department of vital statistics found me sitting up in bed, staring at the wall. She wanted a name for the birth certificate, but Stan and I couldn't agree—couldn't agree whether to spell the name of our broken dream "Spencer" or "Spenser," couldn't reconcile that this had happened to us, couldn't predict how it would change our lives. At night after the visitors departed, the nurses wrote in charts at their stations. A panel of fluorescent lights brightened my room, and a winter wind rattled the icy windowpane of my sanitized hospital room. The hospital employees donned coats, ventured out into this blackness and drove home to the responsibilities of other lives. I remained useless, captive to my post-partum infirmities and mental lethargy. My tender, swollen breasts were over-brimming with milk and I yearned for the child, but he might not even live. I prepared for another pilgrimage to the neonatal unit, to ascertain whether behind all this disappointment, there really was a baby.

Outside the neonatal unit, I washed my hands, fastened the yellow sterile gown behind my neck, and paused before the portals of the automatic doors. Inside, the beeps and buzzes sounded like a cricket chorus. A nurse announced to the staff that another baby had been flown in on a Lifestar helicopter. I hobbled to the corner of the room where I had last seen Spenser in his isolette, with his name lettered on a small banner overhead. The space was vacant. At first my heart pounded, but then I braced myself for the worst. So he had died, and nobody had told me that, either.

"What happened to Spenser Gardner?" I asked a young man with a white jacket.

"Oh, we moved him against the other wall, with the babies who are out of critical condition."

The features of the room softened, and the starkness of the bright lights blurred. I rushed over to him, relieved to be reunited with my little elf. His long little body and strange face had a forlorn appearance, yet after all, he was my child.

I decided to hold him, and dress him in the soft blue sleeper I had purchased. A nurse assisted me in lifting him out, so light and so long, and resting him in the folds of my sterile gown. He warmed my lap as I bent over to kiss his forehead.

"Hello, you," I whispered. Suddenly, as though he were a puppet whose string had been drawn, his mouth elongated into a huge smile. No other facial muscles moved. After a few moments, the smile collapsed, but we had bonded as mother and baby.

Even though it might be he and I against the world, at that moment I decided that I was going to love him no matter what. Despite everything, we would find a way, even though it probably would not be easy.

I was discharged a few days later, but Spenser stayed behind in the neonatal unit. As I was getting dressed and packing things into my canvas tote bag, the phone rang.

"What time should my parents pick you up?" Stan asked.

"Stan, I'm glad that they came, but I really want to go home to my mother for a few days," I said.

"But they drove all the way from Springfield, both of them. They're at the house," he said.

"I know, but after what I've been through the last few days, I just want to be with my mother and be taken care of."

"No, they're coming to get you."

When I dressed Brendan to come home from the hospital and lifted him straight up, my mother exclaimed, "Watch out," thinking his head would wobble, but he stiffened, straight and strong as a board. This time I rode alone in the wheelchair; the baby I left behind scarcely had the strength to move.

Stan's father lifted my bag into the trunk of the car. Dr. Gardner's sandy hair, interspersed with white, was covered by his grey felt cowboy hat on that brisk January afternoon. Neatly dressed, he wore a cotton button-down shirt, belt with a large gold buckle, jeans and cowboy boots. In the aisles of the drugstore and later in the car, I kept a conversation going, because even though he had specialized in pathology, as a medical doctor he might have some insight regarding Spenser's condition.

When we turned the corner onto the dirt road and passed the houses and fields starkly delineated by the bright daylight to our new house, I realized that the sun had probably been shining like this all day. But even though there was a world beyond the confines of my hospital room, I was tormented with worry, and yammered on and on about Spenser.

Dr. Gardner drove straight ahead, his hand on top of the steering wheel. With the same measured deliberation with which he phrased his other comments, he then stated to me, "One contributing factor toward birth defects is advanced maternal age."

In the front seat next to him, I crumpled into a heap, held upright by the seatbelt. I was forty years old, after all. So this was my fault? Was he saying that I was an old, imperfect mother who had deliberately caused her child's disability?

Reeling from the impact of his comment, I said nothing the rest of the way home. When the car coasted to the front door, I did not follow him inside, but turned the other way and headed up to the field on top of the hill, seeking solace among the expanse of sere fields, once lush with butterfly milkweed, Queen Anne's lace and waving grasses during the past summer. Under the panorama of the open sky, I wailed and sobbed.

Stan's parents didn't come looking for me. Even when I came back in through the front door, I was still stunned by the comment and said nothing to either of them. I now realize that they were hurting too, that they expected another healthy, robust grandchild, and were also searching for words to answer the well-meaning voices suspended at the other end of their telephone line.

Becky. I yearned to call Becky, my friend at the office, who had asked me every day about the pregnancy and brought me some baby items, but I couldn't find her phone number, and couldn't even decide whether to call her. I was trapped in my own house with Stan's parents, clawing for an exit, with Stan at work and Brendan in daycare.

Stan's mother moved silently through the house, doing what she could. When Brendan was born before Christmas, she had come to stay, preparing meat loaf and mashed potatoes for lunch, when a peanut butter and jelly sandwich would have been sufficient. I even glimpsed her standing on a chair, cleaning the dust from the chandelier. Now she was offering her services for our second child, but

Spenser's circumstances were totally different. I appreciated her and did not want to hurt her, but as I paced around the house, taking deep breaths, I teetered on the edge of hysteria, so when I came downstairs and found Stan's parents huddled near the dining room table, I lit into Stan's father.

"Advanced maternal age? Do you really think I wanted this to happen, that I would have done this on purpose?"

Stan's father clasped the back rungs of the dining room chair. His mother turned in a circle, as though she had just remembered her next errand.

"And as for all of your male chauvinism, I'm sick of it, sick of it, and I've been sick of it for years. Yes, I love working at my job, and no, I don't plan on staying home, and you don't accept that. You've never respected me for who I am."

Stan's father had no response to my incessant tears.

Stan was wrong; I should have gone home to my mother. Once I grew silent, we all listened to the ticking of the clocks.

In the dining room, the small portable crib with the Pooh blanket awaiting Spenser was empty. Light streamed through the windows onto the white crib in Spenser's bedroom, brightening the aqua green of the lace-trimmed comforter. The diapers and terrycloth sleepers lined the building block panels of the changing table, and the wooden rocker that I had painted lavender stood in the corner. The choo-choo train, intended for Spenser, chimed "Happy Days Are Here Again," but far away in the hospital, he could not hear the mechanized, magical notes of the music box.

Now the message of a voice which had said to me, nearly audibly, the day before going to the hospital, "A normal child is never going to sleep in this crib," made sense to me. As I had tucked the corners of the comforter into the crib I had wondered, would he die? The pregnancy had been uneventful, the heartbeat in utero and sonogram had prompted no concerns. I had even clicked on my cross-country skis and traversed the yard a few days after the due date, but no, Spenser would never be a normal child.

Chapter 6

The Verdict

Within days of Spenser's birth, the doctors in white coats wanted answers. I didn't want my child to be labeled, and resented their wheel-of-fortune diagnoses.

Sotos syndrome. Marfan syndrome. Fragile X. They scribbled notes in their charts, slapped them shut and left to make their rounds. I stayed behind, eyes downcast.

I was in denial because I expected a normal child, but a thin, wizened baby with a nasogastric tube took his place.

On a windy but sunny day in early February, my sister and I descended the grey concrete steps in the parking garage of the University of Kansas Medical Center in Kansas City, carefully balancing tiny sleeping Spenser in his car seat. The wind blew against the glass tower, and when we scurried across the street to the main building, white paper scraps flew wildly around the curbs. We had an appointment with Dr. R. Nick Schondel, division director of endocrinology, metabolism and genetics.

Dr. Schondel, a tall man with thinning grey hair, leaned against the examining table in his white coat. He looked at me through his glasses.

"So were there any complications during the pregnancy?" he asked, arms folded across his chest.

"No, none at all. This was totally unsuspected."

"Any problems or complications with the delivery?"

"I pushed for three hours, and then I had to have a C-section."

"Hmmm," he flipped the pencil around in his fingers. "Were you exposed to any toxic substances?"

"I cleaned the oven, but held my breath every time I sprayed the fumes."

He and all the other medical personnel who were trying to crack the code of why this wasted little wraith lay before us in his blue knitted jacket—instead of a fat, squawking thing—asked all the same questions.

Really, there was nothing. My sister, still wearing her parka with the fake fur ruff, pulled the requested family pictures out of a manila envelope, to discover if whatever Spenser had was somehow slipped into the gene pool. The three of us gathered around the black and white images arranged on a metallic table. Did our grandfather have a long face and large skull? Did our father have an unusually large forehead? Once beloved pictures were now suspect in the relentless investigation of this perfect crime.

Dr. Schondel whipped out a tape measure and wrapped it around my skull.

"Your skull circumference is rather large," he stated.

Spenser slept with his eyelids sealed, oblivious to all the apprehension surrounding him.

"He's not always this quiet. From about two to four in the morning I'm pacing the floor with him," I said.

"They're perverse that way." Dr. Schondel chuckled.

I did not share all the secrets of what transpired late at night, when I awoke to his muffled cries and pulled my heavy body, still disabled by the cesarean section, down the stairs to his crib. In night's blackness, I could not see the bruised face, but could feel his skull against my forearm, and smelled the fetid aroma of urine evaporating from his damp sleeper. Spenser cried, but would not feed. When I positioned him to accept my nipple, he squirmed, but would not latch on. He then cried weakly while I wandered through dark rooms with the moon shining in from the crescent window, my bare feet treading on cool wooden floors. Finally, still hungry, Spenser quieted, and I would lay him down on the crisp white sheet and pull up the coverlet trimmed with lace over his thin body. Within days my breasts, initially tender and bursting with milk, dried up without a trace.

Dr. Schondel, grasping the edges of the yellow tape measure between his thumb and forefinger, measured the distance between Spenser's two pupils. The black notches formed a track bridging his nose.

Dr. Schondel glanced over at the nurse. The moment had come. Without speaking, she carried the baby out of the room, and Dr. Schondel followed, so that he could do more measurements, and come up with a verdict.

"Sotos syndrome." The room came back into focus with a doctor who was decisive, but carefully wielded the power of the truth. For me, having any diagnosis was shattering. I had prayed that this doctor would assure me that my infant was normal.

"What does that mean?" I shrieked. Dr. Schondel's lips started moving, and his eyes lit up as one conversing. I heard maybe every eighth or ninth word, sometimes single words, sometimes a group of them. Big hands, big feet, may be clumsy, large head, advanced bone age, possibility of cognitive developmental delay, of developmental delay, developmental delay.

"Does that mean he's going to be mentally retarded?" I blurted out. Dr. Schondel's head and shoulders were in stark relief against the white wall. I had no more defenses.

"It's too early to know with certainty," Dr. Schondel said.

During late nights, the household asleep, I prayed in the garret overlooking thick woods, "Let him be normal, let Spenser be a typically-developing child, please God." But underneath the supplications was an aching chill. I ran from the truth, but it was still there, an elfin ogre with gleaming teeth, the nightmare of fairy tales. At times Spenser's bright eyes focused on me as he sucked his pacifier with little, rapid motions. Other times, his eyes glazed over as he craned his head back toward something I could not see. That vacant expression sent jolts through me.

As late as the Victorian era, and certainly before, the common folk believed that evil fairies exchanged healthy infants for sickly or deformed weaklings, and called these disabled babies "changelings." Even though science now offers medical explanations, when confronted with an imperfect child, it is reflexive for mothers to feel tricked, disappointed and disgusted to some degree. They may also feel betrayed by their body, or blame themselves, for producing a child who will never be classified as normal. My Spenser definitely qualified as a changeling who had trafficked with fairies.

A few days later, I sat in the television room with Spenser's hard skull pressing my forearm against the wooden arm of the chair. Outside the picture window, a red cardinal flitted across the expanse of grey, bare-limbed trees, while juncos hopped among golden, dead grass. The voices of soap opera characters made the only sound in the house. My in-laws had gone back home, and my husband Stan was at work.

A manila envelope arrived from KU Med Center, with a follow-up letter from Deirdre Crandell, genetics counselor, and Dr. Schondel. The letter stated, "After examining him we feel that there is a possibility that he has a condition called Sotos syndrome. This condition is a condition which rarely occurs in families and generally is sporadic. Clinic features involve a large head, large hands and feet, advanced bone age, and a variety of other problems some of which are described on the enclosed information." I didn't want to read this, didn't want to read this.

The letter continued, "Occasionally, children with this condition have developmental delay, however, this is not a definite feature."

Enclosed with the letter were pictures of babies diagnosed with Sotos syndrome. Naked except for diapers, rectangular black boxes blocked out their eyes. I read the captions under the pictures. This baby, with a winning smile, had an IQ of 60, that one, propped up on weak legs, 70.

"How can they know? These are just babies!" I yelled at the piano in the room. Spenser slept, and I studied his still features for symptoms, such as premature eruption of teeth. With my forefinger I shoved aside his lip to examine his smooth pink gums, finding a little white blotch on the gum ridge. Of course it was milk, but in my irrational mental state, I thought it was a tooth.

The last remnants of optimism drained out of me and spilled all over the floor. Spenser had Sotos syndrome. This clinched it. I didn't even have the energy to rock, to make the hinges of the stiff chair squeak.

The front door swung open. Stan, dressed in his tie and jacket, took one look at me and froze. The afternoon light from the picture window outlined his profile.

I lifted the manila envelope from the telephone stand, and dropped it.

"They sent some information about Sotos syndrome. I think from reading this that Spenser has it."

"What does this mean? Is that baby retarded? Is one of us going to have to quit our jobs to stay home with him all of the time?" Stan shouted.

My hand was draped over the arm rest, in the same pose as when I had dropped the envelope.

During most of the early afternoons, when Spenser was taking his nap, I sewed curtains for the television room, blue and white for the picture window that overlooked grey trees and dead grass. I couldn't get much of anything else done. When Spenser woke up, I rocked him, his head pressing my forearm into the wooden arm of the chair, and watched soap operas.

During an episode one of the actresses was giving birth. On an examining table, with her coiffed hair, only slightly mussed, and closed eyes crowned by iridescent dark lids, she tossed and emitted weak noises from a mouth that formed a lipsticked circle. In a moving tableau, the painted faces of the actresses, together with the handsome actors, spoke lines that encouraged her to push. She responded by thrashing with more intensity and wailing. The crowd erupted into laughter and cheers. I waited for the congratulations to abruptly halt as I wished upon her the show-stopping silence of unexpected tragedy.

A man smoothed her brow. Of course it was a normal, healthy baby. The troupe with the painted masks hugged and kissed each other. "Whose eyes does he have?" said a man in harmonious baritone. "Who does he look like?" came from an aging actress with a raspy voice.

Glued to the animated screen, I willed the baby to be deformed, to die. I despised the actress simulating birth, absolutely hated her. I not only raged at this woman, but also the screenwriters, for never daring to imagine an alternative outcome.

Unlike the actresses who preened themselves for their artificial dramas, I usually wore sweats and did not bother with makeup, except when I had to get out of the house for Spenser's medical appointments, scheduled several times a week. After my six-week maternity leave with Brendan, I had been anxious to get back to work, to check off accomplishments that could be measured in cases closed and investigations completed. With Spenser, eight weeks did not seem long enough to mope around.

My drab appearance in the mirror further chipped away at my ego, and reminded me of the strong correlation between how we feel about our looks and our self-esteem. Not that feeling pretty is entirely subjective. Our confidence is also attuned to that split second of recognition when the faces of others we encounter either warm up or display indifference to us. Many women feel oddly bereft when they reach the age that strange men quit staring at them on the street. Our faces open doors for us, or slam them shut, more than we would ever like to imagine.

"Who does he look like?" friends would ask when I answered the phone.

Of course they all wanted to know. Even though it's only common courtesy to ask, most newborn babies look the same anyway. You can distinguish babies of different races by their skin color, but that's about all. When Brendan was born, the nurses could have brought me a different baby every time the first three or four times he was delivered to me, and I wouldn't have known the difference. Black hair, white face, tightly-sealed eyes, pouty little mouth, fat cheeks. Typical newborn. Asleep, with no emotion.

After Spenser was born with Sotos syndrome, I didn't know what to say. Should I have told them that with his slanting eyes, broad forehead, long face and pointed chin, he resembled E.T., the extraterrestrial of movie fame? His cheeks were also bruised from the botched forceps delivery. Should I mention that also? What would the etiquette books advise?

When I brought Spenser to his numerous medical appointments, I had an attitude, because at that point I could not wrap my mind around how much extra time, expense and effort a disabled child would demand. So I silenced my inner doubts, clung to false hopes that Spenser's problems could be attributed to his rocky birth, and glared with hostility at those with white coats who told me differently.

Within the next few months, Spenser was seen not only by local medical personnel, but also the University of Kansas Medical Center for follow-up visits. We wound our way around the complex. I set my jaw as we drove past the "well-child" clinic, searching for the building for infants who had complications.

I set Spenser's car seat down so I could present my health insurance card to the receptionist. Once inside the examining room following an initial consultation, I flipped through the pages of a heavy hard-bound book about genetic disorders. The clinical names and symptoms whizzed by, cataloguing throngs of maladies buried in hundreds of pages. Before I had Spenser, I had only been vaguely aware that any one of a million things can go wrong with a child. I stopped at a photograph of twin boys, who grinned with exaggerated leers. Whatever they had also caused severe mental retardation, so they were condemned to parade through the years in these lurid masks. Judging from their appearances, they too easily could have been cast as changelings in a horrific tale about malevolent ogres.

"It isn't fair! It isn't fair," I screamed at the black book on the counter. As footsteps approached, I composed myself, stretching my mouth into a tepid smile.

On this particular day, the children's clinic was packed. A nurse spoke to a black-haired Hispanic family in hushed, serious tones near the reception desk. For some reason their baby was not gaining weight.

Elsewhere, in front of a brightly-colored mural, a young doctor in a white coat clutching a steel-jacketed file was talking to a young couple. The woman, dressed in a hospital gown, no doubt the mother, looked up at the doctor. She was attentive, but seemed to be too weak to get up from her wheelchair. Her stylishly cut and colored hair drooped, and her pretty features were not accentuated with makeup. Standing next to her, her husband fielded questions from the doctor.

I studied their dress and mannerisms, straining to hear pieces of their conversation, in order to piece together their story. I determined that they were educated young professionals, had some money. Her husband was dressed in khakis and a pinstripe shirt, and a loosened tie, probably on his way to the office after this appointment. It's likely that he worked for a law or accounting firm in a skyscraper downtown, or maybe in a suburban office park off College Boulevard.

The husband discussed his baby with precise gestures and articulate words. Frederick. Apparently the baby's name was Frederick. The young father, smiling, confident and upbeat, was coping for himself and his wife, promising to make this phone call, or to follow up on that detail. This junior executive was on top of his game, engineering everything possible to assure Frederick's successful beginning.

"Take off all the time you need," they must be telling him at the office. Up to a point, of course, if he had already been absent the entire week. I wondered whether he was also wrestling with what to tell them about Frederick. He eventually had to return to the office, to make a living for this blonde wife in a wheelchair and little Frederick, who might have medical appointments stretching before him like a long tunnel in a house of mirrors.

Spenser slept in his grey car seat. By doing only minimal eavesdropping, I could construct the situations of many of the families surrounding me if I chose to tune in. Later the clinic would be remodeled to prevent conversations from being overheard. The only sounds coming from the new waiting room would be the bubbles pumped into a large aquarium in which bright orange fish rhythmically opened and closed their mouths. In order to protect their privacy, the newly-configured room would effectively seal off hurting families from each other.

Spenser's name was called. A cheerful African-American woman sitting by a height chart in the shape of a giraffe weighed and measured Spenser. This room, decorated with bright juvenile posters popping out all over, pulsated with the sounds of other infants and staff performing their intake jobs. Through her smile and easy-going style as she slipped off Spenser's sleeper, this woman seemed to genuinely enjoy her patients. I was stunned. Didn't she know that we were here because he had a horrible diagnosis? Could she love this baby even if he were deformed or retarded?

At the desk, another clerk rattled off familiar questions. Had it been a normal pregnancy? Had I taken any illegal drugs or drunk alcohol? Had I taken any prescription drugs? Had I received adequate prenatal care? Had I been exposed to toxic substances? No, the pregnancy had been uneventful. Yet this woman, cocking her head to the side with her modern hairstyle, did not comment. If I had confessed to any of the sins, she simply would have recorded the information, without judging.

"Just have a seat over there while we wait for the results of the blood test," she said.

I took a seat next to Frederick's father, who was now quiet and pensive. He gazed down at Frederick, who was stretched out on his legs. Sometimes he picked up the baby's arms, and brought them together in a clapping motion. The infant had a perforation stretching from his mouth to his nose, and stared at his father with grey uncomprehending eyes.

"So Frederick was born recently?" I inquired.

"Yes," the father said, "my wife is still hospitalized, so Frederick spent the night sleeping on my chest. That provided a fantastic opportunity for us to bond."

He enunciated his words with the precision of an actor. Bonding. The new politically correct term for interacting with your baby, a buzzword in hospital prenatal classes. All the couples in his class would be delivering about now, and would have two, four, and six-month reunions. What would he tell them about Frederick? I struggled to remember whether in the midst of the high expectations and shared laughter of my prenatal classes, the possibility of a devastating diagnosis had even been covered.

"So what are they saying is going on with him?"

"Cleft palate, but the doctors are also saying that he might be a dwarf."

I remembered the grinning twins in the heavy book, and the barbed stinging of diagnoses that lacerate the dreams of new fathers, and make "bonding" a bittersweet experience.

"Just be grateful it's something they can fix," I said to him, in reference to the cleft palate.

I was called to the desk. The receptionist informed me that the blood test results would be sent to the doctor and I was to make another appointment in one month.

I glanced back at Frederick's father, now sitting alone, surrounded by empty chairs. Most of the families were clearing out for lunch, and even the television had been shut off. The father gazed down at Frederick with agony and longing, as though he were already a memory.

He then grabbed the visor of Frederick's cap, and pulled it down over Frederick's face so he wouldn't have to look at it.

Spenser was not gaining weight, so as February dragged on, I alternated between staying at home and watching soap operas while he slept in my lap, and lugging him to two or three medical appointments per week.

On this particular day, I had spent the entire morning in the hospital, and even though we had made the rounds of the doctor's office, laboratory, and radiology, we had to visit at least one more department. Although I have friends whose eyes light up when they describe their boring medical conditions of minor significance, I have always striven for robust health and fitness, so resented being chained to the medical regimens necessary for Spenser. I recognized that we were privileged to have access to modern medicine, and appreciated what everyone was doing for him, but the other part of me wished I could shut it all off with the flick of a remote control. The medical interventions underscored what I tried to deny, that this birth had not turned out as planned.

The room was empty except for the receptionist seated behind the rectangular wooden desk. I wore my green sweat suit with the three little bears, a gift from my sister, comfortable attire for a post-partum woman who was hanging out all over. Spenser slept on my lap, his eyes tightly shut and face expressionless, wrapped in a thin blanket. Wispy dark brown hair covered his head, which was unusually large, and his sealed eyelids had a slight downward cast. His tiny upturned nose was that of a doll, but he wasn't a doll baby. He was a recent traveler from the other side of the veil who, having refused my breast milk, was growing increasingly emaciated. A tourist here for a brief visit, who might be booking his return. The worry, the shock, the fear, and the loneliness surged through me and I began to cry.

A plain middle-aged woman, swathed in a frayed bathrobe, whose breasts, waist and hips melded together in her midsection, took a seat in the back of the waiting room. The lens of her glasses reflected the overhead fluorescent lights. As if on cue, she began ambling toward me. Once beside me, she rested her forearms on the back of the chair, her hands clasped together.

"What's the matter, Mom?" the woman said in her quiet voice. The stranger's tenderness choked me so much that I could not speak. I sobbed harder.

"Things just haven't gone as planned," I managed to get out.

"I've had four children, two girls and two boys," the woman began in a monotone. "My oldest girl is in Colorado, working for a construction company, doing really well for herself. My other daughter, Carolyn, was on the honor roll. Always helped me around the house, very cheerful about it, without being asked. When she was twenty-one she was killed in a car accident. As for my boys, one is still here in Kansas, but the other one went up to Alaska. I guess it must have been some kind of argument. He was shot in a barroom brawl."

She relayed her personal history as though she were talking about the weather. With her narration finished, her waddling footsteps transported her back to her tweed-upholstered seat, where she waited for her name to be called.

I didn't realize why she had imparted this intimate news to a stranger until years later. She was educating me about motherhood, not the commercial motherhood of advertising that features darling little girls with neatly braided hair, but the more visceral version, in which children's noses may bleed all over the white carpet, or sometimes they die.

In Starkenburg, Missouri there is a shrine dedicated to the Virgin Mary, a powerful icon of motherhood in Christian culture. In this chapel, which I discovered while bicycling through Missouri, her manifestation is as the Lady of Sorrows. Finding the door unlocked, I stepped into a holy place where the morning light streamed through the stained glass windows, and the silence inside the venerated walls was palpable. The votive candles flickered in their blue glass holders, generating warmth and the aroma of melting wax. I stood before a side altar where the Virgin Mary reigns in glory, enfolded in a sheer white veil that encircles her and the Infant Jesus. I could see past her plaster expression to her compassion flowing outward to the universe.

Among these statues of the divine, I suspended my daily concerns and surrendered to the vortex of life, death, and life resurrected once more.

Nor will I ever be alone. Countless pilgrims have journeyed to this altar, who leave behind crutches, a leg brace, the collar of a beloved dog. She hears them, will always hear them, their anguished cries ascending to heaven. The voices of pilgrims, rising and falling, pulsing to the rhythm of the bleeding Sorrowful Mother. The supplicants pray, they gasp, they murmur, they cry. With every new day they chant of dolores, the countless dolores, the infinite dolores of the Virgin Mary, Mother of God.

Chapter 7

The Screening Test

In late March with my maternity leave almost over, I was eager to get back to my job at the civil rights agency. I helped people. Even if the evidence did not support their allegations, I listened to them vent their rage, and as gently but firmly as possible, confronted them with the truth gathered during my travels to the furthest corners of Kansas.

In my office, everything was in its place. A clock honoring me for high production hung on my wall. The case files were arranged in the black file cabinet. In the morning, I spread them all over my desk, but in the evening, I put them back. I kept to a tight schedule, and finished many tasks.

But to the degree that my office cubicle was organized, during maternity leave everything was muddled. The morning would bleed into afternoon, and by evening, I had accomplished next to nothing. Even on the days we ventured out to medical appointments, we received no definitive answers, just a tentative diagnosis, Sotos syndrome, that hung over us like a storm cloud. One morning, I sat on the footstool applying eyeliner while Stan scurried behind me, getting ready for work.

"What if he died? Would it be better if he just died and we started over with another baby?" I asked my reflection. Then I dismissed the thought. That would be a terrible outcome. Besides, there might not be another baby. I was forty years old.

We interviewed a daycare provider with a kind grandmother personality, whose speech was modulated by a Southern drawl. She answered our questions in a clean room with several cribs and toys neatly piled in a box. As we drove away, we agreed that we should hire her, but had not been totally forthcoming during the interview about Spenser, because if nobody wanted to take on a special needs child, then I wouldn't be able to return to my job. We could manage without my income, but money was the least of my concerns. While lounging around the house, I had missed the heady excitement of the rapid-fire responses during fact-finding conferences, interviewing witnesses, and influencing policy through my unique contributions. Luckily, she did agree to care for him.

When he was almost two months old, I bundled Spenser in his little coat, and laid on extra blankets over the car seat. We were bound for the county health clinic, instead of the private pediatrician's office, for his routine immunizations because of insurance complications. I glanced over at Spenser as I drove through the winter landscape of bare trees and patches of snow. Sometimes he appeared to be a normal sleeping baby, but other times he arched his back and thrust back his head with a vacant stare. Although I denied the diagnosis of Sotos syndrome, I couldn't ignore these abnormal facial expressions. Quite frankly, at those times Spenser did look retarded.

At the clinic, the woman behind the glass window gave me a form attached to a clipboard, with a pen dangling from a beaded-metal chain, along with a blank pink immunization card, which she told me never to lose.

As I waited until the nurse called my name, I surveyed the faces of the people surrounding me. One woman, sitting with crossed arms, chewed gum with an angry glare. Another man with a knit cap watched a toddler turning the cardboard pages of a book. They paid no attention to Spenser, and their apathy puzzled me, because I felt like an imposter who was supposed to be hanging out in this clinic with an ordinary child, but had sneaked in an abnormal one instead.

The last question featured a chart indicating weekly family income. Was it less than fifty dollars a week? One hundred dollars a week? I wondered how anybody could live on that, as we made considerably more. But this was the county health clinic. I again assessed the faces in this waiting room, and tried to imagine how difficult survival might be for some of them, who might not have enough food to eat, struggled to keep their utilities turned on, or relied on dilapidated cars for transportation. Perhaps they had problems that were more pressing than worrying about my baby.

A tall dark-haired woman, an acquaintance, sat down across from me. I knew that Maddy wanted to have another baby, a sibling for her blonde five-year-old bean pole who squirmed beside her. Maddy gazed down at Spenser with infinite tenderness, her head tilted slightly. She may have observed his arched eyebrows framing his dark eyelashes, the resolute set of his mouth, his fists curled into balls, clenching and slowly releasing. Her awe intrigued me, because she must have been seeing something that I was overlooking. I had conspired, along with the cold weather and ashen skies, to become a stone dwelling in a grey landscape, in order to wall up my emotions to escape the pain. Perhaps I had been so focused on casting Spenser as a tragedy that I was refusing to let the script play out in any other way.

"Spenser Gardner?" called the nurse who emerged from the clinic hallway, her eyes scanning the multitude of faces.

I smiled for the first time in weeks.

In contrast, Stan was not smiling. In the evenings he refused to budge from the television downstairs, while I fed Spenser, bathed him and put him to bed, along with his toddler brother Brendan. If they had simultaneous meltdowns, I flitted from one room to another, desperate to soothe the crying, while Stan remained oblivious to all the noise. My Spenser was coalescing into a nuanced person—Stan's Spenser was the scary alien we had brought home from the hospital. Not that I wasn't worried about the future, but could not share these concerns with a partner whose glasses reflected the moving images on a screen.

So even though Stan's negative comments during yet another hospital follow-up visit did not surprise me, they caused me to distance myself from him even further. The waiting room was empty except for a young man and a toddler. Another television set flickered in the corner. I shed my winter coat, and waited for our names to be called. Spenser slept in his car seat, tucked in by his Winnie the Pooh blanket with the bright green trees.

"I'm going to go pay a bill," Stan announced. Now alone, I noticed that the linoleum tiles in the floor were tan.

A heavy door opened. "Mr. and Mrs. Gardner?"

I followed the physical therapist to a room with a bright blue vinyl mat on the floor which was littered with toys: blocks shaped in various cubes, balls, a listless stuffed monkey.

"Please give us your assessment of what tasks Spenser can perform," she said as she leafed through the chart. "I'm looking for his birthday."

"January 30." The yellow sheet, the Denver prescreening developmental questionnaire, had questions such as can your child lift his head? Can your child roll over? Spenser lay on the vinyl mat on his back, deathly still. He opened his eyes when the occupational therapist loosened his blanket. I perused the questions, then focused on the print with growing panic, and read them again. There wasn't even one question I could honestly answer affirmatively. I glanced up at the sound of Stan's voice.

"Where were you?" Stan demanded. "I came back to the waiting room and nobody was there. I didn't know what happened to you, where you went." I remained silent throughout his fit.

Spenser laid on the mat, surrounded by the stationary toys he had not touched or moved.

"That baby isn't going to play with any of those toys," Stan said.

"But he had a very rough birth. I dilated too quickly and then pushed for three hours. They used a forceps on him. He had to be in the neonatal care unit." As I rattled off excuses for the physical therapist, deep down I feared that none of them made any difference.

When Brendan was a baby, he met all the developmental milestones. From the time he first said "Momma," instead of a transition period filled with baby babble, Brendan formed complete sentences with a noun, verb and direct object. He would sit in his high chair, with his chubby legs sticking straight out and arms folded on the tray, and expound on various subjects like a talking oracle.

Our friend Sharon, hearing this speech from a baby whose head was barely covered with hair, shrieked with amazement.

"I can't believe he's talking that well. Listen to him!"

Stan and I looked at each other, drawing blanks. Because he was our firstborn, we had no idea what to expect. Brendan kicked his legs and sucked on his fist.

On a wildflower identification walk when Brendan was about three, he could name plants which the adults had forgotten when the trail led back to the starting point in the windy meadow.

"Um, what was that one again?" a woman asked, pointing to a white, lacy plant.

"Queen Anne's lace," Brendan said with authority. Cat's claw. Indian paintbrush. Poppy mallow. We would point, he called out the name. He knew them all.

"That kid is bound for Harvard," the woman said.

I had already started a payroll savings plan for Brendan's college tuition. Before Spenser, I had never anticipated that any baby of mine might not go to college.

At the daycare, and at home, Brendan would argue vociferously if anything displeased him. This statesman, this pompous little orator, could be difficult.

"That kid's going to be a lawyer like his father," the daycare provider stated.

I demurred, but she was right. Brendan's potential was limitless.

My memories of Brendan faded as I contemplated Spenser lying on the hospital mat. I couldn't will Spenser to lift his head, to roll over, to be a healthy baby. I could arrive at the office early so I wouldn't miss any phone calls. I could schedule two or three conferences in the same location to minimize travel, but I couldn't control this mysterious malady that caused Spenser to be surrounded by toys, but rendered him unable to play with them.

Chapter 8

At The Office

The Monday morning in early April when I returned to work as an investigator at the civil rights agency had finally arrived. I fished around in my closet for a loose-fitting business dress that would accommodate my post-partum waistline. Because we dropped Spenser off at the home of the wonderful daycare provider that we had interviewed, I did not feel conflicted about leaving him. Back in my cubicle, nothing had changed in two months. I requested new case file assignments, and got down to work. As for the nagging tapes about Spenser replaying in my mind, drowning them out, at least during office hours, was a relief.

I was glad to be reunited with my former colleagues, but also guarded because I didn't know how many details of Spenser's "developmentally delayed" condition I should reveal. Underneath my insulating layer of rationalizations, I could not shake that I was responsible for his disorder, because he came from my body. Throughout his life, I would always feel somewhat guilty about his awkward gait, or his phrases uttered in a nasal, dysphonic tone, because our children are reflections of ourselves.

A brisk wind rattled the window adjoining my cubicle. The fluorescent lighting shone over the carpeting, desks and cubicles, which were uniformly steel grey. Above muted ringing telephones, the front door slammed.

"How are you today, Mikayla?" the receptionist asked.

"On my way to heaven and enjoying the ride," Mikayla declared as she swept into the office. "I am blessed in the name of Jesus."

The education specialist had complained that Mikayla proselytized and that religion had no place in a state government office. I wasn't offended, because Mikayla was about the only person who inquired about Spenser. I wondered what everybody else was thinking, because nobody bothered to get the facts from me. Maybe they didn't care because they had their own busy lives, or were too embarrassed to bring it up. Perhaps they sensed that misfortune might be contagious.

One day I stood in the copy room, surrounded by manila files and filing cabinets, waiting for the Xerox machine. Mikayla grabbed the collated material from the tray. After she pushed the start button, the machine resumed its heaving and clacking. She wore a tight-fitting sweater dress, and her ears were studded with tiny diamonds. Her hair was pulled back in a chignon. She glanced up at me.

"My mother had to be taken to the hospital again last week for her diabetes. My brother told me to get down there because it was a serious attack." She paused to sort some papers, and pressed the start button again.

"The next morning when I went into her room, she was sitting up and eating breakfast." She tapped the stack of papers on the table. "I just had to praise His name."

She paused and looked at me directly.

"And you, Margaret, with Spenser, all you need are two or three gathered together in His name, and you easily have that many."

I shifted my weight from one leg to the other, and leaned up against the table. The Xerox machine trays moved up and down as the copies spun out, collated and stapled.

"I believe in it, Margaret, I believe in the victory that He promised. And I am going to be there to claim the victory with you." Mikayla's voice swelled when she said the word "victory." Then she gathered up her papers and left the room.

I had known Mikayla since I was first employed by the commission as an investigator, before I married Stan. Devoted to her church, she treated others with integrity. Although my religious denomination does not emphasize evangelism, Mikayla and I shared a bond of faith, and a belief in miracles, that with God all things are possible. With

Mikayla I could share my innermost desires and would find acceptance. When I was hugely pregnant with Spenser, I could hardly wait to tell her about an amazing statement that came out of Brendan's mouth.

"Do you know what Brendan said to me last night, out of the blue?"

"What?" She waited for my reply, her eyes smiling and her lips slightly parted, as we stood before the reception desk. Brendan had just celebrated his third birthday.

"He said to me, 'Don't worry Mama, Jesus will help you get your baby out.'"

The smile left Mikayla's face and she became very solemn.

"That's amazing, Margaret, and it's a blessing, a blessing that He imparts His word even to small children, and they understand it, sometimes even better than adults."

True to her promise, Mikayla did stand by me at the very end, as one of the mourners at the funeral.

Chapter 9

Believe

Because Spenser continued to crane his head back and stare vacantly, his primary care physician suggested a consult with Dr. Dan Webb, an ophthalmologist, to see if he were blind.

A blind woman worked in the snack bar of my office building. Katy always had a smile on her face, and as she shuffled behind the counter from the cash register to the food receptacles, she cocked her head from side to side. Her eyes, only the whites visible, apparently saw nothing. She spoke rather loudly, and knew everybody.

"How's your baby? You just got back from maternity leave, right?" Katy stated, her hand extended to receive my change.

"Now they think that he might be blind."

"Oh boy. I remember my mother telling me that when I was born, she knew something wasn't right, but when the doctor told her I was born blind she cried and cried and cried." Katy hobbled away, her hand trailing the gleaming stainless steel of the counter.

Dr. Webb examined Spenser in a darkened room with an illuminated screen. He pulled out an instrument with a tiny beam of light and shone it into Spenser's dilated pupils. Then he took Spenser away to another room while I waited.

"He isn't blind," Dr. Webb stated, with a hint of impatience and sarcasm that suggested he wondered why Spenser was ever referred to him.

One less thing to worry about, but in that spring of 1991 when the winter thawed, and I changed him from long-sleeved sleepers to onesies that exposed his limbs, his bony, emaciated body had a grotesque appearance. In a photograph, I propped him up in a red wagon. His skeletal skull was the largest and most dominant part of his body. Deathly pale, he resembled a wizened old man, barely holding on to life. At the same time, the television broadcast images of starving Kurdish babies being buried in Iran, their young mothers heavily veiled as they lowered their tightly bundled babies into their graves. I mourned for these mothers, and for Spenser, who seemed to be kept alive by grace alone. We could have found him dead in his crib any morning, another predictable outcome for babies with one of those strange-sounding diagnoses listed in the thick medical pages of the pediatric book of horrors.

When I wakened to breast feed Spenser in the middle of the night, he would cry and refuse after a feeble attempt. Even later with a bottle, he regurgitated most of whatever he did consume. In the nighttime shadows, the expression on his little scrawny face alternated between serenity and the contortions of a monster. Alone and afraid, my nagging suspicions resurfaced, that he had this horrible diagnosis, this Sotos syndrome. Every night, Spenser and I wandered through vacant halls, gliding through rooms and chill drafts like ghosts, stalked by abject horror.

Spenser kept losing weight. Whereas his weight was at the fiftieth percentile when he was born, on May 20, his weight was at the fifth percentile even though I was feeding him all that I could.

During a visit to the office, my friend Jean held Spenser and bestowed him a kind, knowing smile. Being best friends with Jean was like having an older, wiser sister. Of moderate frame, she wore a feminine blouse, tight skirt and heels. Underneath her short auburn hair, her face was shaped like a heart.

"He's starving," she said in modulated tones. "He wants some food."

"Jean, I just can't deal with one more thing. I take him to the doctor's office several times a week so they can weigh him, we've had so many appointments with specialists . . . ," I explained as my voice trailed off. She sustained her adoring gaze.

"Mom," she insisted again, "he wants some food."

"I don't know. I just assume with all this attention on him they're doing all they can," I said.

However, Jean turned out to be right. The medical preoccupation with Sotos syndrome masked Spenser's life-threatening condition of wasting away. At her urging, I voiced my concern to the pediatrician, who didn't think a gastroenterology consult was necessary, so I made the appointment when he was on vacation.

Speeding toward KU Med Center very early in the morning, trying to make an eight a.m. appointment, I bumped into the car in front of me when I turned off I-70 at the Seventh Street exit. Although the bumpers absorbed most of the shock, when the driver, a grey-haired middle-aged man, ran his fingers along the smooth metallic whiteness of his car, he detected a barely perceptible ping.

"I'll call my insurance company about this. Do you have your card?" The man was not rude, but his ego was inseparable from his car.

I provided the information in the drizzling rain as the traffic sped by us, never disclosing that I was on my way to KU Med Center with a very sick child, not that the driver necessarily would have cared. Years earlier, when a vehicle slid through a snow-packed intersection and rammed into my car, I told the shamefaced people who emerged from their car to forget about it. Nobody was hurt, and the hassle of getting estimates, filling out paperwork and taking the car to the repair shop wasn't worth it.

After I parked on a side street, I snaked my way through the winding hallways of the sprawling medical center until I found the gastroenterology unit. Although the lights were on in the offices, no one had shown up yet. Down the hall, a technician wheeled a patient into an examining room. I collapsed into a chair, grateful for the respite of sitting still in the empty unit.

Within a short while, a nurse laid Spenser on an examining table and noted his skin tone, palpated his abdomen, and listened to his heart and respiration. She listed the present history on the chart as vomiting and cachexia, a term which means general physical wasting and malnutrition. She then ushered us into the office of a dark-haired doctor with dark-rimmed glasses, Dr. Alden Rose, a pediatric gastroenterologist.

"Susan, Susan, do we have that chart?" he asked as he lifted one file, and finding nothing underneath it, tossed it aside.

Susan leaned over him, opened a chart, and pressed the pages down.

"We'll be taking a look, doing an upper GI endoscopy, which means we'll put a tube down his esophagus. Spenser will be mildly sedated," Dr. Rose stated.

"Can I be with him?" I asked.

"No, Susan will show you to the waiting room," he said.

In the waiting room, with voices coming from the television and vinyl chairs in symmetrical rows, another mother was camped out with her knitting. Her daughter Racquel, a dark-haired girl of eleven or twelve, propelled herself in a wheelchair. Raquel appeared to have a healthy upper torso, and to be alert and engaged, but her legs were atrophied.

"So you're here for your daughter's medical consultation?"

"Spina bifida, she was born with spina bifida," her mother explained to me without hesitation after Racquel was called into another room.

"So how . . . ?" I fidgeted in the chair. "How have you coped with that situation?" She dropped her knitting into her lap.

"It's just a part of who she is, but she's so much more than her disability. She really likes to draw. Her teacher even recommended that her work be displayed in the art show. Then she has causes that she is passionate about, such as saving the environment and helping animals."

Mentioning next to nothing about the spina bifida, the mother continued describing Racquel's interests and vocational aspirations. I had never envisioned what Spenser might become due to my preoccupation with his medical problems, but while listening to this mother chat about art, animals, and living things, it dawned on me that Spenser might have a future.

I was summoned back to Dr. Rose.

Acute gastric esophagitis. I gawked at the films, which meant next to nothing to me, until Dr. Rose pointed to ugly, dark red ulcerations in the gastric lining, probably present ever since the nasogastric tube was removed in the pediatric intensive care unit. Dr. Rose prescribed Tagamet and beefed up his formula. I still have the formula recipe stored in my kitchen cabinet, alongside the glass measuring cups. I'll never get rid of it, this documented evidence that Dr. Alden Rose saved Spenser's life.

After only a few weeks of these feedings, Spenser filled out like a helium balloon. On our old oak table in the dining room, I colored flowers, a sun, and some grass in bright, primary hues with crayons. Thank you, I wrote to the doctor. Thank you, thank you, thank you.

The photograph in our Christmas card that year featured a smiling Spenser, bulging out of his red and white Christmas suit. The accompanying card, a Mary Engelbreit drawing of Santa Claus, was simply inscribed "Believe." For at least that festive, joyful season, I kept the spectral Sotos syndrome at bay. Spenser wasn't disabled. All his problems could be blamed on the esophagitis.

CHAPTER 10

Jean

At least ten years after Spenser died, Jean moved to Washington state. Because she played a major role in Spenser's childhood, I flew to Seattle in order to add her pieces into the larger puzzle of his life. We connected in the main lobby. She was the same petite, smiling Jean.

"Your hair is more grey," she said to me.

A few days later after some sightseeing, Jean leaned back in her recliner with her feet propped up. I perched beside her on the couch. Outside her picture window, the tall mountains with rugged vegetation stretched into the clouds.

"What do you remember about Spenser's birth?"

She smiled, grasping the mug of coffee in her hands.

"He was not ready to be born. In the weeks leading up to the birth they decided it was important to take him at that time. They had some dumb ass reason. You went through endless godawful labor."

The white golden retriever sprawled before us on the carpet.

"What are your first memories about him?"

"The first time I held him was at Becky's wedding. When you handed him to me, he was fussy. I asked him, 'What's the problem? Why are you crying?' 'Please tell my mom that I'm starving to death' is what he communicated. He was getting just enough nourishment to keep himself alive and so much love from you, he didn't die. He knew who I was. You and I were close."

"How could he communicate that to you?"

"He just said to me, 'Tell my mom I'm starving to death.' I'm in touch with my guides and I told them to go to the ends of the universe to find what this child needs to survive. They brought back such powerful spirits that their force had to be buffered, funneled through me. I remember when I picked him up an incredible fusion of energy flowed through me. My guides told me that if I did not get him help he would not live. I remember just screaming at you, when you believed the doctors who did not know what they were doing."

Whom should I have listened to if not the doctors? Spenser sometimes saw two or three specialists per week. But Jean did stand in front of my cubicle and say, "He's starving to death," while for me it was just one more thing to deal with.

Jean has always expressed that she is in touch with her guides, especially an American Indian woman Jean referred to as Mona. Jean consulted her for health matters, and she came in handy when we needed a parking space. Guides were not part of my frame of reference before I met Jean. I was skeptical, but did not think she was crazy. Of course, other coworkers in the office did.

"After you came back from the consult at KU Medical Center and he got on Tagamet and a special formula, he went gangbusters. His healing spirits came back and periodically gave him infusions. After his first birthday, he sat on my lap and let me know he was doing well. He did not want to die. He truly wanted to live."

"Do you think Spenser knew he was disabled?"

"No," Jean asserted, "Spenser was not disabled. Spenser's mind was good and strong and clear. His physical development was just slightly behind the rest of him. At times he would explode because he could not get his body to do what he intended."

"Realistically, Jean, he had an IQ of like 70."

"No, that's not right. Spenser was not stupid. He was not disabled. There was a gap between what his mind and body could do."

"He had the diagnosis of Sotos syndrome."

"He was terribly aggravated by his lack of nourishment. For every week he did not get what he needed, it took him a year to catch up."

Outside the window, the mountains were sunny from one angle and dark and cloudy from another. A rain shower pelted the yard even though the sun was out.

Jean rearranged her robe over her knees. "I'm not questioning he had Sotos syndrome, but what happened was like a brick wall in front of him. I truly believe that if Spenser had lived to be twenty-five years old, he would have been a normal individual."

"What about school? He was not at grade level in some subjects."

"They held him back. He was not able to make the translation so they could understand it. I could understand him."

It would be easy to dismiss Jean's sentiments as denial, or wishful thinking, but there were some paradoxes surrounding Spenser's disability. For example, in late May after he died at the end of April, Spenser was posthumously awarded honors in reading and spelling at his school's final assembly. Honors, at grade level, not a watered down curriculum designed especially for Spenser.

Jean rearranged her robe. "You were a wonderfully nurturing mother. He would not have lived if you had not loved him as much as you did. Even though you did not recognize the physical thing going on inside him, you recognized his value to the world. That's what kept him going."

I gripped the warm tea mug, steamy and aromatic in my hands. "Why did he leave us?"

"He was always living on borrowed time and he knew that. Think about the way he embraced life. I don't remember him having angst toward anyone. I'd say he's pretty happy right now."

"What would he be doing if he were alive now?"

"Acting, of course. I communicate with him in that grove of evergreens in the yard. That is where I am mostly likely to see him."

"What does he look like when he appears to you?"

"He's wearing a cap with a visor that is yellow, red and blue, along with kids' jeans and a polo shirt. I first saw him in August. After I had surgery in October I saw him every day."

After I left the living room, I crossed the yard to the grove of evergreens. Off to the side of their yard, the grove is an open area surrounded by a circle of evergreens. The vegetation crackled under my feet. I can't say I sensed Spenser's presence here in this grove, but when I do, intense emotions surge through me, like an electric current. A source of energy. A source of light.

CHAPTER 11

The Hospital Visit

In the office, my mind wandered as I read a detailed position statement from a company. Today Jean was travelling, so the office seemed a lonelier place. At about noon, I put my leftovers into the microwave and turned the knob for two minutes. Job announcements and memoranda were posted on the tack board. Nothing new.

Rick, my former supervisor, stirred his soup after he took it out of the microwave, and as the steam rose from the Styrofoam bowl, he was about to say something. I had had a long history with this man, who once suggested that he and I avoid the Hilton, but find a quiet little hotel so we could save money on expenses at an upcoming training conference. He sexually harassed every woman in the office at one time or the other, regardless of her age, race or weight. He received occasional slaps on the wrist for this behavior in an agency which investigated complaints of sexual harassment and imposed subsequent fines and penalties on employers. I worked with all kinds of people at the agency. All kinds.

Clutching his plastic fork and napkin, Rick scowled as he looked out of the window, sighed, and sat down again.

"The question I have," he said, his voice breaking with tension, "is what we're going to do about the office lunches."

I turned to notice the frown clouding his steely eyes.

"Some people want to continue having it every month, and other people say they're tired of it, don't want to have to bring in potluck," he continued.

I listened to him, and realized that he expected a response to this weighty question.

"Well, the people who want to participate can continue to come and those who don't, won't," I may have answered. Maybe I wasn't even that nice. Maybe I really blew up, because I no longer had any patience for much of the trivial garbage that had consumed countless hours of deliberation before I had Spenser.

But now that my duties had changed slightly, Rick was no longer my supervisor. My new supervisor, Bill, was tall, well-groomed, and always dressed in a suit. He was also an ex-Marine with two or three tours of duty in Vietnam, so he often told stories about the war.

"I can remember riding back from town, passed out in the wagon, with gunfire and grenades exploding all around us," he told us once when we convened in the break room. "It's a wonder I'm still alive."

"Then why did you ever go to town?" My amazement resulted from having a female perspective.

He gave me a dead pan look for about five seconds.

Bill was calculating but also gentle, and he had a quiet way of supporting me, although others warned that my loyalties might be misplaced.

On the day of my annual job evaluation, Bill sat behind his desk in a suit and tie, a large window behind him silhouetting his head and shoulders. Because I was taking Spenser to several medical appointments per week, I had not completed enough investigations to qualify for an outstanding evaluation. There's no arguing with numbers. I had not met the standard.

"You're having all these appointments, but when he gets older, he won't remember none of it," he said, sensing my anxiety.

He opened my personnel file and handed me his completed evaluation for my signature. He had checked the box, "Outstanding."

"Bill, I don't deserve this. I just missed it. I don't have enough cases."

His face registered no emotion.

"I know that, but I marked you outstanding for the extra work you have done for Barbara in the intake department."

There may have been a few afternoons that I helped Barbara with some phone calls.

I studied his face. Not a muscle flinched. Not even a twinkle in his eye. His mind was made up.

"Right," I said, signed the evaluation, and handed it back to him.

I never did know how Bill could keep such a straight face. A few years later, I sat with Bill in another waiting room of St. Vincent Hospital, where Brendan and Spenser were born, and Spenser was treated so many times. Bill's son had broken his neck in a car accident, faced paralysis, and was fighting for his life.

"Margaret, we're going to beat this thing. Todd is going to walk out of here." Wearing a pullover sweater with his elbows resting on his knees, Bill looked at me as though he could see to the bottom of my soul. I intuited that Todd was never going to walk out of there, and that Bill was clinging to the hope that if he wished it with enough conviction, he could make it so.

The next day, Mikayla, Kim, Barbara and I took an extended lunch hour, and brought lunch to his wife Dorothy, mother of his son.

We found her in the waiting room, staring down at the nubs of the grey carpeting. She seemed to be very far away. Without shedding our coats, we waited for her to lead the conversation.

"You know, I remember the first time that Bill came to the house," she said. We clutched the takeout food with grease marks on the bag.

"I was supposed to go to my girlfriend's house that night, but then this date with him came up. He drove around the block a few times. I don't know why, because he certainly knew where I lived." Her eyes sparkled, but she was focusing on something we could not see.

"Sally and I had been good friends for quite a while. She was at the house that night. Bill came into the living room," she continued. We struggled to follow the logic of her narrative, but she was skipping around too much for her story to be comprehensible. She regaled us with stories of their courtship as though she were a gay Southern belle, and we were her subservient admirers, attending to her every whim.

We stayed longer and offered her the food, which she declined. She did not come down from this reverie, but waltzed through every moment of their first dates, never mentioning their child who lay in peril in the adjoining intensive care unit.

We did not ask about her son, and glanced at our watches. It was time to go back to the office, and we never took off our coats.

"I don't know if Bill and Dorothy realize how completely their lives will change if Todd is confined to a wheelchair," Barbara remarked as we approached the elevator.

Todd did eventually leave the hospital, but in a wheelchair. As we headed toward the hospital parking lot that day, I thought that Dorothy's ramblings were disoriented, even peculiar, considering that she seemed to be in a time warp that separated her from her son's accident. Now I think I understand. When faced with the chaos of intense crisis, we start at the very beginning, because if we can trace through our limited logic how we arrived in the middle of this maelstrom, we can restore order. Dorothy was asking herself a simple question: How did all of this begin?

Along with Dorothy, as I construct his story, I attempt to decipher the mysteries surrounding Spenser's earthly existence and untimely passing. His photograph in a frame with embossed flowers, a drum and a cello is next to my computer. The young child, with platinum blonde hair, silk against a broad porcelain forehead. An impish smile. In another picture over my desk, he looks like an angel, ethereal, not of this world. I ask him, "Spenser, what happened?" His unchanging expressions blend in with the silent, stationary furniture in the room, so my question goes unanswered.

But unexpected tragedy never makes sense, and defies classification into our rigid systems of logic. We're left grasping our desiccated corsages and yellowed prom programs years after the event, in the dark without a clue.

CHAPTER 12

The Big Yeller Dog

When he was about eight months old, Spenser was getting weekly physical therapy because he could not sit up. On the bright vinyl mat, the physical therapist laid Spenser on his side. She showed Spenser how, if he walked himself up with his arms, he could attain the sitting position. I doubted he could do it, at least not for a long while.

One subsequent evening after dinner, I herded the children into the television room. Brendan walked, but Spenser, I had to carry. The night through the picture window was a solid black. Because Brendan was crying, I had my back turned away from Spenser.

When I turned to face Spenser, there he was, sitting up on the gold shag carpet, beaming his brightest smile. He had done it, all by himself, surprising me with a positive outcome.

Several months later, when Spenser was just over a year old, Stan was stretched out on the couch, which was upholstered in a green Oriental pattern. Spenser, wearing his green and white-striped sleeper, stood up. His body undulated slightly, as though the ground were shifting beneath him, but his knees locked, and he maintained his balance for about five seconds. Once again, Spenser seemed so proud of himself.

Stan sat up from the couch and swung his legs to the carpeting. This wasn't necessarily supposed to happen. Our frame of reference was of a disabled baby who probably had some syndrome, and might never walk, but the evidence was insurmountable. He was standing, had grown so tall. Then Brendan tackled him, and as they tussled in the folds of the blue curtain, Spenser wailed his characteristic "whaaa" sound that signaled Brendan was bothering him.

In the hallway is a baby picture of Spenser taken after he could sit up. One knee is cocked and the other is straight. His hands are clasped together, and he is smiling at the camera. I reveled in buying wonderful clothes for happy, toddling Spenser, matching caps in the bright primary colors of red, yellow and blue.

Jean and I took Spenser to a neonatal follow-up visit at the hospital. As he toddled in short even steps past the nurse's station, he held out his arms as though he were tyrannosaurus rex. Dr. Siddington had not seen Spenser since his dismissal from the neonatal care unit. When Spenser advanced toward him like a wind-up toy, Dr. Siddington jumped back several feet, as though he had seen a ghost. This was not the same child who lay weakly on the mat, unable to play with any of the toys a few months earlier.

In the march of the ensuing weeks, I could almost feel the earth inclining toward the sun. As it journeyed in its arc across the sky day after day, Spenser reflected its golden rays as his abilities grew.

"This disability thing, it isn't going to be so bad," I said to my sister when she called. I stopped the late night journaling and constant mantra of prayers. I should have taken the time to relate to those kids in special education, to learn that this boy loves chocolate ice cream, or that girl is deathly afraid of spiders. They also live in this crazy world, and how they deal with the crosscurrents defines what kind of people they become, just as it is with us.

More importantly, we were having fun with Spenser. He loved the zoo, the children's museum, the library, dressing up as a jack-o'-lantern for Halloween. We would make accommodations for him if necessary, but so far there was no need. As my anxiety lessened, it became easier to treat him as a typically-developing child. The unknown other, the changeling, was being exchanged for a human child of my own.

So when Spenser was two and we returned to KU Med Center for a follow-up visit with Dr. Heidi Adams, a clinical geneticist who had been following his Sotos syndrome, I was ready for what she had to say. This young woman with honey-colored hair that reached her shoulders had two young daughters of her own.

"He has it," she stated.

I didn't flinch because it didn't hurt.

"So, tell me again why you were uncertain of the diagnosis before?"

"A telling characteristic of Sotos syndrome is advanced bone age, and his early nutritional difficulties and possibly the placental infarct prevented it."

"Actually, I'm glad to hear that. Now that we know what we're dealing with, we can made sounder decisions," I said. "If I were to have another baby, what are the chances it would also have this syndrome?"

She shook her head. "Really, that's just about impossible to predict."

Dr. Adams and I talked about all the funny, unexpected little things that Spenser was doing, and then it was time to drive back. Unlike other drives home from KU Med Center, I wasn't mentally rewinding tapes of worst-case scenarios. Instead, on this hot July afternoon, I planned to head out to the swimming pool.

So Spenser's official diagnosis was Sotos syndrome. It is estimated to occur once in every 10,000 births, and possibly results from an autosomal dominant inheritance pattern. Affected children are characterized by advanced bone age, advanced growth in early childhood, an antimongoloid slant of the eyelids, a pointed chin or moderate prognathism, a large, dolichocephalic head and prominent forehead, poor motor coordination and verbal and motor delays. Do with it what you will.

But most importantly, the gloomy prognoses forecast at the time of his birth never materialized. He did walk and did talk, albeit several months behind schedule, but he eventually did everything his way, and it was just fine. Then, of course, he danced to music, and shattered a bowl on the floor, and ate spaghetti, and all of the dark hair he was born with was replaced by a silvery golden blonde. He toddled around in his red corduroys with the train appliqués and smiled at everyone. Nobody frowned at him. We must not have told him about the dire predictions, the dark clouds surrounding his birth, or maybe he wasn't listening or didn't care. He was too busy living his life, but he did weather continual health problems. His nose was always runny. He drooled. His words were nasal. It was as though he constantly had a cold, and for a time every night I hooked a green plastic mask to his face, held in place by an elastic strap that went around his head. We rocked and read stories while the respiratory therapy machine hummed and produced the steam that he inhaled. Despite his challenges, he surveyed the world calmly, with his slightly labored breaths, and lymph nodes swollen the size of walnuts just under his ear lobes. It was inevitable that this child would have to have ear tubes.

On the last day of December, the offices of the ear nose and throat specialist glowed like a gold band near the top of a tall medical office building, enveloped by a thick, damp fog. The waiting room was peaceful, a respite from the cold. Tired from the demands of the day, patients waited for their appointments while they sat passively in their chairs, motionless, like characters in a dream. I relished reading magazines under the softly glowing overhead lights.

Spenser wore a tall, cone-shaped hat fastened under his chin which the daycare provider had made because it was New Year's Eve. Spenser cruised to a low table and rearranged the magazines.

"I go to a New Year's party," he said to a man dressed in a three-piece suit who was absorbed by the pages of his newspaper.

From over the pages of my magazine, Spenser scurried to the end of the row of chairs, crouched down to pick up a small toy, and brought it back to the table.

"I have a New Year's party," he said in a low voice to a teenager, who rested his sleeping head on the arm of the chair.

"New Year's party," he droned, as he set the waiting room straight with his purposeful tasks.

I did not have the heart to tell him that he wasn't going to any New Year's party because Stan and I were grateful for the chance to stay home and rest.

New Year's party. New Year's party. He wore the hat proudly, with a quiet dignity. Nobody laughed at him. In the medical office, he was celebrating New Year's Eve at his party without the trappings of the streamers, the confetti, the chorus of "Auld Lang Syne." He never needed permission to make his own way in the world, to possess his quiet insistence and determination.

Dr. Lee spoke in staccato. He was a short man with peppery hair who wore yellow scrubs. Because his English was difficult to understand, a nurse stood at his side to translate.

WALLKILL VIEW FARM
15 STATE RT. 299W
NEW PALTZ NY 12561
*** (845) 255-8050 ***

THANK YOU !

DATE 08/30/2019 FRI TIME 17:33

PRODUCE	$1.67
SODA or WATER 11	$2.99
DEPOSIT	$0.05
SODA or WATER 11	$2.99
NYS TAX	$0.48
TOTAL	$8.18
CREDIT CARD	$8.18

CLERK 1   000210   00002

WALMART ALWAYS LOW PRICES

WEST TH STATE ST

NEW PALTZ NY 12561

*** (845) 555-0808 ***

THANK YOU !

DATE 08/30/2019 FRI TIME 11:33

PRODUCE $1.81
500Z 1T WATER 1T 400Z $5.25
DEPOSIT $0.02
500Z 1T WATER 1T 400Z $5.25
VAT.TAX $0.48
TOTAL $8.18
CREDIT CARD $8.18
CLERK 1   012000   50000

"We do operation Monday," Dr. Lee stated. It was a Friday.

"So Monday," Stan extended his hand in a rolling motion, "several weeks from now?"

"No, in three day. Monday. Be at hospital six a.m."

Spenser was crying when he woke from the anesthesia. A nurse dropped him into my arms and told me to take him out into the hall.

We went out into the corridor, a busy intersection of the hospital. Streams of people filed by, some dressed in surgical scrubs, others in street clothes. There was talking, voices, the constant din. A jackhammer sputtered across the courtyard in the distance.

Spenser stopped crying. He jerked his head around, and looked over my shoulder. I listened for something out of the ordinary. He yanked his head back to the left, shifting his weight in my arms. I registered voices, a blue jay shrieking outside, just ordinary people making their usual sounds, but for him, he was hearing a whole new world. With every successive layer of his medical problems that was peeled away, Spenser emerged with greater clarity.

Although our schedule was still crammed with medical appointments, Spenser was on a trajectory to healing and wholeness that could not be suppressed. I didn't know whether to attribute his transformation to medicine, miracles, or a combination of both.

For example, there was the incident before Spenser's appointment with the speech pathologist. The winds of late spring were pleasantly cool, blowing the dust into the bristled welcome mat before the front door. Spenser played outside on the porch without a jacket. I could hear the screeching sounds as he pulled his yellow metal dump truck across the cement.

I hoisted the ridged tube of the vacuum system onto my shoulder and trudged up the stairs. The noise drowned out the sounds of Spenser's truck, only for a moment, as I vacuumed the orange Persian rug.

I dropped it to check on Spenser. From the deck, I could see him playing right below me. He looked up at me and smiled.

There might be time to clean the bathroom. I misted the glass mirror with a spray of vinegar and water.

I again pushed open the sliding glass door to check on Spenser. This time, he was gone, as were the sounds of the metal dump truck. Only the breezes jostled the trees.

I bounded down the stairs out onto the front porch. I surveyed the gardens, the driveway, the sloping hill behind the house. He had vanished.

In the east is a pasture with high grass, that ends with a creek that winds its way through a thick tangle of trees, and then to the north, the neighbors have a trash dump, a cavernous hole with sharp, rusty metal edges jumbled up among broken glass and spines of deer carcasses. In the west where the gravel driveway leads up the hill, a truck rumbled down the road. Any of the undergrowth could swallow a small child. How far could he have travelled in fifteen minutes? Or was it a half hour?

"If I have to call the sheriff, Stan will kill me," I said to the rock wall.

I listened to my intuition as to which way to sprint, which has spoken to me as far back as I can remember with a guiding voice, neither male nor female, or of any recognizable person, just a voice.

That way. I charged up the hill, my breaths becoming more labored as I met the sharp incline, and passed the fruit trees to the dusty gravel road. I dashed past the cedar tree, situated in the middle of an otherwise treeless pasture.

At the bottom of the hill, Spenser was hiking at a good clip in the middle of the road, with our yellow Labrador retriever, Beau, trotting along behind him.

Men were sawing trees, littering the road with some fallen branches. As I ran to Spenser, a man with a grey tattered shirt regarded me as I panted.

"He was just coming along, walking down the road, with that big yeller dog," the man said after a moment. I scooped Spenser up in my arms.

The next day I rushed into Jean's cubicle.

"Jean, Spenser got away from me, and started down the road, with Beau following him. He could have been hit by a speeding teenager!" Her phone rang. She told the receptionist to take a message.

"He never would have been hit by a speeding teenager." She swiveled in her chair to face me. Her brooch was pinned at the top of her apricot blouse.

"Why not?" I sat down in the green vinyl chair next to her desk.

"The teenage boy would have been run off the road instead." Jean's auburn hair was feathered softly around her smiling face. "His guides are protecting Spenser."

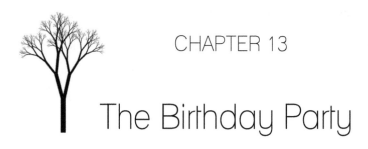

CHAPTER 13

The Birthday Party

Even though we now grow organic fruits and vegetables and I always have adhered to a healthy diet, my mother was never averse to taking the kids to McDonald's. So one spring afternoon, not long after his escape act, Spenser, seated in his high chair, tore open the plastic encasing his Happy Meal not far from a cascading sheet of water. My mother and I chitchatted while Brendan ate his French fries.

Before Spenser was born, in another McDonald's when I was travelling, a young mother and father ate with their child, also seated in a high chair. They pulled the wrapper off his hamburger and positioned the straw so he could drink from his paper cup because the child had noticeable, pronounced physical disabilities. Other customers, seated at adjoining tables or in line, either shot him furtive glances, or stopped in their tracks to gape at him. The young couple paid no attention to the gawkers, but continued tending to their child with dignity. For them, sitting with their child in a McDonald's restaurant must have required tremendous courage.

Throughout history, those with physical or mental disabilities have been alternately revered or spurned. Oedipus regarded Tiresias, the blind oracle, with esteem, whereas hallucinating persons, believed to be possessed by demons, were tortured. The fairy tales of the Grimm brothers abound with dwarfs and giants who have secret knowledge, and access to otherworldly realms. Because of their peculiarities, those with disabilities unsettle us, and whatever we cannot understand, we fear.

When I was a Brownie scout, our troop made party favors for children with disabilities at a foundation for crippled children. Standing in the hallway in our crisp, brown uniforms, we gripped our gifts of decorated cardboard stuffed with trinkets and candy. Waiting outside, we could see the handicapped children seated in a semi-circle in the day room. Most were in wheelchairs. Others had feet and hands twisted into unnatural poses. Some drooled with their mouths open, their heads supported by a head rest. A few emitted low, unintelligible guttural sounds.

"Now when we're allowed to go into that room, you will choose a child and present your favor to him," our Brownie leader instructed us.

We shivered in that hallway, because we were terrified of them. When the signal was given, I darted into the semi-circle, threw my favor toward the feet of one of the children, and sprinted back out as fast as I could.

My mother's voice interrupted my recollection of how cruel I had been to that child. "Have you seen the new children's section at the library?" she asked.

"Yes, I think they did a good job," I said, wondering how the wall of water in the McDonald's operated.

Young children began congregating at a long table off to our side. Apparently they were celebrating a birthday because colorful helium balloons were tethered to the table with tinsel. A young woman set out a tiered chocolate cake topped with candles, with ice cream next to it.

A little boy, carrying a present wrapped with pink paper and a purple bow, approached Spenser.

"Hi, Spenser. How are you doing?"

Spenser beamed him his smile. Then the little boy assumed his place at the table while his father helped him take off his jacket.

My mother and I conversed about our next garage sale, plans for the summer. Another small girl arrived with another present, then another little boy sauntered into the restaurant, stopping to greet Spenser.

Once the little guests were all assembled at the long table, a woman scooped out the ice cream and lit the birthday candles. The children's voices blended into an excited prattle.

As I glanced over at them, I pieced together that I knew all of them from somewhere.

Spenser's preschool daycare. They were all in Spenser's class, and he hadn't been invited.

Or had he? Some parents didn't send birthday invitations through the mail, but stuffed them into the cubbyholes, where they mix with a jumble of construction paper artwork. The invitation could have dropped to the floor, never made it home. Yet my doubts remained that this mother had purposely excluded him from the party.

I didn't recognize the hostess, but I watched the scene over Spenser's shoulder as he held his hamburger, and I could envision a steady stream of future birthday invitations arriving in elementary school, when Spenser would realize he had been excluded.

I made a plan, and decided that if Spenser were not invited to future parties, I would inquire with a syrupy voice, "I'm sorry, but we must have lost our invitation to Brandon's party. Could you fill me in on that date and location again?" Of course the hostess would apologize for the oversight. If not, I would explain to her that there was no reason Spenser could not be treated as a typically-developing child.

Perhaps it was because of my proactive attitude, but in all the ensuing years I never had to make that phone call.

But even though I was developing coping strategies, and I perceived that Spenser's prognosis brightened with the passing months, if Stan had anything to say about Spenser it was negative, so I had stopped seeking support from Stan.

Did I detest him because of his attitude toward Spenser? I wasn't happy about it, but I was increasingly reconciled to the fact that I could not rely on this man for support. Besides, it was always so comforting to curl up next to a warm body at night, and he had an endearing way of standing in the shower, dripping wet, waiting for me to hand him his towel. Also, I'm an eternal optimist, believing that there is always hope, and sometimes he did astonish me. He surprised me when he consented to attending a Families Together conference for parents with children with special needs on a wintry day several months after the birthday party. Besides functioning as a support group, Families Together provides education and information about available services for special needs children. So we bundled up Brendan and Spenser, strapped them in their car seats, and proceeded to the Holiday Inn. A colorful clown with an orange mop of hair greeted us, and escorted our children to another room.

We found our conference room, filled with other parents, where we sunk into the peace of having no other pressing responsibilities, or the demands of small children.

Yet there was a leaden aura of sadness that hung in the room because our young children would never be classified as normal. Some would require a wheelchair, and consequently an adapted car with a levitating platform, wherever they had to go. Some children with limited self-help skills would require nearly around-the-clock care. Other parents were saddled with staggering medical bills. Most were juggling jobs, households and other children in addition to the one who demanded so much. The facilitator entered the room and invited us to introduce ourselves, along with our child.

"Hi, we're Shane and Tracy, and our son Brian has Down syndrome." Tracy smiled and gave a quick little wave. She had very long brown hair that hung over a cotton dress with puffy sleeves. Was she even twenty? Her husband cut a handsome profile, but was likewise very young. Both children themselves really, and this Down syndrome child was their firstborn. By bearing a Down child so young, Tracy defied the statistical correlation between Down syndrome and advanced maternal age.

A man with hair slicked with oil and a grey car coat said, "We're Lou and Mary, and our daughter Brianna has spina bifida." Spina bifida is a neural tube defect, that almost certainly causes paralysis below the waist. To avoid it, women in my prenatal class were warned not to take hot, soaking baths during pregnancy. To this mother, it happened anyway.

Next in the round of introductions was an older man, with grey hair shaved close to his head. "We're Ed and Sandy. We raised four healthy, normal children, absolutely nothing wrong with them, but then we adopted this one, and my gosh, what a mess," he said. "Like I say, our own biological children are healthy and normal, but this boy might have Fragile X syndrome, they aren't sure yet."

I clenched my teeth, and thought to myself, "Get the hell out of here. Who do you think you are, bragging, rubbing in the fact that your own genes are impeccable, as though any of these people deliberately chose to be in this room?"

In the stillness, I continued the internal rant. "No, you're perfect, and aren't you noble to take on this problem, you son of a bitch." My mouth remained shut. It would not have been politically correct to express such thoughts in an assembly where we were to accept everyone, without judgment.

Actually, in the wake of losing a child, cognitive thinking is easy to contain and defuse. The surprise attack comes from unbidden emotions such as anger or grief that strike from the rear. Not so much after he was born, but since Spenser died, I sometimes flare with jealousy when I come across a mother and child playing patty-cake, totally immersed in each other. Or when I witness the couple who videos their child's every action, or when I read Christmas letters about nothing other than the child's accomplishments. Then the evil thought enters my head, "What if he died?" and I have my answer. Their lives would be ripped apart.

As the large group disbanded for the breakout sessions, I watched Shane and Tracy disappearing down the hallway. With her crisp cotton dress and flowing partly-braided hair, she resembled Dorothy travelling down the Yellow Brick Road. They walked as though on air, because their movements were so quick and lively, yet held hands, as a token of their bond to each other. Perhaps they had been high school sweethearts. As I watched them, I prayed that nothing would ever shatter their innocence.

Later at the banquet, I deliberately positioned myself next to an outgoing dark-haired woman. As the waitress filled our water glasses, she talked about her twin girls, now two years old. Elena was typically developing, and Eleanor had cerebral palsy. She had the same dreams for both girls. Yes, Elena would certainly go to the prom, and eventually get married, but Eleanor would too. Just a few little adjustments along the way. All her teachers said so. They all wrote cards at her last birthday party, describing a variety of Eleanor's unique qualities.

"Are you finished with this plate?" the waiter asked.

"Yes," she answered. Either this woman to my right was a fool, or I might consider becoming more hopeful myself.

It was dark as we drove home. I don't know what Stan was thinking, but as the headlights broadcast light into the fog, I imagined a future scenario where maybe things really wouldn't be so bad. I had been knocked off this pinnacle any number of times after attaining it, but the conference shored me up. Maybe I would find a way to really accept him, be happy, and to say to hell with all the obstacles.

Because Families Together had informed us that the public schools were obligated to offer preschool services to children with developmental delays, I took Spenser to the screening in our school district. Maybe he wouldn't need these services because he would catch up. Yes, he had Sotos syndrome, but because those affected exhibited a wide spectrum of abilities, maybe he would be on the higher end, and eventually no one would even notice.

The bleachers in the gymnasium were shoved back against the wall to allow room for the parents and young children running around. When immersed in this chaotic scene, rather than playing with the other children, Spenser jerked around on the floor, propelling himself in a circle with his legs. His face was contorted, and he screamed unintelligible sounds. The director of special education services, a stylishly-dressed woman with a scarf wrapped around her neck and a gold necklace, approached him.

"That one," she said motioning to Spenser, "is definitely eligible."

Of course we had been found out, because as a young child Spenser rarely blended in. To me, his vocalizations and movements were unique, distinctive, and a textbook illustration of developmental delay. It was no use to admonish, "Spenser, stop it!" because I could not have prevented him from being himself; that same self which caused me to cast my eyes down at the lacquered wooden gym floor, readjust my jacket, and proceed to the table to fill out the enrollment forms. Despite their declarations that they have totally accepted their child's behavior and no longer register the stares of strangers, I question whether any parent of a disabled child has been able to extinguish the very last trace of discomfort or embarrassment. We are, at an instinctual level, tribal creatures who take our cues from others.

Not long afterward, Barbara, the intake manager, was on the telephone in a cubicle across from mine. She preferred pants over dresses, and had a short no-nonsense haircut. Her oldest daughter was pregnant.

"Yes, what they call the alpha-fetoprotein level is elevated, so the child might have Down syndrome, but that won't make any difference at all." I knew her well enough to know that she was faking. "No, absolutely no difference at all, because we will love that baby no matter what. With all the advancements, it's not as bad as before." The rising voice of a walk-in at the front desk drowned out the rest of her conversation.

A week or so passed, and because of her latest news, Barbara had a series of people to call.

"Yes, Maude, we had a terrible scare. An absolutely horrible scare that the baby might have Down syndrome, but it turned out to be nothing. The baby is normal."

What about loving that baby no matter what, Barbara? Apparently some children are easier to love than others. So even though I was adjusting to Spenser's disability in small increments, I occasionally cringed.

CHAPTER 14

Kindergarten Roundup

Brendan and Spenser attended Chippewa Elementary School, but there was something about it that worried me. Within sight of the playground were huge clouds that billowed into the sky next to a tall brick building. It was a power plant that burned through large heaps of black coal.

Brendan told me that on the playground the kids speculated that there was a giant that lived in the huge building, and that it was haunted. The pervasive invisible toxic fumes that seeped into the air concerned me.

I knew that the public could access a listing of the emitted compounds, but I did not recognize the names of any of the chemicals, and had no yardstick with which to measure the impact they had on the air my children breathed.

Marty, a friend from college who majored in chemistry, would know about such things.

After Marty studied the report, he seemed to indicate that most of the substances, although not desirable, were not extremely dangerous. Or maybe he did say that some of the substances weren't so good. All I knew was that—as a concerned mother—I wanted to do everything I could to shield my children from harm. But realistically, what could I do? Were the emissions from the coal-powered power plant a sufficient reason to transfer the children to another school? Everyone in the vicinity was breathing the fumes. It's no secret that we are poison-

ing the planet and inhaling or ingesting toxic substances that are causing respiratory problems and cancer, but how many people even make
the connection, or seem to care?

So, I had reached an uneasy truce with the emissions by the time
Spenser was eligible for kindergarten roundup. In the gym at Chippewa Elementary School, parents sat on folding chairs between the
two hoops on the basketball court, enveloped in the din of animated
chatter. With the wooden bleachers folded up against the wall behind
them, the principal, the school nurse and two kindergarten teachers
smiled from their table.

"Welcome to kindergarten roundup here at Chippewa Elementary
School," announced Mr. Hodges, the principal, pushing his chair out
as he stood. Listening to the confident voice of this large and affable
man, I could envision many happy school days for Spenser. I later
learned that this principal, Mr. Hodges, greeted students in the morning, wrapping some in friendly bear hugs. He played with students on
the playground, pushed them on the swings, and knew every student's
name.

After the school nurse reminded parents about immunizations, a
third grade class came in to serenade us. I watched a girl with long dark
hair and a tank top, and a boy with downcast eyes mouthing the words.
What would Spenser look like, what would he be doing, by the time he
was in the third grade?

The parents milled around the refreshment table, waiting for their
children to emerge from the breakout sessions with the kindergarten
teachers.

I cornered Mrs. Quinn by the cookies and punch bowl.

"So how did Spenser do?" She already knew I was his mother.

"Oh, just fine." She smiled and looked at me with her jade green
eyes. I took a bite out of an oatmeal cookie. She didn't seem to have
anything more to say.

I edged closer to her, and blurted out, "But you know, Spenser
has Sotos syndrome." I waited for her reaction during the gap in our
conversation. Her vacant stare indicated that she did not understand.

"Is that supposed to be some kind of a problem?"

The loud voices of talking parents were punctuated by the shrill
shrieks of babies. Although there was nothing unusual about the kin-

dergarten roundup, I was disoriented by Sandra Quinn's innocence in wondering whether Sotos syndrome, which had caused us untold grief, was considered to be a problem.

She smiled and waited a beat. "No, I'm sorry, I just don't know about this, never heard of it," she inserted into my silence.

I wanted to believe we did not have a problem.

Sandra Quinn was Spenser's kindergarten teacher in the fall, and the following year he transitioned to first grade by spending a half day in Mrs. Quinn's class and a half day with the first grade teacher. Spenser adored Mrs. Quinn.

I was horrified to realize that perhaps his teachers had spent more time interacting with him through focused activities than I, in my pre-occupation with getting to the next meeting, making deadlines, doing the laundry. I promised myself that later we would find more time to deeply engage with each other but, for Spenser, that day never came.

So several years after Spenser died, I interviewed Sandra Quinn in her classroom at Chippewa Elementary School. Mrs. Quinn sat in a low wooden chair, dressed in a Nordic green sweater that matched the green in her eyes, which were penetrating and very expressive. She laughed easily and her emotions were never far below the surface.

"What do you remember the most about Spenser?" I asked.

She leaned forward with her elbows on her knees. "The thing that stands out most about Spenser is that he enjoyed acting out, not in the behavior sense, but that he enjoyed doing little plays and being characters. When he was the great big billy goat, the troll, or papa bear, he would really try to get his voice and impression to match the characters. At recess, he would be a pterodactyl, and that climbing thing on the playground was his nest. He would fly around with his wings and that is something we did together." She smiled as she extended her arms and swayed as though she were flying through the air.

"I think he was frustrated that he could not do some things as well as the other kids. That's when I would get the looking away."

"The looking away?" I asked.

She jerked her head to the side. "There were times he would indicate, 'Stop, I don't want help.' He was proud, and headstrong. That's typical with kids. Rather than fail, they just don't do it. With him it was that looking away."

Her voice became animated as she remembered another incident.

"When he was making the transition into first grade, doing half day kindergarten and half day first grade, in his mind he was a first grader. The first grade class wore shirts, 'Mrs. Baker's Bunch.' When I said something to him in the afternoon, he faced me, put his hands on his hips, and announced, 'I am in Mrs. Baker's bunch,' then turned very dramatically and walked off."

Mrs. Quinn sat up and put her hands on her hips. I scribbled notes of our conversation on a white note pad.

"I do remember that he called me an 'asshole' once, but I don't know if you want to put that in the memoir. There were kids bustling around, catching buses and as he was leaving I said, 'Bye, Spenser,' and he answered, 'Bye, asshole.' Mrs. Sheridan was standing there and I said, 'Did I hear what I thought I heard? I think he called me an asshole.'"

Spenser knew better than to use that kind of language. Maybe he didn't know what the word meant. Or when he was expressing his independence, maybe he did.

She clasped her hands together. "He did come off as a confident child. He was not a follower. He just loved the *Toy Story* characters. If that just didn't warm the hearts of everyone, when he was Woody singing that song in the talent show. Getting up there showed a tremendous amount of confidence."

The hallways of the school were still by this time, and outside, the darkness descended.

Mrs. Quinn gazed off into the distance. "Honestly, I don't remember anyone making fun of him. In terms of his future, I thought wonderful things for Spenser. I did a little reading about Sotos syndrome, and how they had a pretty good prognosis and would grow into their bigger hands and feet. A few years later when I went into the special education teacher's room and saw him reading, he was on a roll. Then when I saw him on stage, it was obvious he had the drive to make something of himself, was not one to sit back and let the world go by."

"Do you think he would have carved out something other than a minimum wage job?" I asked as I gripped my pen more tightly.

"I could have seen him in high school involved with plays, either backstage or onstage. No, I don't picture him cleaning rooms. You could see his real love of performing, his creative side."

Mrs. Quinn concentrated on his potential, but as the self-conscious parent of a disabled child, I may have been too focused on his limitations, because we carry around a ton of emotional baggage surrounding the disability. In our insecurity we may be magnifying flaws that others hardly notice. Stan never imagined any rosy outcome for Spenser, but articulated that he could foresee Spenser picking up towels at the Y, or doing a similar menial job. His low expectations caused friction between us, but mine were probably not much better. But then again, my mother had taught me never to disparage any kind of honest work, so Spenser forced me to confront my elitist attitudes. I guess I was a snob. Mostly, because Spenser never progressed beyond being a child, I never looked that far into the future, so it may have been unfair to ask others questions that I never asked myself. Perhaps I was seeking affirmation, for someone to assure me that his life had meaning, that he made a difference, and that had he lived, it all would have turned out fine.

After I thanked her, I tunneled down the long brightly-lit hallway, past the student art pictures posted on the walls, pushed open the automatic door and was enveloped in the night.

CHAPTER 15

The Gathering Storm

There is a point when the summer turns into autumn, and we can almost pinpoint the day. Perhaps it is when a few brown curled leaves crackle under our feet on the road, or when the sun seems to have descended from its zenith in the sky. The fertile, flowing days of late May that portend a leisurely summer lingering before us reach a climax, and too soon we find ourselves on a downward slope.

August. The beginning of August. It rolls by every year; and every August when the boys were in elementary school I bought new crayons, scissors and glue sticks, and sorted through school clothes to see which were outgrown. School started way too early in mid-August, but I knew I wasn't going to change the system.

At my desk on a late afternoon in early August, I paused to study the calendar. I had tons of vacation time, but Stan was buried under some crucial cases and we really hadn't discussed any travel destinations. What if I took off an entire week to spend at home with the boys? I twirled my pen, wondering if I was being reckless and impulsive, like when, much younger, I contemplated going off to live in Boston with a man I barely knew. The daycare provider would not be pleased about losing a week of income, and I might have to pay her anyway, but before I ever dug through papers to find the contract, I decided that spending the time with the boys was worth it.

On Sunday night before the vacation week, a fierce rainstorm knocked out the electric power. At the oak dining room table, a candle glowed over my sheet of paper outlining the events of the week. With the rain and thunder rumbling in the background, I was transported to a rocking chair in my parents' house, trembling with excitement as I curled up with a Nancy Drew book late at night. The first few pages were the best, because the mystery had not been solved. Instead, all the intrigue and wonder loomed in the future, just like tonight, when I charted the unexplored territory of our coming adventures. Monday the zoo. Tuesday the library. Wednesday a picnic in the park. Thursday tie-dying shirts. Friday exploring the creek.

Every morning, I did some housework before we set out. I left them watching a video as I threw some clothes into the washing machine, or vacuumed a room. We did not leave the house before ten or ten-thirty, but I did keep to my schedule.

On Wednesday, we munched on some fast food in the shade on a wooden park bench. A slight breeze lifted a wisp of Spenser's blond hair. I brought my hand down on a wrapper to keep it from blowing away. Down below us, some older boys dribbled and shot baskets;. across the street behind us was a small shelter house, and a sidewalk flanked by hostas leading to an old train engine. We wandered toward it, with no concern about time, or having to be somewhere else. The engine was stout, black, and stationery, a relic. Brendan scaled the step into the engineer's cab, but I had to lift Spenser onto it. The rest of the car was blocked off with metal bars, so there was nothing further to explore. We meandered over to a swing set and some playground equipment. I pushed the boys in the swing sets, listening to the squeak and whine of the cables as the gravel crunched beneath my feet and the sun set lower. We drove back home.

On Thursday I set up the dye containers on a table on our sunny deck. The white t-shirts had been laundered and dried, and I glanced at the instructions on the small white bottles of Rit dye: a bright red, gold, forest green, magenta.

"Look boys, we're going to tie strings around knots in these shirts. What colors would you like?"

Brendan stood by the container with the red dye, and plunged in the shirt, but the activity did not actively engage the boys. Something irritated Spenser and he started crying and charging around like the bees that flew from the rose bushes to the flower gardens.

On Friday we took the blue and white patchwork quilt down to the creek with peanut butter and jelly sandwiches. The branches of the trees tossed overhead. Water bugs propelled themselves over the surface of the water in still pools, their legs moving like oars. The boys took off their shoes and socks, and balanced on the slippery rocks as they stepped carefully through the shallow water, tottering from one side to the other to maintain their balance. The sun left its mid-day station and sank toward the horizon, and nobody was in a hurry. There were no distractions, only life lived moment by moment with the boys. So the week ended, and the next Monday the usual routine resumed. Why don't I have abundant still shots of memories recording similar weeks, more time set aside for existing only in the present?

A week later, as I hurried down the streets of downtown, something was off kilter. School was starting Monday, so the summer was over. Not feeling well, I wondered if I were coming down with some virus.

I drove by the old black locomotive in the park, and drew a quick breath. It was so forlorn and stubborn, daring to sit still while everyone else sped by. It was also shrouded with tenderness and so much heartsick longing. Next year at this time, Brendan and Spenser would be a year older, and we would never pass this way again.

Now that Brendan and Spenser were school age, I immersed myself in their childhood activities. During October, I sewed elaborate Halloween costumes, stitching away at the sewing machine past midnight. Spenser as a toddler had been a rabbit, his pink face and blonde hair framed by a rabbit-ears hood in a plush, white fabric. Later he was a pirate, and then Peter Pan. I decorated spider cakes for the class parties, and helped pass out treats after they bit apples swinging from strings. Brendan started playing the violin. Both were in Cub Scouts. After work and a hastily consumed meal, we'd rush off to a school activity or lesson nearly every evening. It was hectic, but I was following the script that we should do everything possible for our children.

Stan, however, kept his distance from activities with the kids, but it was not always so. Spenser's birth marked the demarcation point of when his involvement ended. When Brendan, the normal healthy baby was born, Stan whisked him off on Saturday mornings for the class for new fathers, but he never attended a similar class with Spenser. I found a photograph of Stan holding Brendan under a crab tree bursting with pink blossoms, and another one of me and Brendan with snowflakes falling around us. I'm wearing a pink pastel ski jacket, and Brendan is wrapped in a green padded jumpsuit, his arms and legs sticking out stiffly like those of a scarecrow.

In contrast, Stan didn't take many pictures of Spenser as a baby or toddler. He dressed in his suit and tie every day, went to work, and returned home. I drove the boys to their activities while Stan watched television, or puttered around the house. I would stay up late; he'd go to bed earlier. However, Stan did the majority of the cooking and grocery shopping, stemming from an incident in our upstairs apartment when we were newlyweds, when Stan sat at the glass dining room table and pulled items out of a brown paper sack.

"Why did you buy frozen green beans? Canned green beans are cheaper," he said.

I turned around on tiptoe after stuffing a bag of rice into the top shelf.

"No reason. My mother always bought frozen vegetables, and aren't they more nutritious, less processed?"

"A box of macaroni and cheese. Another waste of money. You can make it from scratch."

"But who's going to?" I opened a cupboard door.

Over my shoulder, his arm plunged again into the insides of the sack. "Almond extract. When will you ever use this?"

"Sometimes for baking. Sometimes recipes call for it." Once more the sack crinkled as he fished out another item during his monotonous drill.

I turned to face him with my hands on my hips. "Okay, if you don't like it, you do the all the grocery shopping from now on."

Although his nitpicking irritated me, that we had to save every penny was inscribed in our unwritten code. Even as our incomes increased, it was difficult for us to be generous with each other, to splurge for the pure joy of it. Because we were unable to meet each other halfway over a can of green beans, when faced with Spenser's disabilities, we were really on opposite shores.

Each of us struggled with Spenser's disability. When Spenser was a baby, I journaled late into the night, but Stan and I did not cross our borders to console each other. Any attempt at communication with him would be met with either a silent stare or antagonistic comment. But in those wee hours, I was undergoing a metamorphosis that Stan was not, so that when Dr. Adams confirmed the diagnosis of Sotos syndrome, I could see through the disability to Spenser, the flesh and bones child. Spenser smiled all the time. He kept striving. I don't recall that Spenser ever said, "I can't."

On the other hand, Stan articulated that he was embarrassed by him and that his disability was a cruel trick that the cosmos had played on us.

Another photograph. Spenser is four and Brendan is seven. They are both facing the camera, wearing lifejackets and clutching canoe paddles, with the blades framing the backdrop of a bluff overlooking a rapid river. Both are wearing caps, and their legs stick out from large swimming trunks that balloon around their bodies. I'm swept back into a family summer trip to Arkansas, when we floated down the Buffalo River under a bright sun that reflected off white sand. The canoe slid through the water seamlessly, leaving the barest ripple in its wake. Peering down over the gunnels with the water as clear as glass, we could see pebbles of tan, maroon, and black embedded in the sandy bottom. Together in that canoe, propelling ourselves forward with minimal effort, nobody was arguing, not even Stan and I.

Arkansas is brimming with mysteries, and long-forgotten secrets that hover around the remains of dilapidated cabins decomposing in the woods. We explored dark, cool caves with stalagmites and stalactites beaded with moisture. As we wove our way through the winding roads, around every curve was a sign advertising some tourist attraction, some oddity created by the confluence of woods, cave and stone in those Arkansas hollers.

One morning as we set off from a trailhead leading into the woods, we climbed over small branches and large rocks that obstructed the path. Because Stan and Brendan walked ahead, the gap between them and Spenser and I widened.

"Stan, please don't get so far ahead. Spenser can't walk as fast," I yelled into the woods. Spenser navigated his way around a large rock with his hands. Although Spenser was absorbed in the adventure, I worried about getting lost or separated. Stan had the car keys and the maps.

"Stan, please wait up!" I yelled more loudly. Now I heard nothing, not even the sounds of others trudging through leaves. We finally caught up at the trail's destination, a waterfall surrounded by boulders that fell into a huge, dark pit.

"Stan, can we have fun together? I have to stay with Spenser and he can't keep up with you and Brendan." Stan didn't look up and made some comment about where this waterfall was on the map.

That afternoon Stan and Brendan went swimming in the river and I stayed behind in the cabin while Spenser slept on a bed in the loft. As I read a book about life choices and transitions, I paused between the lines to ponder where my life was heading.

I desperately wanted a third child, but Stan did not. Perhaps I reasoned that a third child would somehow compensate for Spenser's disability, that Spenser was something of a half child, and with another whole child we would have an achiever who filled us with pride. My mother advised against it.

"You're getting too old. You might have another one like Spenser," she would say.

I was not getting too old. A number of celebrities, as well as ordinary women everywhere, were having babies in their early or even mid-forties. As for waning fertility, I had no problems becoming pregnant with either one of them.

Or perhaps I wanted a third child because I was so enthralled with pregnancy and babies. Despite the nausea and fatigue of the first trimester, pregnancy was like waiting for Santa Claus for nine whole months. The intense love I had for my children was off the charts, and I wanted to magnify that bliss.

At the office, I confided my difficulties to Mikayla, who took the time to sit with me, listen and understand. My pain was reflected in her dark eyes, and sometimes for a few moments we prayed together, in hushed voices.

The following fall, Stan and I travelled to England, where I had lived for several months before I was married. In every cathedral, in every small chapel, I lit a votive candle and prayed for another baby. It would take a miracle because in response to my fervent wishes, Stan wouldn't touch me. One night while Stan slept in the bed at my side, I sat gazing out the open window into the moonlit sky. I was not happy. Remembering the girl who had visited this country fifteen years before made the return bittersweet. Then my future had beckoned like a painting of a garden bursting with blooming flowers, and all I had to do was step through the frame by marrying my graduate school boyfriend after I returned to the States. But instead of leading to marriage, children, and a resumed career, the relationship ended, and after several years of desperation and loneliness, I finally met Stan.

I wish I could say I found some resolution as I sat curled in the chair in that cozy bed and breakfast inn, but after I closed the windowpane and got under the covers beside Stan, the same tape played through my head, that I loved my children, my job, and my friends, but did not love my husband. I maintained the charade of my marriage by convincing myself that three out of four are good odds because nobody can have it all.

The excitement and variety of my job compensated for my lackluster marriage, and I received affirmations for exceeding the required production quota as a civil rights investigator with every evaluation. Every case presented a new cast of characters with a unique script. The scenarios behind sexual harassment complaints ranged from being amusing, to brutal and vulgar. Budding office romances could sour, and solidify into hatred.

At a factory, I interviewed an assembly-line worker charged with sexual harassment by a co-worker. As I questioned him, the machines whirred and clanked behind us.

"Did you make inappropriate comments to her?" I asked.

"Yes," stated the sandy-haired man. His response caught me off guard because when confronted with adverse allegations, witnesses generally issue blanket denials, or allege that they have no memory of the incident.

"Did you slap her on the buttocks?"

"Yes," he stated point blank. My questions became even more frank, and as I scribbled his responses on my white legal pad, I could foresee very definitely recommending "probable cause" for sexual harassment.

"I have no further questions. Thank you for your time," I said, extending my hand.

"Now do you want to hear what she did to me?" the man asked.

I sat back down and resumed taking notes about a birthday cake she had baked for him with a pronounced phallus. As for her inappropriate comments and times she touched him, I could not record them fast enough.

However, this case was the exception. Most women did not welcome the harassment.

Another man charged with sexual harassment was a true gentleman. He had asked his employee if he could kiss her when they were alone together in the storeroom. As a respected family man in a small town, rumors of the investigation were affecting his marriage.

I sat across from him and his attorney in his office. He wore a cardigan sweater, and his eyes were laced with pain. After asking the preliminary questions about his job title and dates of employment, I took a slight breath and broached the question, aware that I was lacerating wounds.

"Did you ask to kiss her when you were in the storeroom?"

"No, I didn't,' he answered with a burst of energy, "and I'll never, never, never, ever do that again!"

A few months later, the female investigators sat at long tables covered with tablecloths in a hotel conference room for a training session. We munched on cantaloupe slices, strawberries and grapes as we listened to a life coach.

"Now I want all of you to write down where you see yourself in five years," she said. "In order to ever realize your goal, you have to visualize it first."

I adjusted my blank piece of paper.

"Do you want to be a supervisor? How high on the organization's ladder do you want to climb?"

I stalled, because I was satisfied with my present job. As a supervisor, I would be confined to the office while my subordinates were out investigating complaints. The life coach pointed to the notepad on the easel.

"But don't only think about your professional life. Think about your personal life as well. What goals do you have for your family? What will that look like in five years? Ten?"

In five years Brendan and Spenser would be five years older, and in ten years, ten. Being their mother and a civil rights investigator summed up my major goals.

"So, ten years. You have to prepare for it now," the life coach said, holding her pointer with both hands.

I scribbled on my note pad to look busy. In ten years, I wanted to be in the exact same place.

With the passage of a few years, I was still content in my roles, but Stan was in therapy and on antidepressants. I watched him out of the corner of my eye, in between my career, the children, volunteer activities, the housework. We passed each other on the way to the microwave, or the car. At times we argued, but mostly spoke in low intonations about paying the propane bill, going to visit his parents for the weekend.

One evening in the church parking lot, a couple whose children were the same age as mine walked ahead of me. Dressed in jeans, they slung their arms around each other as their hips swayed back and forth, linked by a bond that was natural and instinctive. I clutched the zipper of my parka as the sharp teeth of the tines bore into my palm. They were in love. Stan and I were not.

At home under the chandelier at the oak dining room table, I inclined toward Stan in his flannel shirt, cuffs rolled up on his forearms. He wiggled his toes in his stocking feet, and read from a questionnaire from his therapist.

"Would you say that I find social interactions energizing or draining?" he asked.

"Draining, because you tend to be introverted. Interaction exhausts you," I said.

"What is my attitude toward new projects?"

"Wait a minute. Doesn't that therapist ever want to talk to me? After all, I'm your wife."

Stan ignored my question, proceeding with "How do I deal with disappointment?"

In church I prayed about ending my marriage, but had to consider Brendan and Spenser, so vulnerable and innocent. Influenced also by my volunteer job of resolving custody disputes, I visualized the woman I was working with. Trim, fit, and impeccably dressed, she was an adjunct at a university, but she and her ex-husband were fighting over custody of her children. She had to drive sixty miles to meet them at a truck stop on the interstate and, once in the car, her daughters were resentful of being uprooted from their friends. She had remarried another man, whose English she corrected, who was also wrangling with his ex-wife and children. Stacks of unpaid bills, contested real estate transactions and ongoing court appointments topped the situation off. Early one morning, the telephone rang.

"Margaret, I have been reduced to nothing," she sobbed on the other end of the phone. Her comments had been so guarded and circumspect the last time we had met. Although she was confronting challenges, I rationalized that her professional, tailored appearance reflected how she was efficiently managing it all. This telephone call revealed that her life was a complete mess. I did not want to be in her situation, so again I decided to stick it out and make the best of it. With any luck, I might be a young widow.

I first sensed that something unsettling was brewing in early May, when the veterinarian detected a tumor in our dog Beau.

"We'll have to do exploratory surgery and biopsy the tumor," the vet said. "If it's benign, we'll remove it and the dog should be fine. If it's malignant, we'll sew him back up and make him comfortable."

As Stan stood by the dog pen, he seemed uncertain, slightly lost, as the wind blew up dry leaves that swirled around him.

"You might consider whether it is worth spending all that money on a dog," he suggested, regarding me with a deadpan expression.

"I'm not going to sacrifice Beau due to lack of money. If I have to I'll cash in some of the college savings bonds," I answered.

The second clue occurred a week later when I agreed to be the committee chairperson for Brendan's Boy Scout troop.

Stan appeared and stood under the frame of the doorway, listening to the phone conversation.

"You might want to consider whether you want to take on any additional duties at this time," he said.

"Well, but I should get more involved. Why let everybody else do all the work?" Stan disappeared into the other room.

In the middle of the month, we visited a botanical garden in Kansas City, blooming with the tulips and hyacinths of mid-spring. Stan went off with Brendan, and I remained with Spenser. After a few futile moments of trying to find them, Stan appeared with two hamburgers, one for himself and one for Brendan.

"Why didn't you buy food for all of us? What the hell do you think you're doing?" I exclaimed.

The rest of the afternoon was a repeat of Arkansas, with Stan far ahead on the winding paths with Brendan, while Spenser and I struggled to keep up. In the car, I seethed all the way home.

On the last day of school, Spenser rode the little yellow school bus for preschool students with disabilities for the last time because in the fall, he would be in kindergarten. The bus driver, a middle-aged woman who often wore sleeveless white blouses, had picked him up from school and driven down our long, winding driveway to our doorstep every day.

The garden was flooded with late afternoon sunshine. Spenser descended the three steps, dressed in his blue t-shirt and plaid shorts, his arms laced through his little backpack.

"Just a minute. I want to pick you a bouquet of flowers," I called to her. I stepped over the ox-eye daisies and teetered on a rock in the stone path. As I cut through a swath of dame's rocket, Stan charged out of the front door.

"I'm leaving for Springfield," he said.

"What? Why now?" The motor in the school bus idled.

"I told you. I'm getting a truck from my parents' house."

"Can you wait? Can you wait for just one minute until I get these flowers?" I stepped past the marigolds, balancing on one foot as I reached for another blossom. Stan backed out and sped up the driveway.

"Here," I said, thrusting the stems into a vase for the bus driver. "I hope these hold up for you. Thank you so much for all you've done for Spenser."

She reached forward from her seat and took the flowers. "If there are any problems on the regular bus, if anybody makes fun of him, you just call the school. You call the school, and I'll keep driving him." She backed out of the driveway, for the last time.

A few days later, Stan called me at the office. From the eighth-story window I could see the squares of more windows stacked vertically on another wing of the same building.

"Hello," began his familiar voice, "I was wondering if you could get off and come home a little early today."

"Yeah, I don't know why not. Most people have gone home and I'm at a stopping point." I glanced at the clock behind my shoulder. Three-thirty p.m. No voices emanated from the grey cubicles, no one popped popcorn in the microwave. It was a Friday, right before a three-day weekend, Memorial Day.

Before leaving I dropped by the office of a friend, an elegant woman with dark hair pulled back into a chignon, and a face painted like a china doll, highlighting huge, dark eyes. The corners of her mouth crinkled when she saw me.

She had left her first husband after he was charged with embezzling from his employer in order to support his cocaine habit. This happened right after she finally became pregnant. Now she was dating Mitchell, a friend that I knew through Stan.

"I think I'm going to take off. Will you see Mitchell this weekend?"

"Oh, no," she said, unclipping her earring, "that's over."

"Why?"

"He's buying a house, and I don't figure anywhere into the equation."

"But that doesn't mean that you can't visit him at his new house, that you can't continue your relationship," I said. "He's never been married. It's a big step for him. He just needs more time."

"No. I can read the writing on the wall," she answered with her head turned away and gaze directed toward the window.

I knew that Mitchell adored her. I reminded her that he had dressed up as a rabbit for her daughter, but she would not listen. For her, there had been too many disappointments, too much disillusionment. Even a wonderful person like Mitchell could not convince her to trust any man again. She was done.

I changed from my heels to tennis shoes, grabbed my plastic bag and my briefcase, and pushed the elevator button in the hall, thinking about how broken relationships leave casualties. I also wondered why Stan wanted me home early. He'd been to see his parents, so maybe they bought Brendan and Spenser bicycles.

Memorial Day weekend. Traditionally the time to pick strawberries. Some, ripe and squishy, exude a pungent aroma, while others, white and small, resist being plucked. Whenever I was home from college, I would boil strawberries and rhubarb together in a steamy pot, pouring in a heap of white sugar, to make tangy jam. As the elevator descended, I remembered other Memorial Day weekends, unlike this one with overcast skies, which had begun with splashy sunlight.

But it had been a cold spring. The strawberries weren't ready yet this year. On this Friday afternoon of grey, gusting winds, I pulled into the driveway to see Stan on our front porch. He sat on the wooden bench, looking at me as if he had misplaced something of value, and was waiting for me to find it. He almost never sat on the porch, least of all the wooden bench. I followed him to the green table in the middle of the basement floor. He pulled out a typewritten document.

"I have decided that I can no longer survive in this marriage and am seeking a divorce." The reflection from his glasses obscured his eyes.

"Of course, the house will have to be sold," he continued. The jumbo crocus bulbs, gold and purple, the peach trees, once mere whips but now spilling over the driveway, the perennial plants, chosen after hours of poring through catalogues, paraded before me.

His hand trembled slightly as he shoved the document toward me. "I've prepared this and want you to sign it."

I had no intention of signing it. I scanned some of the typewritten words—words that were wreaking havoc on the timbers of the house, the innocent pets, the bright shining faces of Brendan and Spenser.

He spoke slowly, but I only comprehended every fifth or sixth word. His expression never wavered. He was absolutely sure. Was I not even entitled to an advisory opinion regarding the end of my marriage? But this had been fermenting for a long time, started growing late at night as I read, journaled, and prayed about Spenser at my desk that overlooked the darkened oaks while he slept.

"I've rented an apartment in town, paid the deposit," he droned on.

Part of me watched this scene play out as though I were sitting in the audience, with my attention focused on Stan, the actor speaking on the stage. I then remembered the similar pose he struck when he warned me about spending money on the dog's surgery. With calculated insistence, like mice gnawing in the chilly spaces under the eaves, he had plotted every detail of the separation in advance.

I pushed back my chair and dashed upstairs. The maroon couch, purchased when we could finally afford a decent piece of furniture, gone. The needlepoint chairs, embroidered by his great aunt, gone. The kitchen table, gone. The brown chairs that circled it, gone. The upstairs living room, once plush with furniture, was stripped and bare.

"Where's all the furniture?" I screamed.

"Now, Margaret, this is no time to get irrational and be upset. I've come to this decision and was hoping we could talk it through calmly." So this explained why he was in such a hurry to get down to Springfield on Spenser's last day of school. He needed the truck to move the furniture.

I pushed past him and yanked open the drawer of the blue hutch. The checking account, all of it withdrawn, with the exception of eighty-six dollars and thirty cents. The savings account, leveled to zero.

"I'm leaving now," he said, as I turned to see him standing in the kitchen.

"What about Brendan and Spenser? Aren't you even going to tell them in person?"

"I'll tell Brendan if the bus brings him before I leave, but I'm not waiting around to tell Spenser."

"You what? You can't even stay until I drive over to the daycare to get Spenser?"

The recessed light over the microwave shone on top of his head. With his arms crossed, he stared at me as though we had never had one conversation. After fifteen years of marriage, he had become a stranger.

"One last thing," he said, "you need to call the telephone company and get the service put in your own name or they will disconnect it by Tuesday. I'm no longer responsible for your bills."

The shadows of evening lengthened. The place under the area lighting where he had been standing in the kitchen was vacant. The house, stripped of essential furniture, was no consolation. I was now a single mother, alone with the boys: Brendan, eight, and Spenser, five.

I rushed outside and jogged to the top of the hill in order to process what had just happened. The familiar scenery, the open fields and wide expanse of trees in the distance seemed askance, slightly off kilter. The shadows were menacing, eerie, almost pea green, the way that the air is charged right before a tornado. The woman who lived across the road opened her mailbox. I barely knew her, but rushed to her side.

"My husband just left me. He left me just now and I don't know what's going to happen next," I said to her, as my voice mounted and tears started to spill. Before she could empathize, her mother drove up, which ended our conversation. For her unsuspecting mother, it was just an ordinary day, but I had been walled off from the mundane, and would not sleepwalk through the routines of daily living without sheer panic for a very long time.

After dark, the music from a loud rock band blasted from a beer party next door. Every word of the vocalist, and every chord of the bass, reverberated off the wallpaper in the boys' bedrooms. As I traced the melodies of familiar songs, it was comforting to know that there were people nearby. My senses were heightened, attuned to the harmony of the music, the spicy aroma of the spring night air, the velvet blackness hovering over the house, the loneliness that was seeping in through the windows. I did not want to turn off the lights because I was terrified, quivering within the protective structure of the room, wondering from which direction the next calamity would strike.

CHAPTER 16

The Forgotten Years

The next morning, the boys and I started our life without their dad. Because the kitchen table was gone, they ate their cereal perched on stools behind the breakfast bar. Although Stan usually did the grocery shopping without the children, now that we were running low on staples, it was up to me.

Confronted with a smorgasbord of enticing snacks packaged in all shapes and colors, Brendan and Spenser went into overdrive. Spenser dashed away from me, and Brendan grabbed potato chips and soda pop from off the shelves, resulting in quarrels. Because we didn't have the money for junk food, every calorie had to be nutritious. As Spenser pushed the shopping cart, an elderly man dodged out of his way to avoid a collision. I could see this was not going to be easy. They were, after all, only eight and five.

With almost nothing in the checking account, I was broke, and would have to cover the mortgage, the utilities, food, Spenser's daycare, and everything else without Stan's salary. Plus, I had to enroll Brendan in summer camps. Because I could not afford the educational zoo camp he attended in previous summers, I located a camp for economically-disadvantaged children at Louden Elementary School.

"So there is no charge. No charge whatsoever?" I asked the woman over the phone.

"No, no charge," she said.

After Memorial Day weekend, I resumed the routine of getting up early, dropping off the boys, and going to the office. Later in the week, I drove to a track meet, the site of the camp field trip, to pick up Brendan for a medical appointment.

I scanned the large, roving crowd of active children for Brendan. His camp counselor appeared from behind the bleachers.

"Yes, he's around here somewhere," he said, making a sweeping gesture with his arms.

Brendan was not over by the track where runners lined up for relays, at the concession stand, or in any group. Not dressed for the outdoors, I trudged from one location to another, my heels sinking into the soft earth. With the sun beating down on me, I rubbed the salt from my perspiration out of my eyes. I glanced at my watch. I would be late for the appointment if I could not find Brendan. I searched again for his counselor.

"I can't find him anywhere."

"Well, I just don't know what to tell you," he said, shrugging his shoulders. He blew his whistle and corralled a group of children into a line.

Quite confident that Brendan was not at the track meet, my only alternative was to drive to their point of departure, Louden Elementary School. The playground was deserted, but there was Brendan, along with another boy draped over a swing seat, who pushed himself off the ground with his legs. The irritation from missing the appointment paled in comparison to my amazement.

"Brendan, why didn't you get on that bus this morning? What happened?"

"I went to the bathroom and when I came out the bus was gone," he said.

"You've been here all day? What about this other little boy? Will his mother be coming at five?"

The boy did not respond, but smiled at me as he rocked himself on the swing, his hands gripping the chains.

I suppose you get what you pay for, but how far could I trust the universe to protect my children? The incident reinforced the panicky voices inside my head that I could not quell, that we were exposed, alone, vulnerable, and that something terrible might happen.

Within the next few weeks, Stan and I worked out a visitation schedule. Now I would be without them on Tuesday evenings and every other weekend. I spent those weekends cleaning the entire house, doing laundry and going grocery shopping. On Tuesday evenings, I pulled the car under the carport and turned off the ignition. After rifling through the mail, I leaned my head against the car window and dozed off as it grew darker. I could not make myself go into that empty house that had no boys and would stay in the car until it was almost time to pick them up at eight.

As the summer dragged on, we got into a routine. Every night I stood over the kitchen sink, loading up the dishwasher at about midnight, after rousing myself from the rocking chair in Spenser's room. There was always one more dirty dish, another casserole pot to soak, a few stray serving spoons strewn over the counters.

When I finally had time for myself, I would climb the stairs to lie down, still dressed, just for a few minutes, until I woke with a jolt at three or four in the morning, only to change into my nightgown and get into bed.

I wasn't as worried about Spenser's disability. We were managing. Spenser never really caused me any problems, but Brendan did. At dinner, the three of us huddled around the plastic picnic table I purchased from Target. Spenser, framed by the white wallpaper with a morning glory pattern, chattered away, but I wasn't really listening. Brendan would interject an obnoxious remark, so I would drag him out onto the deck for a time-out. Spenser would sit at the table, watching Brendan go back and forth, his head turning like that of the mystified meadowlark perched on a hay bale that traced flying model airplanes as they flew through the air one summer at camp.

As for the family dog, the tumor was benign. Beau lived for several more years in good health, so the money was well spent.

CHAPTER 17

Whitman Concert Hall

Not that I had to worry about Brendan and Spenser running away from me in department stores or other public places. When they were too old to be carried or pushed with their legs dangling in the child seat of the grocery cart, they hovered near. Whenever I looked down at them, their wide, trusting eyes, framed in chubby faces, met my gaze. I decided to make a game out of it anyway, especially now that we were on our own.

"Now boys," I said, after the dinner dishes had been rinsed and stacked into the dishwasher, "we're going to play a game called 'Strangers.' We're going to pretend that we're walking in a store, then I'm going to break away from you and become a stranger, and after that I'm going to find you again."

They waited for my next sentence, saying nothing. I took their hands. Brendan, on my right, came almost to the middle of my chest. Spenser, on my left, came up to my waist.

"Okay, boys," I said in a sing-song tone, "look at those peaches on the shelf. They're nice, but we're going to buy the bananas." We walked in a small circle in the living room, past the wicker settee, then strolled past the floral couch.

Then I broke away from the grip of their small hands and charged down the stairs to the basement. In the coat closet, I rummaged around for a large woolen cloak. I hesitated, debating how to complete the costume. A rubber Halloween mask of a wizened monster lay on the top shelf. I pulled it over my head.

"E-e-e-e-r-r-r," erupted the loud, guttural cry from my throat. I ascended the stairs, stomping with loud footsteps. From the living room, the boys screamed.

"A-a-a-a-w-w-w-w." With greater intensity, I articulated the sounds of a monster as I barged into the living room, with my hands arched over my head. My fingers pointed downward like piercing nails as I hovered over them.

"A-a-a-h-h-h," they wailed, as they backed into the cushions of the couch. From the two ocular openings of the mask, I gauged their level of terror. Their cries careened on the adrenaline rush of this horror spectacle, but yet their faces were smiling. They could see that I was their mother, assuming the guise of an evil mother, a changeable alien.

I again fled the room, returned to the closet, and ripped the suffocating mask over my head as I draped the cloak onto a hanger.

"Boys, boys, where are you?" I sprinted up the stairs. "I couldn't find you, and I worried that a monster would get you. Brendan? Spenser? Are you all right?"

I found them standing in the living room, on the rattan rug, as silent as statues.

"Now don't get away from me again," I said as I took their hands. "Let's stay together in this store, and not get separated."

I never wanted to lose them, never wanted to be separated. They belonged near me, always.

By August, having figured out how to pay for quality daycare, I exposed Brendan and Spenser to music, dance and theatre at the Fun Factory.

Before the children were born, I had been quite the actress in local theatre productions. I loved it, loved it, even when my character got doused with water, and I stood shivering in the wings in a smelly, damp raincoat and drooping hat, fatigued to the bone.

I adored being behind the footlights, knowing that the audience probably couldn't see the saliva from the actors' mouths as it sprays in an arc through the air, launched by precise articulation. You can't see the audience very well through the footlights, so you don't feel exposed knowing that your first grade teacher, gynecologist, or the president of the company is staring at every move you make. The many blurred faces morph into a huge sleeping beast that grunts and grumbles, occasionally roused by the cackling electricity of pandemic laughter. Besides, it isn't you up there on the stage, the you who crosses the street in the morning rain to catch the bus, it's the character. When I donned my costume and makeup, it was the character who struck the pose and said the lines when the lights came up. I don't know where my soul went, but I disappeared.

When I was Joanne in *Vanities* by Jack Heifner, rather than fret about forgetting my lines as I stood behind the side curtains before my entrance, I took deep breaths and sensed the presence of spirit.

In the green room hang pictures of the grand dames who founded the theatre many years ago. Behind the glossy acrylic paint of their portraits, they smile at each nervous actor mouthing his lines. Or they watch the ingénue, her eyes lined in black and pert mouth painted red whirling in her bathrobe, searching for her stage prop. One of the faces in the portraits had been a gracious lady, a high school English teacher and stunning actress whose beauty transformed everything she touched. In a letter to the editor in the local newspaper, her relatives lamented that she did not live long enough to see the splendid new theatre. How proud she would be, they wrote, having invested so much of herself in it. How sad that they do not know that she is still there every night, waiting in the wings with every actor in that liminal moment when he cloaks himself in the character before he strides onstage.

So then when Brendan was born—Brendan the best and brightest, who spoke in complete sentences when he was two, Brendan, so stunning that I caught strangers looking at him in the grocery store—of course, would be the actor. I searched for signs when the daycare provider carried him onstage for the preschool Christmas program. He clung to her, sleepy from a nap. After the piano finished hammering out the carols and the children filed out, Brendan stood on the platform facing the audience.

"He's taking to the stage like he owns it, look at him," I said to my mother. Yes, I thought to myself, he is a natural. I have my actor.

By the time he was six, Brendan did not like sports. On sunny autumn days on the soccer field in his shiny blue jersey, Brendan ran away from the ball whenever it came near him.

So much for sports. I had done my obligatory duty as a mother of a boy, and now I could involve him in the really exciting stuff— art, music and theatre. Spenser could go along, but I did not harbor the same expectations for him because, after all, he did have Sotos syndrome, and in the theatre world, let's get real about how snarky actresses can be. If you're late for a cue or miff a line during a scene they may blackball you, and as for someone who may drool slightly or occasionally look retarded, they would cut him dead.

In any case, I dropped both boys off at the Fun Factory camp. Back home in the evenings on our outside deck, they rehearsed their butterfly number as twilight fell.

"I am a butterfly, see my beautiful wings," the scratchy music sang to the pungent blossoms, the birds nestled in the lush leaves, and a sliver of a moon peering through the trees. The boys jumped and sang until it was time to steal away from the intoxicating night, into the fluorescence of artificial lights where I started their bath.

At the end of the week, the fledgling thespians showcased what they had rehearsed with a grand finale performance. I found a seat in the darkened auditorium of Whitman Concert Hall, climbing over little brothers and sisters whose arms and legs shot in every direction. After the audience hushed, Brendan's musical number was announced. I scanned the distant group for his face, but when the music commenced, I struggled to pay attention, still preoccupied with the day's problems at the office.

Then Spenser's group filed onto the stage. Suddenly, there was Spenser, gleaming, radiant, glowing from within. The footlights and overhead spots magnified his face, and his smile seemed permanently affixed. Because of his height he entered in the back row, but he did not remain there. Instead, he nudged his way into the front row, and the children parted to let him in. Perhaps it was the light reflecting from his platinum blond hair, or because my heart leapt to him through the darkness, but I was mesmerized by how Spenser, front and center, stood out from the rest of the group. Surely everyone in the audience was focused on this bright, happy child, shining with confidence, riding the same ray as the music. All the other children blurred together. Were they there at all?

When their number was over, the children turned and began filing off, first the front row, then the back. Instead of leaving the stage with his group, Spenser was glued to his spot like a mannequin, standing erect front and center, his face radiating a permanent smile. The next group of children emerged from the wings. Spenser stood alone on the stage. Finally a woman from behind the side curtain escorted him off by the shoulders, and the audience murmured muffled laughter. Although he was gone, in that liminal space behind the footlights, something of him remained. I had never seen him so happy. So it was not to be Brendan, but Spenser fulfilling the role of my son, the actor.

Years later, I forced my feet into first position as Janine demonstrated ballet technique at the bar. Stretching forward, her long straight brown hair fell over her head as her hands made contact with the floor.

After the lesson, when the dancers sat on the sidelines untying their toe shoes, she and I lingered to talk.

"You know I teach at the Fun Factory during the summers," she said, standing with one knee bent.

"Brendan and Spenser were at the Fun Factory one summer, but that was a long, long time ago." I said.

"How long ago?"

"You wouldn't have been there. It was, wow, maybe fifteen or twenty years ago."

"What year? I have been there a long, long time," she said, drawing out her words.

"Okay, it was the summer that Stan left me, twenty years ago."

She paused, as though doing a quick calculation. "I was there."

"Really? Then do you remember Brendan or Spenser Gardner? Spenser? He had blond hair, and a disability?"

She squinted up at the corner. "I do remember one special little boy with blond hair. Do you have a picture?"

I searched in my wallet, and found a small thumbnail portrait of Spenser, the last school portrait he ever had.

Janine held the picture. Then she screamed.

"Oh my gosh! Of course I remember him. He totally threw himself into everything we did," she said, holding the picture. "He loved dancing. He loved acting out stories. Some of the other kids held back, you know how it is. But not him. He was the most enthusiastic one in the class."

Now Janine and I have coffee together regularly, and have pieced together other former situations when we were leading parallel lives, but never knew each other, until now. While waiting for the barista to prepare our chai lattes, we discovered, among other coincidences, that when I was in a theatre production, and a fellow cast member confided that she discussed her troubled marriage with "the neighbor across the street," that neighbor, of all the people in the world, was Janine. Whenever we meet, we have so much catching up to do, but then again, so much of what is unspoken does not need to be articulated. It is as though we have known each other for a very long time.

Somewhere along the way, I stopped believing in coincidences, and computing the odds of running into a person you haven't seen for years who has an important message for you that changes the course of your life. If you were to further compound your probability theorem by encountering that long lost person in a shop or office you'd never been in before, you would be hard-pressed to deny that there is someone who is watching over you.

Blessed with enriching day camps and gilded evenings that faded into darkness without a murmur, we drifted through the summer. We ate peanut butter and jelly sandwiches down by the creek on the tattered blue patchwork quilt. We read bedtime stories every night, chosen from the armloads of books we gathered from the library. I was on automatic pilot, going through the motions. By locking into the routine, I shoved aside the nagging fears that swirled around me like wisps of invisible smoke. I could tell myself that we were managing financially, but dismiss that we had next to nothing in reserve. I could obliterate that I was lonely, and yearned for the companionship and caress of a man. I could pretend that I would never run out of energy, even though I was exhausted.

In late August, the elementary school sponsored their annual "Back to School Night," an opportunity to introduce myself to their teachers. Because I didn't have the money to spare for a babysitter, I brought the boys along and hoped that they would be fine on the playground.

Washing my hands in the restroom as the evening waned, Spenser and Brendan appeared at my side. Spenser's eyes were red and he was crying.

"Brendan, what happened?"

"Some boys threw sand in his eyes." Brendan always spoke the truth, in calm and measured tones.

"Some boys what? They threw sand in his eyes?"

I knelt down and examined Spenser's eyes, which were very red. Spenser made whimpering sounds, and seemed incapable of speech.

"Where are these boys? Who are they?"

"I don't know. They all ran away," Brendan said.

"They aren't in your class? You don't know them?"

Brendan shrugged. I simmered with rage, as involuntary violent mental images of knocking the stuffing out of those boys crossed my mind.

Brendan has always been a cool, detached child, and he rarely shows his emotions. He shuts himself in his room and reads for hours. He graduated from high school with straight A's, but he confessed to me, during his last school break, that he's started to realize the importance of relationships. During his junior year in college, and at my request, he sent me his recollections regarding the playground incident.

I printed off his e-mail:

"Now that I finally have time and am in the mindset, I will tell you what I can about the one episode I clearly remember where Spenser was tormented. It was just me, Spenser, and a handful of other boys outside, as you were doing something inside the school, perhaps PTO, I'm not sure."

"Back to School night," I said out loud, as I leaned back in the chair.

"A fair number of the kids at Chippewa knew that Spenser was different, based upon not only his behavior but the appearance of his face and head. Most kids did not bother him, though I must wonder whether this was due to adult supervision."

So I never should have left them alone on the playground.

"Realizing that no one was around, these other boys about my age walked up to Spenser on the swing and began to taunt him with hateful words, saying 'retard,' 'stupid,' 'dummy,' and 'bighead.' After they had approached him in this way, he started to run away. Seeing that this was their chance to get after the boy who seemed to get all the special attention, they then proceeded to start picking up sand from the playground and throwing it at him. One boy got in front of Spenser and threw the sand in his eyes, another dumped it in his pants, all the while chanting and jeering at him. Finally, after doing this for some minutes, the boys shoved Spenser to the ground, kicked more sand on him, and then left."

I closed my eyes. I could hardly stand to read this.

"Brendan, Brendan," I said to the e-mail, "why didn't you try to defend him?"

"These boys were a bit older than me, and outnumbered me. If I had the courage to confront them, they would have had special anger for a person who would actually stand up for a 'dummy,' and I could have been seriously injured. I essentially had no choice but to take the middle road, not joining in on the abuse but watching the evils they carried out."

"No, Brendan, you could have screamed for them to stop without touching them. You could have run for an adult before any further damage was done. You had other options," I said, with my voice rising, even though there was no one else in the room. I could feel the sand in my eyes. I could summon up the wrenching defeat and rejection Spenser must have experienced. The clock chimed the quarter hour.

Brendan, the incident on the playground is like a cocktail party, where people sip their wine in upscale living rooms. We've all been to those parties, making small talk, piling stuffed mushrooms and fruit slices onto our plates. Then someone, impeccably dressed, makes an unexpected comment that initially seems totally out of character, which maligns women, or those with disabilities, or those of another race. If it's a real zinger, we can feel the reverberations tingling inside of us. We gauge the territory. Maybe we summon the courage to speak up, and maybe we don't.

"But you have to say something, Brendan." I slid the e-mail off to the side, and turned off the computer. "Brendan, you have to say something."

Out of the condolence cards we received after Spenser's death, one stands apart, and enabled me to piece together more fragments of how his peers perceived Spenser. On a white sheet of typewriter paper, folded in half, Connor, a sixth grader, inscribed his cover: "In Loving memory of Spencer Gardner," and drew a heart balloon with Spenser's name in the center.

Dear Mr. and Mrs. Gardner,

We are very sorry that a such traggic thing could happen in the world. We all suffer in life but some suffer more. I never thought a good person could die like Spencer at such a young persons age. I think it is sad that god had to put you through this but at least we all know he is going to a place were god can take care for him forever. In all of our hearts, Spencer is a person we will all will have memory of. This is my way of showing my sorrow to you.

Everyone, well not everyone, but some people, use to make fun of Spencer. I never thought much of it until now. I've learned that it's not what is on the outside or even the way they act, its on the inside that counts. Now I know that people aren't what they seem. They can be more different than you imagine. Death can be a problem that forever stays with you but somewhere someone will always care just as much as you. I wish that Spencer could of grown up and be able to have fun and to do stuff that kids do. Death always makes you remember how important life is and to not take things for granted or just because it's their. From now on every time I take stuff for granted or want more, I'll think of Spencer and how fragile life really is.

I just want to say one more thing, I will forever remember Spencer as the best kid I ever knew for he has always been kind even in the roughest times.

Your friend,

Connor Manning, 6th grade Chippewa

That "death can be a problem" is an understatement, but the letter is charming because it was written from a child's perspective, and reminds me that not only was Spenser a child, but his world was mostly populated by other children. In our haste to cross the threshold into adulthood, we discard patches of our innocence. Through death, Spenser is crystallized as a child, allowing us to set in stone lofty notions such as that Spenser had "always been kind even in the roughest times," while dismissing any nagging doubts as to whether his transition to adulthood would have sullied his beneficence, because he would be pilloried by cruelty and rejection.

I sighed, and filed the letter back into its slot in the accordion file, then got down on my knees and shoved the box with Spenser's memorabilia back into the closet. Outside my window the last scarlet leaves were falling from the maple, and the branches of the trees on the hillside, now mostly bare, tossed in the wind. Considering that it was early November, the weather was unseasonably warm and sunny, but these days wouldn't last, so Brendan and I planted tulips yesterday in the garden atop the rock wall. We plunged the metal bulb planters into the ground, positioning the bulbs in the cool, dark soil. Submerged in the earth, the tulips won't see the sunlight again until their green vegetation emerges after the frozen winter. When they arrive in the mail in a few days, I'll be planting one-hundred and twenty daffodils for naturalizing. I want to bury them all, to thrust one bulb after another into the dark earth, where they will lie dormant until they are resurrected in the spring.

CHAPTER 18

The Dance

In November the divorce was final. Because Stan owed me alimony, I was able to keep the house. So, the three of us hung on. A few weeks before, the Scout troops visited a pumpkin patch on a warm October day. More photographs of Brendan and Spenser, on top of a hay wagon piled with pumpkins. The orange of the pumpkins, and the blue and red colors of their clothing blazed in the bright sunlight. But inside my chest a dull ache pulsated, because I couldn't deny that I was a single mother, that Stan and I were not at the pumpkin patch together. The other fathers knelt, and took pictures. They grabbed their toddlers by the hand, and called, "Come here, Maddy, let's get an apple cider."

The little things were piling up, and everything was becoming more difficult. Alone in the house late at night, there was nobody else there to attend to a child's nightmares, to fix a leaky faucet, to discuss whether Brendan really needed braces. The daily grind was wearing me down, nipping at me like an army of mosquitos, as I grew weaker.

On the fireplace mantel is a church directory picture of me, Brendan and Spenser. The photographer told Spenser to sit on my lap, but he threw a fit, wrinkling my dress. He wanted to be a big boy, so he stands with his hand on my right shoulder, just like Brendan on the other side. I have on a red dress and string of pearls. Brendan and Spenser wear ties and long-sleeved shirts. We are smiling at the camera, but there are three of us, and not four.

A little entry in the newspaper, in fine print, announced the divorce. Until the divorce was final, dating was out of the question for me, because it would not have been fair to drag a new person into my unfinished business. But after November, I started looking at men in the elevators, wondering which ones were available.

By mid-January, the weather was uniformly misty, cold and grey. In contrast to the winter weather outside that entombed the high-rise drab building where we worked, inside the animated telephone conversations of my colleagues livened up the scene. From my cubicle, I could hear Barbara taking complaints, and Marilyn, the education specialist in the cubicle next to mine, scheduling a presentation. Also recently divorced, she and I were becoming closer friends.

"Margaret, it's time you got out. Let's go to a contra dance together this weekend," she said, swiveling around in her chair to face me.

"What is it?"

"You change partners so you don't have to be paired to one person the whole evening. I'm meeting Jack there, that guy I told you about, but I'm trying to slow things down. I don't want to give him the impression we're on a date. You and I should go together." Her clear blue eyes, framed by wavy blonde hair, were convincing.

When we arrived at the gymnasium of the elementary school, the band, consisting of a fiddle, guitar and string bass, rehearsed the strains of English country tunes and Scottish jigs. As more dancers arrived, people milled around the gymnasium floor, drifting into small groups that formed and then scattered. Strangers returned my open smiles. In their faces I could read anticipation, and a hint of insecurity. The ambiance seemed casual yet congenial, where anything could happen.

Not knowing anyone else, I shadowed Marilyn, whose attention was diverted by Jack, an earnest young man with dark hair and glasses, who would not leave her alone. From the sidelines, I watched a dapper young man whisk a woman around the basketball court in his arms under the bright lights. Although he was dressed in a long-sleeved plaid shirt and vest, with his finely executed steps and graceful flair, he danced as though he were a professional ballroom dancer in a tuxedo with tails.

"Oh, Marilyn, don't expect me to dance like that," I said.

She smiled and disappeared into the crowd with Jack. From then on, I was on my own. The music started, and I did the steps to the lively jigs as best as I could. Do-si-do. Join hands. Promenade. If I went the wrong direction, my next partner would grab me by the arm and set me straight. Thus I was passed on, from one man to the other, with a frozen smile on my face.

When the band took a break, some of the dancers, fanning themselves, gravitated toward the open door and vanished into the cold January night. I was overheated, never should have worn a wool skirt and long-sleeved turtleneck. I wandered through the crowd, then found myself facing the ballroom dancer. He grinned at me, with his feet spaced apart, his hands clasped in front of him.

"Hi, I'm Tom," he said.

"I'm Margaret."

"What?" he asked, leaning closer.

"Margaret," I replied. He was tall, with an aquiline nose and handsome features. His medium brown hair, parted on the side, was swept across his forehead. He had an athletic build that resembled a wedge, with a broad chest and strong arms that tapered into narrow hips. He nodded in response to my comments, while still smiling broadly.

"So, what do you do?" I asked, raising my voice over the din of the crowd.

"I'm an in-house attorney for Allman Mutual Insurance," he stated.

"An attorney? Really? Where did you go to law school?"

"Harvard," he said. "Where did you go to school?"

"I went to Grinnell." This man had possibilities, so I actually had the apparent good luck to meet someone interesting. Asking for the next dance, a waltz, he drew his arm around my waist, and pulled me closer to him as we whirled around. He cocked his head to catch the melody, and hummed the tune.

"So where do you live?" he asked me.

"Out in the country."

"By yourself?" He arched his eyebrows in surprise.

"With my two boys." He would eventually find out anyway, that I had been married.

"So have you been married?" I asked him, sensing strongly that he had not, because he possessed the aura of innocence of those who have never been through a harrowing relationship.

"No."

I became fearless. "Why not?"

"I guess I never found the right person," he said.

"It's never too late," I said.

I grabbed my coat after several more dances with other partners because I did not want to seem desperate by hanging around for him. But back at home, in front of the mirror, I stepped up on my toes with my arms resting on an invisible partner, and twirled around while swaying to the rhythm of a waltz. Even if this man never held me in his arms again, another one would.

On Monday morning, Jean set her coffee mug down on my desk. Behind her, others passed the doorway of my cubicle.

"I met two men at the dance this weekend who seem to be possibilities." I scooted closer. "One is Tom and the other is Cedric."

A smile spread across her face.

"And the thing about Tom," I said, but the phone started ringing. I picked up the receiver, and then put my hand over the mouthpiece.

"It's him." Still retaining her broad smile, she collected her coffee cup and left the cubicle. I breathed in short puffs as I listened to his disembodied voice inviting me to a concert.

Because the concert was in the town where he lived, I drove to his house, a suburban split-level in what had once been the newest section of town. The neighborhood revealed its maturity through the towering evergreens, oaks and maples that formed a canopy over his street. It was halfway dark when I rang the doorbell. The door opened, and there he was, wearing his aviator glasses, a plaid shirt, sweater vest, and khaki pants. As he led me up a half-flight of stairs to the kitchen, I noticed that the rooms had almost no furniture, which told me that he had not established a home for himself, but a place to crash when he wasn't working. I sensed a vacancy in his daily life, somewhat akin to the one I was experiencing as a single mother, but not identical to it, because if he'd never had his own family, he might not miss it. The light from the kitchen spilled onto the polished wooden and linoleum floors. Outside the windows, the boughs of trees swayed in slow, undulating motions.

"Yes, this is the kitchen, and then upstairs, the bedrooms." His voice cracked slightly.

In his red sports car, he drove us to a folk music performance of lively Celtic music. I rested my hand on his knee. He tapped his hand on his leg and nodded in sync to the beat. On the drive back home, he tuned his radio to a classical music station.

"So, have you been employed for very long as a—what was it again?" He reached out to adjust the dial.

"Civil rights investigator. Yes, I guess about fifteen years. What brought you to the Midwest?"

"I got tired of the winters in Buffalo and wanted something warmer, so hired on with a firm located in Kansas City after law school graduation."

"Is your family still living in Buffalo?"

"No, my parents retired to Florida and I have one brother in California and another in Montana."

We continued the drill of reciting the most obvious, superficial facts about ourselves, but other than classical music, I had no idea what this man was passionate about, where he stood on the political spectrum, or what kept him up at night. I tried in vain to get past the guardrail of his refined, yet shallow posturing. Certainly the conversation was cordial, for him probably enjoyable, but as we sped along through the darkness, I experienced the loneliness of trading the intimacy of a long marriage for the superficiality of a first date.

Back at his house, I slid a heavy wooden piano bench away from his upright piano, and warmed up with Czerny exercises. I couldn't play any classical pieces from memory, so resorted to climbing the scales in a rigid, prescribed pattern.

Upon hearing the piano, Tom darted from the room, sifted through stacks of music, and returned with some show tunes, along with his mandolin, penny whistle, and drums. I stumbled through "People Will Say We're in Love," creating a cacophony of wrong notes. He did not seem to care. I noted the time on my watch.

"Well, it's late." I was paying a babysitter.

"You have to go now?"

I started up the stairs. He rushed past me, blocking my access to the front door, then grabbed my shoulders, and kissed me. I kissed him back, answering with my suppressed longing from all the mornings that my head lay on a tear-stained pillow.

He followed me out, and leaned against his car with his arms crossed in front of his chest, smiling. I turned the key in the ignition and put the car in reverse. Obviously he was interested, but I had no guarantees, because the father of my children had left me after fifteen years of marriage, and passion had not stopped other men from taking off. Knowing how much I could grow to care for this man, I was scared stiff.

CHAPTER 19

Perils

At the end of January, on a day that was warmish and windy yet a thin pane of ice clung to the creek, I was cleaning the house while Brendan and Spenser played outside. I swept up the last of the wallpaper scraps of the floral-flocked pattern adorning my redecorated bedroom. Through the open window, Spenser shrieked. At the window, the sound reached me again: a bellowing, an agonized cry, not their normal play sounds.

I tramped through the dead stalks of vegetation leading to the creek. Brendan stood on a large, flat rock that parted shallow streams flowing past it. Spenser sat in a deeper pool, the water up to his chest. He was almost six.

I stepped into the oozing mud and yanked Spenser out of the creek. As I lifted his body into my arms, sheets of water fell from his jeans and shirt.

"Brendan, Brendan! Why didn't you try to pull him out? Why didn't you come and get me?"

Brendan stood on the rock in his green jacket, hands in his pockets, and shrugged. He was nine.

Hot bath water rushed out of the faucet. I stripped off Spenser's wet clothes, stiff like cardboard from the water and slime. Outlined against the glistening tiles of the bathtub, Spenser shook as if he were convulsing. His lips had a bluish tint.

Hypothermia. In how many more minutes, or seconds, would Spenser have lost consciousness and sunk under the surface of the water? In that creek bed with the sun glistening on patches of ice, Brendan might have watched him slip away from us.

I don't blame you, Brendan; you were only a child. I'm the one who was responsible: a harried, overextended single mother, who shuttled the boys to violin and scout activities after working all day, and crammed all the housekeeping chores into evenings and weekends.

On Tuesdays I had a free evening during Stan's visitation, but because I mourned being in the empty house without the boys I surrounded myself with people in the public library. Ensconced within the tall shelves of books, I could hear those in the adjacent reading area rattling the pages of newspapers. Sometimes a child scampered through the maze of the bookshelves, and then vanished after dropping a book with a loud thump.

My father would journey to the library to read on late wintry Sunday afternoons, as darkness set in beyond the tall windows. On several walls, the library now has vertical rows of blue leaves inscribed with the names of donors and those memorialized. I often stand before my father's leaf and touch the letters of his name. Now one of the blue leaves bears the inscription of "Spenser Thomas Gardner."

During the visitation evenings, I sensed that my father spoke to me through the words of the books, so sitting in the aisles with my elbows propped on my knees, I read about divorce. I learned that it is not true that every unhappy family is different, because relationships end according to a predetermined set of behavioral patterns. Often one person wants out, and the other doesn't, may not even realize the partner is unhappy. Before the final split, there is often a fight to end all fights, as though the couple, in one final desperate spasm, bludgeons every last vestige of whatever love existed between them in order to kill it dead.

On the subject of dating after marriage, a popular book, *The Rules*, featured a gleaming diamond ring edged in flowers on its cover. It advised that if you want a marriage proposal from an honorable man, you should follow the mores of your grandmother, rather than the egalitarianism of feminism. Do not chase the man. Let him pursue you. Be cheerful, light-hearted, and busy with your own affairs. Do not cling. Do not bring up the subject of marriage. Withhold physical intimacy. A promising kiss will suffice.

I reflected on my earlier relationships, when I received embarrassing proposals of marriage from men I considered to be mere friends, whereas the heartthrob with whom I was physically passionate would not commit. Maybe there was something to these rules. Maybe despite necessary and valid feminine advancements in education and employment, the basic biochemistry between men and women that governs love and marriage cannot be altered. I decided to follow these rules with Tom, because I had nothing to lose, and everything to gain. Tom was charming, refined, well-educated and wealthy. If he married me, Brendan and Spenser would have a stepfather, we could be a family again, and the financial and logistical problems of managing my life would be solved. I could not allow myself to envision, even for one second, the envelopes from mutual fund investment firms that were stacked high on his counter, because my anxiety level would skyrocket.

In those stacks, I also perused *The Unexpected Legacy of Divorce* by Judith S. Wallerstein, which dispels the myth that children easily adjust to divorce. Instead, by illustrating the divided loyalties, the interrupted schedules, the increased stress, and the battles projected onto future graduation, marriage and christening ceremonies, Wallerstein asserted that divorce leaves scars that last a lifetime.

To illustrate the chaos, Wallerstein provided a poignant example of a little girl who was frantic because no one fed or watered her rabbit while she visited the non-custodial parent. I grieved for the little girl. I grieved for the rabbit. I grieved for all the insults, deprivation and pain that Brendan and Spenser were experiencing. I never wished this for them. To compensate, I did my best to fashion the perfect Christmas, replete with decorations, cookies, visits to Santa and presents. We dyed Easter eggs, which I hid outside the house. I baked them elaborate birthday cakes, and hosted parties at the skating rink or bowling alley. I volunteered for their school parties and school committees, but at night, I was totally exhausted. I worried that I would not be able to continue this pace. Our marriage had been far from ideal, but being divorced was worse. I deeply resented Stan for thrusting me into these circumstances, which I never would have chosen.

I glanced up from my book at the clock on the library wall. I needed to be at Stan's apartment, a few blocks away, in ten minutes. He lived in an apartment building close to downtown which had a history of robberies and at least one murder. I rang his doorbell, and his garbled voice came through the intercom.. He had never invited me up, and the heavy wooden door was always locked, so I huddled in the mist. Behind me, cars whizzed by on a major traffic way, and across the street, the red neon lights of a Walgreen's drugstore blinked in the darkness. Stan, Brendan and Spenser appeared behind the panes of the wooden door. After acknowledging me with a brief glance, he pushed Brendan and Spenser through the door, which locked behind them.

Once outside on the sidewalk, Spenser fell down on the pavement, throwing a tantrum. With my purse falling forward over my shoulder, I grabbed his hand and tried to pull him to a stand. A man with a dark beard, worn coat and hands thrust into his pockets approached us, who smelled of tobacco and whiskey.

"Do you have a quarter you could lend me?" He surveyed me with distant eyes.

"No, I really don't," I answered, yanking Spenser with increased force.

With wobbling steps, the man kept going down the sidewalk. I hustled Brendan and Spenser into the car, and locked the doors. Stories overhead, behind his sealed windows, Stan would not have heard our screams had there been a violent confrontation. Because we had nothing to say to each other, he did not even linger at the doorstep to make sure I made it safely to the car. Naturally I was frantic, but survival mode left no time for lamenting that Stan had a lump of coal where a beating heart should have been. The boys and I simply would have been crime statistics, having been thrown into a place where we never would have found ourselves but for the divorce. Stretched beyond our limits, lacking resources, worn down and run over, we were easy prey. This is how people fall through the cracks.

CHAPTER 20

Reconciliation

I f you would have asked me after the divorce why Stan and I were no longer married, I would have reported that he was selfish, rigid and controlling. He called me scatter-brained, lacking common sense, and lazy, which I vehemently protested.

"Lazy? He called you lazy?" my sister said at the time. "Girl, you never sit down."

But then the years passed. We were never meant to be married, but through our bond with the children, mutual acquaintances, shared history and common interests, we became friends. Now, I'll call him with a short question about Brendan, and we'll talk for several hours, candidly, about anything. Certainly surviving the death of a child negates pettiness and puts even a failed marriage in perspective, but even more importantly, if being a friend to everyone is a thread woven through Spenser's personality, how could I not honor him by making peace with his father? I decided to interview him about our marriage and Spenser.

On a summer day, Stan swung on his front porch, his right side in profile, while he was reading. I approached the gold stucco two-story house with white impatiens flanking his front steps.

"You walked," he said, somewhat startled.

I glanced at my watch. Ten thirty in the morning. It would be two in the afternoon before I left Stan's house. After several years of reflection, I'd say that the main cause of our divorce was our inability to communicate effectively with each other without defensiveness or volatile emotions.

Inside of his house, we sat on opposite ends of his maroon couch, which once belonged to both of us.

"So you saw *The Sound of Music* last night?" I began.

"I did, and it got me to thinking about how things have changed in the thirty-two years since I first came to this town. I was thinking about how this is my life and things aren't going to be much different from now on because it's been largely written." Stan wore khaki shorts and a steel grey polo shirt. He occasionally flexed his barefoot toes.

"It brought back a flood of memories for me," I confessed. "Do you remember how I was nominated for best supporting actress for being Frenchy in *Grease* but the woman who played the Mother Abbess won. It's pretty hard to trump 'Climb Every Mountain.'"

"Indeed." He nodded. I noted that Stan still has the same expressive eyes with long lashes.

I sat up straighter on the couch.

"What were your impressions when you first met me?" I asked.

He turned toward me with an amused look. "We were in the University Heights clubhouse. Somebody mentioned going to Warehouse Stage on the Levee and you picked up on that, started talking about being in *Vanities* with the three women. You were being a bit theatrical, and animated. It kind of perked you up."

"Were you ever in love with me?" I asked.

"I'd say so, yeah. Of course, it's a waxing and waning thing."

This surprised me, until I thought back to the nickname he had for me when we were first married, "Roo."

"What went wrong with our marriage?" I asked him.

"Well, of course that would be multi-determined," he began, slightly jutting out his chin, "but the straw that broke the camel's back for me was your wanting another child."

"But then Spenser died, so it would have been a wash. Why were you so opposed to it?"

"I don't know. I'd have to speculate today." He searched for the answer. "It had something to do with the extra work, extra money, exhaustion. But then my feelings do vacillate. Now I look at our office manager who has three grown children and willingly embraces being a grandmother. But the other end of it, with our young secretary, is that the children are sick, she's constantly busy with them and misses work. It's hard to look back fifteen years, but it was too much. Then again, maybe it was just me being lazy and selfish."

I glanced at the oil painting of yellow chrysanthemums that hung over his fireplace, which used to hang in our sun room. He swiveled to look directly at me.

"I do think that very few people have the patience and tolerance to be good parents. Of course we all have our talents and strengths, but I do not think I am one of those parents, and for the most part, you aren't either," he said.

I wrote in my notebook as quickly as I could, but my writing was not a diversionary tactic because his assessment of my parenting skills did not anger me. I did not agree with him, but could accept that he had a differing opinion. I relished his honesty.

"So . . . Spenser," I said.

Stan nodded. "How different life would be if he were still here. A month or two before he died I came to the decision that I would probably have to dedicate a chunk of my life to him, and that would be my role in life."

I had never heard this before. "You would take care of him?" I asked.

"Yes, however fleeting, I had an awareness that my lot in life would be to take care of him, knowing this may not have been the life I wanted, but this is what I'm going to have. He never would have been able to live completely by himself. I decided I needed to get involved with the developmental disability community. So when he died, my future changed."

All the German beer steins, in vivid bright colors, once on top of our hutch, were now ensconced inside his built-in book cases.

"I will say this, my life became easier, but then again, who knows what journeys he would have taken me on? It would have been very hard." He reflected for a moment. "I'm not sure I'm strong enough. I'm not religious, but from the perspective of religious values, one might say, 'Well, Mr. Gardner, you weren't up to the task.'" His eyes widened with the realization.

No, he wasn't, but I no longer hold that against him. We simply are what we are, born with certain traits, and struggle to chisel self-improvement designs onto our personalities like a sculptor who tediously chips away at rock.

"Do you ever visit the grave?" I asked.

He glanced again toward his front door that opened onto the shaded porch.

"I haven't been there in two or three years, and I guess the primary reason is that I don't think about him very much. What is that going to accomplish? Talking to the dead, it's just superstitious magic. Why do people visit graves anyway?" He lifted his hands in an exasperated gesture. "So, I don't see a need to make a physical pilgrimage. I'll occasionally have dreams and he is always the age he was when he died, but they are much less frequent. You can't control when memories of Spenser pop up in your head, but no, I feel no compulsion to visit the grave."

"I don't think that Brendan has grieved Spenser's death." Stan agreed, but was only momentarily sidetracked. Reflections, philosophies and conclusions kept tumbling out of him.

"There was a time I believed," he continued, "that we might visit him in the afterlife. But of course there's no evidence of that."

"So do you think you'll ever see him again?" I asked.

"No, of course not." He looked directly at me, his face frozen for a moment in a conciliatory smile.

I glanced at my watch.

"So in thinking about Spenser's life, would you say the positives outweighed the negatives?" I asked.

Stan gave a quick laugh. "Well, you'd hate to go on record saying the balance fell to the negatives. Wouldn't you want to have the ideal child with all the attributes: beauty, brains, affability? Sure, because we live through our children and they are a reflection of ourselves. I like my challenges in incremental doses, and Spenser was a huge jump."

I wrote quickly, recording all of this, some of which I had only intuited, but had never known before. He suddenly leaned forward and turned to face me.

"Margaret, I wonder how you became the better person? I fall short. I'm not that strong. I'm kind of weak. I don't know that I was up to all the challenges. It was more than I could handle."

He never would have acknowledged this while we were married. Because we heard footsteps and voices approaching, this comment remained suspended in mid-air.

"Oh, here they come." Stan started for the door. "Probably from some church. I'll go tell them I'm not interested because I'm an atheist."

After their polite conversation faded away, he sat back down on the couch. "Spenser took me places I did not want to go, literally and figuratively. Like that time at the skating rink, when all three of us were falling down. You just had to swallow hard for him, the things he couldn't do, like throwing a ball. It's disappointing, makes your life harder. Who wants that?" He put his hands on his knees. "But now I'm just repeating myself."

I shut my notebook and tossed my pen back into my purse. "I've got to get going. Someone is waiting at the library, and I hope he's not starting to feel abandoned," I said.

"Oh, that's right," he laughed and saw me to the door. "Nice talking to you."

I wish I could have stayed to talk longer. After you've been married to someone for fifteen years, had two children together, and one of them dies, you know him quite well and have much in common.

CHAPTER 21

Courtship

For my second date with Tom, I spent all day cleaning the house, which is my fallback when I'm afraid that my best will not be good enough. I could not control whether this man would ever love me, nor was I an attorney with his salary, but presenting a freshly-mopped kitchen floor I could handle. Tom pulled into the driveway, so I rushed downstairs. Behind the windshield of his red sports car, he studied how I stood on the porch in front of the house, as though he were watching everything in slow motion. Then he emerged from the car, looking very distinguished in his navy blue suit. Taking two steps toward me with his fingers on his lapels, he surveyed me from head to toe and back up again.

At the reception, when he introduced me to his business colleagues, we sipped champagne, lined our plates with hors d'oeuvres and engaged in pleasant small talk. Alone again after the performance, he helped me into my coat, opened the car door, and drove forward with his eyes on the road, very guarded. I wondered if he had any sexual drive. Saint Thomas, as I sometimes referred to him with Marilyn or Jean.

Our third date was a polka dance in Strawberry Hill, a Croatian section of Kansas City. Tom taught me the waltz, polka, foxtrot, and rhumba. With my mind jumbled from the different steps, I hoped to outlast the band, but the shrill accordion and tamburitzas reeled with perpetual energy. During the break, he introduced me to his friends

Sid and Lana. He had held me in the darkened ballroom but once back in the car, he kept his eyes on the road.

"So how do you know Sid?" I asked.

"He plays the tuba. I've seen him in a tuba band," Tom answered, waiting for the red light.

"Oh, how did he meet Lana?"

"I don't know."

"Well, how long have they been together?"

He shrugged. "I don't know that either."

Men usually don't know. I guessed that Lana, recently widowed, probably felt the same ambivalence toward these dances that I did. She dressed up, showed up, and performed the steps with a blank facial expression. When Sid extended his hand, she followed, like an automated doll. I suppose Tom enjoyed sharing ethnic folk dancing with a new partner, and I did tell myself that it is important to expand our horizons. I also reminded myself that I was fortunate to be dating this man, even though I lacked the energy for the incessant lively dancing and found the music to be jarring. Whenever I was with him, I had two children at home who missed their mother.

Stopped at another red light, Tom concentrated on driving as the radio began playing Rachmaninoff's "Piano Concerto No. 2." Animated by the music, his baritone voice broke the silence as he crooned to the melody. Then in a moment of tenderness, he reached out to stroke my cheek, and ran his fingers through my hair. I crouched down in the seat, daring to hope that in a candid moment this man was revealing his true feelings toward me. He then turned back again to the steering wheel, and fixed his eyes on the road.

This weekend routine of attending musical concerts and folk dancing continued for the next several months. I would find a babysitter if it was not Stan's visitation weekend, get dressed up, apply makeup, and plaster a smile on my face. With Tom, I did not discuss the temperamental washing machine or how many dirty socks were piled up. I scarcely mentioned the boys at all, sensing that he wished they did not exist, because he never asked about them, or suggested meeting them. Yet at folk dances, sometimes sitting apart from the others, before I stumbled through all the impossible steps and Tom whirled me around into nauseous dizziness, I would gaze at the polished wooden floor, and long for Brendan and Spenser.

I had figured out that marriage would be the best thing that could happen to both of us, but Tom talked only of music and trifling subjects. I envied Marilyn, because since the first contra dance, Jack had been hounding her about getting married, and didn't mind if her kids were along on their dates. Tom really wanted nothing to do with Brendan and Spenser. So I smiled, and I danced, and I waited.

On our fourth date, we sat at my blonde oak dining room table, eating oatmeal cake. I turned the pages of a seed catalogue.

"I'm thinking of planting two more peach trees this year," I said. My words did not seem to register with him.

"Would you like to sit on the couch?" I led him into the darkened living room, not knowing what to talk about next.

As soon as we sat down, he grabbed me into an embrace and smothered me with kisses. I undid the top button of his shirt, and stroked his hairy chest. I undid the second button, then the third, and then pulled his shirttails out from his pants. When there was a respite to the kissing, I sat on the edge of the couch as he reclined with his head on the armrest. As he beamed at me with an expression of arousal and joy, he revealed his kindness and gentleness lying underneath.

The physical attraction we ignited in each other was typical of the breathless, romantically-charged early days of a relationship that is headed somewhere. While staring at some piece of paper in the office, I was transported to the first time his hands ran all over my body. Because we came from similar families and educational backgrounds, falling in love with him was a predictable outcome. I knew that we were a match, but he did not. He told me about several of his serious previous relationships with women who wanted to marry him. He did not reciprocate their feelings. Would he ever want to marry anybody? Would he ever decide to marry me, or would he discard me like he did them? How long should I wait? He was having a good time; I was separated from my children and paying for babysitters. The stakes were very high, so I was tap dancing as fast as I could through all of our dates.

"Do you know what really impresses me about you?" I ran my hand down his cheekbone.

"What?"

"The fact that you sing and play music at your church every week."

"Really?" He laid his hand on his heart.

"Yeah, I mean, yeah. I'm not going to start quoting the Bible or asking if you've been saved, but it shows that you have substance. Faith is important. It is, damn it. Not some narrow-minded religion that crusades against gays, but a faith that emphasizes service to others and lets you believe you are part of something much bigger than yourself. In my darkest times it has kept me going. I don't see how people get by without it."

"Well, thank you," he said.

After their bath on an ordinary night, the boys and I chose a story. The lettering and pictures of the book came into stark relief when lit by the wall light behind our shoulders. Brendan snuggled next to me on my right, and Spenser, now six, was on my left. Both had wet hair and smelled like baby shampoo from the bath.

While studying the book, Spenser inhaled with audible breaths due to his respiratory infection, and a slight bit of drool trickled from the corner of his mouth. He frowned in sympathy with Bert of Sesame Street, who had been rejected in the story. I reached up to turn the page.

"Nobody likes me, nobody likes me, nobody likes me, because I'm stupid," Spenser said in a sing-song tone, apparently resigned to it. "Everybody hates me, but I like them anyway."

Where did that come from?

"Well, it's time for bed," I said, shutting the book and standing up from the couch. I didn't know what to say, because it was too late to explore all the ramifications of the situation he had introduced. We could talk about it tomorrow, maybe after school.

In their darkened rooms, I tucked them in and we said prayers. Then I waited for Tom to call. After a few moments, Spenser's breath assumed the measured cadence of one asleep. The night-light offered the only illumination in the room. Half dreaming, with my head turned to the side against the back of the rocking chair, I replayed tapes of conversations in the office, of what I still had to do before tomorrow.

The jangling phone roused me from my reverie. Tom's voice sounded more formal, yet also more edgy than normal.

"Margaret," he said, "I've been thinking that even though you are a wonderful woman and we have had some great times together, I do not want to continue a relationship with a woman with children."

My focus went to the place where the white tile floor met the brown wooden cabinets as my chest expanded..

"But you don't even know them. You haven't even met them. You haven't given the situation a chance," I said, twisting the phone cord in my sweaty palm.

"I just, I just," he stammered, "think that it would be better for both of us if we ended it now and I continued looking for a woman with no children."

So, my worst fears had come to pass. I remembered *The Rules*, and combined with what I had learned from past relationships, knew that screaming and wailing would get me nowhere.

"Well, I certainly hope that you change your mind," I said in a frail voice. "I think we could have a great future ahead of us."

As I ascended the stairs, I did not emit more than a few little tears, because I wasn't surprised. My greatest fear had come to pass, and I had been a fool to expect a different outcome. Tom was going to leave me, just like my husband did, and all the others before him.

CHAPTER 22

The Roto-Tiller

The cold and rain dissipated, the weather grew more balmy, and soon it was mid-May, the end of another school year. Between Scouts, lessons, and classroom parties, I had stepped up as the happy, involved mom, bringing in a tray of decorated cupcakes to the Christmas party, or treat bags to the Valentine's party. The cheerful, effervescent multi-tasker, believing, with no rational reason for doing so, that everything would be all right.

On the last day of school, I watched Spenser's class frolicking in the sun, playing tug of war and tossing bean bags. As unexciting as the party was, I did not want it or the school year to end, because the boys and I would go home to a cavernous house with an endless succession of seconds, minutes and hours to fill.

Memorial Day weekend, three days stretching out lazily into the spring. An anniversary, because exactly one year ago, Stan had left me. On Saturday afternoon, I decided to tackle the garden, overgrown with weeds, because the produce could make a dent in our food budget. In the shade of the Morton building barn, the roto-tiller sat adjacent to the riding lawn mower. Knowing enough to pull back the lever to open the choke, I grasped the handle of the pull chord, and yanked. Nothing. I pulled a second time, bringing my hand up past my shoulder. Silence. I tried again, and again. Not a whimper from the machine. Without any mechanical knowledge and insufficient physical strength, it was really hard to live in the country without a man.

Defeated, I headed back into the house, and lay on the couch. I squinted up at the white ceiling, then closed my eyes. As I tallied the struggles of the past year, I stiffened with fear while the house closed in on me as though I were sealed in an alabaster tomb.

"Who do I think I'm kidding?" I said to myself. "I'm broke, I'm lonely, and I can't get this roto-tiller to work!" I considered jumpstarting the relationship with Tom, but my efforts might only dead end into more pain. Although Brendan and Spenser played quietly in their rooms, I would have to summon the energy to feed them, organize their messy rooms, and eventually put them to bed. Hurtling into an unknown future, all I could foresee was the daily grind of arduous tasks, loneliness, and financial insecurity, possibly until the end of my life.

Because my heart was racing, I was gripped by extreme anxiety, yet because I was unable to move off the couch, I was also depressed. Before I could not have imagined how those two contradictory emotions could coexist, but there I was, with my anxiety flooring the accelerator in a car going nowhere.

Once, mercifully, the weekend was over, I returned to the routine of my desk. Just as my work had scuttled my worries about the infant Spenser, I now buried my sorrows in my case files. The morning sped by with returned telephone calls and the paperwork of administrative closures.

By noon, the commotion ceased. I had no errands to run, or invitations for lunch. The dark feelings returned in thundering waves. I did not know how I could make it through another day, another hour, or even another second.

I jerked open the desk drawer, pulled out the thick booklet describing our insurance coverage and dialed the number of a therapist.

"So could you come in a few days from now?" she asked. "Or can you even wait that long?"

"Probably not," I answered.

In the evenings after work, I collapsed into a chair, reading books about loss and grief. Every sentence was a lifeline, letting me know that others, in similar chairs in other bedrooms, suffered as well.

I prayed fervently, almost all of the time. During the noon hours, I was drawn to the basilica on the corner. Inside, it was quiet, cool, and buzzing with unseen spirits. I pulled down the kneeling bench, clasped my hands in prayer, and observed the statuary of the Holy Family, their pastel plaster hands outstretched in adoration. Stained glass windows dotted the sides of the church, and frescoes of angels with swirling robes adorned the dome over the altar. Soon a priest in white robes would enter, make the sign of the cross, read a Biblical passage, perhaps give a short homily. On the street again, in the bright sunlight, the peace of the muted cathedral sustained me.

I attended the vast cathedral nearly every day. Sometimes when I prayed, I visualized an image that had outstretched arms that were clothed in a flowing blue robe. Because I could never see the head, the vision lacked gender, but its essence of compassion and nurturing evoked femininity. She seemed to portend that giving of oneself is holy. Whether she was there to help me, or was teaching me by example, she communicated a simple message: Let love flow through you, through every vein and artery, seamlessly, effortlessly, without even the propulsion of a beating heart.

I attended Beginning Experiences, a support group for those recently divorced or widowed. In the church basement, seated on secondhand couches, we were united by palpable grief.

A woman named Deb, petite and with dark-rimmed glasses, explained that her husband was frequently hospitalized, as was his ailing mother, so Deb spent a great deal of time tending to them in their hospital rooms, while maintaining the household and raising their teenage daughter. Her husband had also befriended an unmarried girl with a baby who lived with them.

"Then one day I discovered," Deb said, "that she was living with us because my husband was the father of her baby."

No one said anything. Her confidence was safe with those who had similar stories to share.

"I just don't know where I am anymore, what I'm doing," said Ann to a blank spot on the wall. Ann was in her thirties and had straight hair that bobbed as she turned her head. "I somehow drove to the grocery store, but then when I got to the parking lot, I said to myself, 'Why am I here?'"

John was middle-aged, with grey hair shaved close to his head. He missed being in his family home, with his children playing loud instruments out of tune. His wife had prolonged periods of depression when she would retreat to her bedroom. One day his wife emerged from the bedroom to announce that she wanted a divorce.

"My friends tell me that I should take a cruise," John related. "But why should I spend all that time and money going somewhere just to be depressed? All I have to do is go up to the top of Bennett's Mound and look out in order to be just as sad."

When it was my turn, I droned on about the failures of my marriage, all of my shortcomings, in an endless stream.

"But what about him?" Deb interrupted. "You sit there saying 'I did this or that,' what about him?"

I faced her, startled into the realization that I was not entirely to blame.

At a Beginning Experiences retreat at a convent in Kansas City, we spent the weekend journaling, commiserating in groups, and diving into our grief. A young, plump woman's husband had killed himself shortly after the divorce was final. A woman's priest accompanied her to the jail where her husband was incarcerated for being with a prostitute. Coming home late Sunday night, as another passenger and I hashed out all we had experienced, we passed the baseball stadium, which meant that we had driven many miles out of our way, but more importantly, we were on the route to recovery. When I got home, I filled up the cat's water and the dog food dish and scouted around. Something had changed. Things were not quite as bad.

So I wrote Tom a letter, because I had nothing to lose. My words pulsed through the pages, as though I were speaking to him, about how with our common interests we could forge a meaningful partnership, that he might enjoy driving home each night to Spenser running to greet him in his Batman costume. I kissed the letter before depositing it in the mail slot.

Within less than a week, Tom called. Holding the receiver as I lowered myself onto the couch, I reveled in his honey voice.

"So you called because?" I asked.

"Because nobody has ever bothered to write me a letter like that," he answered.

So we made plans for the next weekend, another concert, another round of scheduling babysitters.

We were so happy when we were together. That summer, we swam at the lake, with our warm, slippery bodies touching in the dark green water. As we laid on the hot sand, shielding our eyes against the sun, we discovered more about each other. At my house, I played the choppy chords of Praetorius on the piano, while he played the melody with his tin whistle. Afterward, we would pass under the arching trees on our country road, calling to the barred owls as they hooted to each other overhead.

As the summer passed, I went through the motions of dating, enjoying our activities with an undertow of dread. It was not a difficult part to play, even though I was certain that he would eventually leave me, as all the others had done. He still had not met Brendan or Spenser.

The inevitable weekend approached, that Tom and I would spend the night together. To assent with my body, would result in the most intense pain if he withdrew.

I sat in my office on a Friday afternoon, unable to concentrate on the files.

"Barbara, Barbara, I want to be with him, but I am so scared."

Barbara sat on the green vinyl chair in the corner of my office. As a former alcoholic, she frequently counseled girls who were breaking the habit.

"You're terrified because the relationship is going to the next level," she said. "Just fake it until you make it. Fake it until you make it."

"Of course, there's always the chance that I won't make it to the other side, that this will end in complete failure."

She held my gaze. "Of course that's a possibility. There are no guarantees or certainties. Just let go of the outcome, and live in the present as much as you can."

Tom sat at his kitchen table after we spent that first night, wearing his blue gym shorts with his brown hair tangled from the shower. His broad chest and muscular arms were perfectly sculpted and he could not have been more gorgeous.

"What kind of cereal do you like?"

"I guess the raisin bran," I answered. I poured the milk over it and put the silver spoon to my mouth, but I could not choke it down, because my stomach was locked into a vise. My reaction to stress is to tighten up so that I can't even swallow. Since the divorce, I was at least fifteen pounds lighter, and never had the weight to spare. At the office, my friend Lola had noticed.

"Margaret, have you lost a lot of weight?" she asked.

"This dress is slimming," I said with a smile.

"All of your dresses are slimming," she answered.

It was true. At the grocery store I stocked up with the boxed drinks loaded with vitamins for people undergoing chemotherapy treatment because I couldn't swallow anything else. The chocolate and vanilla flavors were best.

One morning I flipped through the pages of a file when the telephone rang.

"Well, were you planning on enrolling Brendan and Spenser at Chippewa this year?" asked the school secretary.

Summer was ending so somewhere at home were the blue enrollment forms. How could I be so stressed that I overlooked enrolling them in school?

Several evenings later, Brendan, Spenser and I shopped for their school clothes at a discount store. I flipped through the racks, looking for clothes in colors that would mix and match.

In line at the checkout counter, I thumbed through the price tags. I was short by twenty or thirty dollars.

It had taken me more than an hour to find these particular school clothes. I studied the writing on the sign detailing what happens to people who write bad checks, but bought the clothes anyway, figuring I had time to transfer money from another account.

I took another risk by explaining to Tom that because we had been dating for six months, it was time for him to meet the boys.

Tom stood by the bookcase. Brendan, nine, wearing a white polo shirt and some khaki school shorts, stood across from Tom without expression.

"Brendan, this is Tom." My voice caught slightly.

"Brendan," Tom said, and reached out to shake his hand.

"Brendan, go get your pictures. Show Tom what you've been drawing," I suggested.

Brendan retrieved the drawings and handed them to Tom.

"Oh," Tom said, examining the indistinct shapes, "so this is?"

"A man driving a car and that's the house," Brendan explained in a monotone.

Spenser demonstrated his enthusiasm for the new guest by running around in the adjacent room. I had informed Tom of Spenser's disability, and figured that as time wore on he would discover its ramifications for himself.

The weekend before Tom picked us up to go to the zoo, I checked the clothes the boys wore, but did not coach them. They anticipated an enjoyable outing; for me it was the ultimate audition. Just inside the gates, we were greeted by the giraffe exhibit. By the time we reached the black bear exhibit, Spenser rode piggyback on Tom, with his arms wrapped around his neck. Tom swiveled toward me, with his arms linked under Spenser's legs. Spenser smiled at me over Tom's shoulder.

"Could you loosen his grip just a little?" Tom asked me. "He's cutting off my air."

"Sure, you just reposition him, jostle him slightly so he's up higher on you," I said, giving Spenser a little boost.

As we were driving away, Spenser started kicking into my seat from his backseat, to let me know he was still there. The boys detected that Mom's speech was more formal, and that she exhibited a tense, artificial cheerfulness during the afternoon, but at least there were no major meltdowns.

CHAPTER 23

Green Beans

E ven though I had to turn the ground over one shovelful at a time, the warming weather drew me outside and I planted the garden. We live in a valley in Kansas, and there's nothing flat or boring about the terrain. Our landscape is that of undulating wooded hills threaded by gurgling streams. The woods are populated with all kinds of creatures, some visible, some in hiding, all magical. Once the loud scream of a woman came from the creek, but no one was there. A bobcat, someone suggested.

A long, winding driveway leads down to the house, snuggled against the hill. The yellow lights coming from the window, which send lone shafts into the woods, are eclipsed by nights of a full moon, when a dazzling white light blankets everything, almost like snow. Stan and I chose this house because we wanted to breed this wildness into the boys: the insistent crickets, the frog chorus which starts on one specific day in March, the cries of a circling hawk. In and of itself, the countryside is a holy shrine.

By mid-July, the garden was teeming with green beans, tomatoes, sweet corn, onions, yellow squash, and zucchini. Because I could not afford a new one, I purchased a used pressure canner.

"It's been the source of many happy memories for us," said the white-haired lady as I handed her the cash.

"Yes, I want to continue the tradition," I said to her. Whenever I preserve food, I feel surrounded by farm women from the past, bustling around steaming kitchens, putting up the bounty of the harvest in amber and fuchsia jars that sparkle in the light.

I come alive between the hours of about ten to midnight. One summer night, the windows were open, letting in the racket of the insect choristers.

I had sterilized the glass jars, simmered the beans in a big pot on the stove, shoved them into the jars and capped them with gold lids and bands. I set them one by one in the canner, and set the large and heavy lid on the circular rim. I turned the lid to the right. It refused to lock. I tried again. I checked the rubber gasket and knelt down at eye level to the lid. I rotated the lid many times, but it would not fall into place.

"No," I cried. "This has got to work. We need this food."

The green beans, lined up in the jars on the red counter, were ready to be processed. I crumpled onto the pink carpet of the bottom stair with my back against the wall and closed my eyes.

"Please God, I need your help now. Not later, not an hour from now, not some unanswered prayer that won't be revealed until tomorrow, now."

My voice continued mumbling in a monotone, with the intonation of a mantra. "Now, God, now. Not later, now."

I stood up, took a deep breath, and approached the canner. I lifted the lid and positioned it over the outside rim. Underneath my hands, I felt the lid swivel into place, slowly rotating, until it locked. For the first few moments, it moved on its own.

I wasn't about to waste any time being mystified. As a divorced mother with two children, I needed all the miracles I could get. Despite the financial troubles, the physical exhaustion, the craziness of relationships, and the problems at the office, I believed that things were going to get better. My faith, clear as a drop of water, sustained me.

Not that my faith magically solved all my problems. Once he perceived that this new man in mom's life was diverting my attention from him, Spenser began sabotaging my blooming relationship with Tom. On a hot day as we drove down a dusty road to the beach, Spenser kicked the back of my seat and ground his fingers into my sweaty back. At a Greek folk dance festival in Kansas City, his shrill scream pierced the room because he wanted a salad. When we stayed in a hotel, he wailed interminably next door. He wanted no Tom, and all of me next to him so he wouldn't be in that alien, loveless room.

As I laid on the starched sheets in the dark, Spenser's amplified shrieks sent a jolt through me, because although Tom loved me, his reluctance to take on the boys prevented him from making a commitment. The boys could not understand how we would be better off, or that I loved Tom. They wanted their mom all to themselves, even a mom who sobbed late at night as she did the dishes with a balance of thirty dollars in the checking account. I flirted with the idea of letting the boys live with their dad, but concluded that if I had to choose, I would choose them, even though I shuddered at the tunnel of loneliness stretching before me.

Many years before, when Brendan and Spenser were both asleep in their cribs past midnight, I spied the headlights of a vehicle descending the driveway. Once in the driveway, the driver killed the headlights and remained in the truck. With my heart pulsating in my throat like the wings of a bird, I crept downstairs for a better view through the front door, but could not identify the faces of the strangers through the darkness of their cab, parked yards away from the porch.

I opened the heavy front door, did a quick dance between it and the screen door, and slipped back into the house. Even though I feared for my safety, I wanted to let these intruders know somebody was home.

With no haste, they ignited the engine, backed up and drove away.

I crept upstairs to the boys' bedroom. The night-light illuminated the small pattern in the wallpaper. Their breathing was barely audible, and they emanated the smell of freshly-bathed children. I realized at that moment that I would have done anything to defend them, even at the cost of my own life. After all, their lives were just beginning, and I had lived forty years. So, when it came right down to it, I would choose the boys over Tom, but I wanted them both.

As I left my car to meet my friend Marilyn on a bright sunny afternoon, I steadied myself with a quick step against the force of the wind. By now Tom and I stood at two and a half years of innumerable dinners in fine restaurants, classical musical concerts, and weekends that I had paid a babysitter. During sleepless nights as the clock struck one, then two, and then three, I warned him that I could not continue this dance indefinitely. With his eyes shut and wrist on his forehead, he would respond with "Can we talk about this tomorrow?"

Marilyn and I ordered our food and took our trays to a table flooded with sun. She and Jack had been married for several years. Her new job since leaving the agency sounded interesting. I sighed, and stuck a French fry into the ketchup.

"Marilyn, what I wanted to talk about today is the relationship with Tom, to get your opinion as to what I should do."

She inclined her head, as though searching for a question.

"So have you found out something about him that you weren't expecting?"

"No, he's still a wonderful man." My stomach tightened. "What I'm concerned about is that we have been dating for two and a half years and he has not proposed to me."

"But as long as you're having a great time, why are you worried?" She painted the air with her straw, as though she were holding a brush.

"Paying a babysitter every other weekend, imposing on my sister to take them for a week during the summer, all that dressing up and going dancing is for what? I want a permanent relationship." I leaned forward over the half-eaten food.

"But he's never been married before. Especially considering that he's in his forties, you're asking him to make a major adjustment." She picked up her drink and took a sip.

"Yes, I can respect that, but he's had time. I just don't know how much longer I should wait." I took a deep breath, and ventured further. "Haven't you read in advice columns about women who waited ridiculously long, like twenty or thirty years, and then they were really old, and had no prospects, and realized they had wasted their lives?"

"Yeah, that's crazy, but if you give him some kind of ultimatum you risk losing him entirely."

"I know that. I know that well, because when I was in my late twenties a relationship was driving me crazy, and when I told him that if we didn't get married it was over, he was gone." With downcast eyes, I averted my glance to the white table top.

Marilyn shrugged. "I can sympathize, but in the end, it is up to you. Just be sure that you can live with whatever consequences come along."

"It's almost," I said as I dragged a piece of lettuce across the paper wrapper, "as though I can see the handwriting on the wall, that it's already doomed, because if you have to force someone, doesn't that mean that he doesn't really love you?" A child darted past us, then held her paper cup to the beverage dispenser on tiptoe.

After leaving Marilyn, I decided not to issue any ultimatum, because I did not have the power in this relationship. But as the summer rolled by, the pantomime I played at contra dances became more forced. By September at the Renaissance festival, as we wove our way through the roving minstrels and the painted actresses with dresses that exposed their cleavage, I counted on my fingers that this was our third Renaissance festival, the third time that I had dressed as a gypsy and danced to Celtic jigs from the time the gates opened until they staged the grand finale against a setting sun.

"Let's go," he said, clutching his program. "This harp ensemble is playing in Dinwiddie Dell in ten minutes. Which way is it?" he said, surveying the moving throngs of people. He wore a white flowing tunic with a sash at the waist, striped pants and odd leather shoes that turned up at the toes.

"I don't know," I answered, poking along on the dirt path strewn with straw. The site of the festival was a maze of woods, bridges and decorated shops. After he found the harp ensemble, I stayed a distance behind, with my arms crossed. He knew I was mad.

Within a week or so, Tom terminated the relationship again because he could not foresee life with the boys. That weekend, the boys and I watched the dazzling costumes behind the footlights at a university play. I had survived other major disappointments. Brendan and Spenser, their faces bathed in soft light, were transfixed by the action on the stage. After all, I still had them, and we were together.

The following Tuesday, Tom called. "Margaret, this weekend is the piano concert in Kansas City."

"You want to go together?"

"Yes, the concert starts at eight, so I'll be by about six-thirty. Maybe earlier, if we want to go to a restaurant." His words sounded forced, with a hard edge to them, as he avoided referencing that this conversation completely reversed his termination of the relationship the week before.

"Okay, that'll be good. Bye."

I was stunned that he had called again, because I had no confidence in myself. I could not fathom that maybe he was too deeply in love with me to be able to leave, and that during our short absence, he may have missed me.

CHAPTER 24

Reversals

A week before my December birthday, Tom and I dined in a restaurant. He occupied himself with cutting the roast with his fork and knife. Even though he remained unsettled regarding his future with the boys, the dynamics between us had shifted. His futile attempts at ending the relationship had been unsuccessful, so perhaps there was no turning back.

I twisted my black and gold class ring over the joint of my fourth finger, and handed it to him across the table.

"You're going to need this to size the engagement ring," I stated.

He said nothing, but slipped it into the inside pocket of his sports jacket. He proposed the following week on my birthday, and that spring he introduced me to his parents in Florida. I had never desired to visit Disney World, because I envisioned nothing but noise and confusion, but after Tom suggested we stop by Disney World while we were down there, it seemed the perfect opportunity for Brendan and Spenser.

When we emerged from the tunnel under the railroad and entered Main Street in Disney World this is where we were in our lives: Brendan was twelve, Spenser was nine, and Tom and I would be married in about a month. For me, anxiety and sadness had been completely eclipsed by a future of endless possibilities as prim and promising as the twentieth-century buildings that sparkled in various hues of every imaginable color. From the rooftops, the towers, the windows, and down to the grating, no architectural detail had been ignored. And the

Main Street buildings were not facades of a movie set, sagging with age or waiting to be dismantled in a few months, but genuine, solid, structurally sound from front to back. Not a single piece of trash blew down the street. The gardens were immaculate, with flowers precisely spaced in mulched beds from which no weeds emerged. The crowds were not rude or jostling. At the end of the street, the magical Cinderella Castle sent spires soaring into the sky, the signature Disney imprimatur which Tinker Bell circles before every Disney movie.

So this was the kingdom I had stepped into by joining with this man. After all the stress, financial hardship and arduous work, I had emerged on the other side. Brendan and Spenser rambled beside me, saying nothing, enchanted by all the sights.

As the weather grew warmer, we ducked into the air-conditioned exhibits. As we watched *A Bug's Life* through 3-D glasses, the blue ants and green grasshoppers jumped out at us, and we flinched when we were doused with mist by overhead sprayers.

After we emerged from the building, Spenser, wearing his olive green short set with frogs, insisted on carrying Tom's red backpack. His blond hair and white tennis shoes accentuated his tan.

"Are we going to Sid's Toy Shop tonight?" he asked.

"Yes, Spenser, but that's tonight. That's part of downtown Disney after dark," I said. We had a coupon for this attraction, where children could create their own toy based on the baby face perched on an erector set that the naughty Sid Phillips had concocted in the movie *Toy Story*.

Next, we attended a *Lion King* presentation in the Harambe Theatre. Dancers, singers and actors costumed with elaborate African headdresses and costumes swarmed onto the stage, twirling around with their microphones to address the audience seated on all four sides. As the music swelled, the animals, the warthog, the elephant, giraffe and lion, entered on festive floats from the four corners. The performers with long manes grew more frantic, until the stage cleared and a female dressed in a white body suit appeared with her dance partner in a sea of blue light. She ran to him and they danced in a ballet pas de deux. Then he hooked a guide wire onto her back and she ascended, twirling, as I dissolved into the music, "Can you feel the love tonight?" She rolled backward into an arch, her sequins flashing, "The peace the evening brings." After she was lowered onto one pointed toe, she and her partner circled the perimeter, gaining momentum, until her partner tossed her away from him, his arm outstretched, and she flew freely again.

We were in this wonderful place, together, a family again. The boys would have a stepfather who loved me. The female acrobat swung around in a wide circle through my tears.

As we left our seats and filed out of the theatre, Spenser asked again, "Are we going to Sid's Toy Shop?"

Yes, Spenser, yes. As we strolled by screaming passengers on roller coasters and souvenir stands brimming with colorful toys, this became his insistent, constant mantra, "Are we going to Sid's Toy Shop?"

As we strolled along an avenue, a stately red-brick Victorian mansion with twin chimneys loomed before us, on the crest of a slight hill. We wandered toward the Haunted Mansion as if mesmerized. As part of the crowd, we were crammed into a room with flickering lights. The chamber had no windows or doors, other than the one through which we entered, which now slid shut. Brendan squeezed my hand as an eerie voice admonished, "There's no turning back now." Even Spenser forgot to chirp in about Sid's Toy Shop.

Once in our seats, during a long, slow journey through the dark, we passed ghostly portraits, phantom dancers, and a disembodied head intoning at the scene of a séance, "Send us a message from somewhere beyond." The disconsolate sounds, the murmurs welling up as though from memory, the flashing visages that shone brightly and then eclipsed into darkness were all stock props of a haunted mansion. Yet this was to be the definitive metaphor for our trip to Disney World, not Mickey Mouse hugging small children, or Spenser whirling by on the carousel, but Spenser separated from us by death, less than a year later, when we would peer into a murky miasma for voices, visions, images, anything that would communicate to us that he was still there.

That evening, we did find Sid's Toy shop nestled in the bustle of downtown Disney World. It was crawling with children and decorated with bright colors, lurid reds and purples, where Spenser proceeded from station to station in order to assemble his own mutant toy. When he emerged with a baby doll's head attached to a robot body, he was content, and we didn't hear "Are we going to Sid's Toy Shop?" for the rest of the trip.

Years later, when I lifted the doll, its two eyes fluttered open and the blue irises of the glass eyeballs directed their gaze at me. I cradled the doll in my hands. Spenser fashioned it by attaching a tan animal foot with bright red toenails as a right arm and a boxing glove to a silver tube as the right leg. He scribbled blue hair with either a colored pencil or crayon over the doll's bald head. I store it in a box with other precious memorabilia: the dinosaur t-shirt he wore to the emergency room, the sympathy cards and letters, the extra funeral programs.

CHAPTER 25

The Wedding

At our wedding rehearsal dinner, Tom and I, seated at the table of honor, picked through our salads as we faced our guests. Henry, our best man, rose to his feet.

"I'm sure that all of you have special stories to share in regard to your association with Margaret and Tom," he stated.

Those assembled twittered among themselves, but no one stepped forward.

"I'm sure there are stories out there," Henry stated. His greying hair was combed back neatly and he wore a suit and tie.

We waited. Spenser sprung up from his seat. His large head, in profile, was topped with the silky blond hair that spilled onto his broad forehead. His face tapered into a pointy chin, and he raised his angular arm.

"I think, I sink, I um, I think," he struggled to begin. His porcelain face was flushed, slightly swollen, his lips chapped. "I think, I sink," he continued without apology.

My stomach tensed as I kept smiling. A bridesmaid, forcing a smile, looked down at the remaining sauce on her plate. The spaces between the moments expanded.

"We thank you for all coming and hope you have a safe trip home and a special thank you for all who came," he articulated. He smiled at every guest in the room, as though he were the master of ceremonies. We all exhaled.

On the June evening of the wedding ceremony, I primped before the mirror in the dressing room with the bridesmaids in their shiny taffeta dresses. Spenser sat on the carpet with some toys. Katie, his daycare provider, figured out how to attach the suspenders to Spenser's cummerbund. Dressed all in white, his skin glowed a rosy tan, and his platinum blonde hair sparkled.

In the narthex of the church as the organist sounded the exuberant "Trumpet Voluntary," I clutched my bouquet of yellow yarrow and purple statice. The candles glowing on the altar and the dimmed lights in the sanctuary shimmered through the gauze of my veil. Following the bridesmaids, Brendan and Spenser, in their white waistcoats, marched down the red carpet toward the priest and the minister. Spenser toppled from one side to the other with choppy steps, as though he were a penguin. Because this was not his customary gait, maybe he thought the wedding procession was another opportunity to play a part. Was he stealing the scene from his mother? Always the actor, always on stage, reminding everyone that playfulness can penetrate the most serious moments.

With one sweeping motion of my skirts, I emerged from hidden view and revealed myself to Tom and the groomsmen standing at the altar. With mincing steps that parted the ruffles of my floor-length gown, I approached the altar. Suspended between the travails of the past and the unknown future, I did not want this short triumphant journey to end.

Years later, the snow blew past the window as the lengthening afternoon grew darker, I found the videotape of the wedding.

I fast-forwarded the tape, as the ushers seat guests in the wooden pews with choppy Chaplinesque steps. At the end of the ceremony, the minister announces to the crowd, "May I present Margaret and Tom Kramar." I slip my arm into Tom's and the audience bursts into applause as my white skirt trails down the altar stairs to Purcell's "Trumpet Tune."

During the reception, the hand-held video camera surveys the room from different angles. Guests, waving and smiling, come in and out of view. An accordion plays "Sunrise, Sunset," as couples sweep across the floor. Spenser nestles himself into the tiered frills of my long white dress, with one hand on my waist. When we cut the cake, he faces the guests with a frozen smile as people clap.

Now I'm dancing with Spenser. I lean over to grasp both his hands, swinging his arms from side to side. His steps are out of synch with the music because he appears to be worried and lost. Next the camera zooms in on me leaning toward Spenser, as he utters words under the noise of the crowd. At the time, I had no idea why he was clinging to me, so in need of my reassurance.

I take the white photo album from underneath the table, shifting my gaze from the television screen to the laminated leaves turning in my lap. Here's one of the four of us, facing the guests before our first dance. Tom, holding up my gloved hand, like a victor. Brendan and Spenser, their eyes red from the flash, face us. Brendan looks angry. Spenser seems puzzled, about to cry. I close the album and immerse myself back into the videotape, where Spenser has buried his tears into the ruffles of my skirt right before the dance of the wedded couple. He locks his arms around my hips and thigh, crumpling my dress. Because he was hobbling me from dancing, Katie, with long, shiny, blonde hair, crosses the open dance floor, puts her hands on Spenser's shoulder, and extricates him from his grasp. Tom and I waltz across the floor, our first dance as man and wife.

After the honeymoon, I stood on the porch when Stan pulled into the driveway with the boys. Spenser's face was partially obscured by the trees reflected in the transparent glass of the windshield. The screen door slammed behind him as he disappeared into the house. He probably ran straight to his room to be certain that nothing had changed. Considering his tears at the reception, he must have feared that after the wedding, he wouldn't ever see me again. It never occurred to me to explain to him that I would never leave him.

In the following relaxed, summer weeks, Spenser accepted Tom's presence in the house. One evening I caught Tom and Spenser facing each other with long sticks. Spenser was posing as Peter Pan, and he had cast Tom as the evil Captain Hook. We were finally a family again, and the leaden weight of stress had slid off my shoulders like an un-fastened cloak. But the euphoria was temporary, because before Tom and I celebrated our first wedding anniversary, we would bury Spenser.

CHAPTER 26

He Never Grew Up

That summer of our marriage when Spenser was nine, he had a choice: he could either go canoeing with his dad in Arkansas, or participate in a summer theatre program. He ate his cereal in the green wooden chair.

"Playhouse in the Park," Spenser answered with a certain smile.

I studied him. "Are you sure?"

"Playhouse in the Park," he answered.

Perched on the wooden stool behind the breakfast bar, I called Stan to let him know the summer plans.

"You can't just enroll him in that summer theatre program," Stan said.

"Why not?" I leaned forward on the bar stool. By this time Stan and I had been apart for four years and much of the acrimony that immediately followed our divorce had dissipated. In increments, we were learning how to communicate with each other, a skill we lacked during our marriage. Now when he made a suggestion, I no longer reflexively balked.

"He's retarded. They shouldn't have to put up with that. Call the director, Jody Hodson. Try it for a few days, and if it doesn't work out, he can be withdrawn."

I was conflicted. Although I weighed Stan's suggestion due to my predilection for trying to please everyone, I did not foresee any difficulties with Spenser's summer theatre enrollment because he was mainstreamed in many of his school classes, and certainly was not a discipline problem, but perhaps I was being overly optimistic. The bottom line was that I had resolved many issues surrounding Spenser's disability and Stan was still struggling. In any case, I made the call.

"Hi, Jody, I'm sure you remember me, Margaret Gardner, from various theatre productions. I'm calling because our child wants to participate in your program, but I should advise you that he does have Sotos syndrome," I stated.

"Well, what does that actually mean in terms of our program?" Jody's stern tone caught me by surprise, because her reaction did not fall into my script. Just like I was speechless with Sandra Quinn years earlier at the kindergarten roundup, if someone responded to the diagnosis in a straightforward manner rather than with sympathy, curiosity or concern, I did not know how to react.

"Well, I guess he . . . ," My thoughts became jumbled. "He does have mild mental retardation, but he's really enthusiastic about theatre, so I suppose that, well, I guess I'm just calling to let you know."

"Well, I guess all I can say is that whatever happens, we'll deal with it," Jody replied.

So the next Monday morning at Gates Park, Spenser slammed the car door and ran across the gravel to his camp counselor, a dark-haired girl with a sporty haircut and whistle on a lanyard.

"Hi! Are you," she ran her pencil down the list, "Spenser Gardner?" Spenser grinned with his broadest smile.

"Okay guy, my nickname is Star, and I'm going to be your counselor for this session. Just put your lunch down over there and in about ten minutes we're going to start our warm-up calisthenics." I laid Spenser's lunch container on top of the green park bench while he did windmills and jumping jacks. He did not look back at me.

Spenser brought home a script from camp that was way beyond his reading comprehension level.

"So, Spenser, this is your script? You want, um, do you think you can read this? Do you want me to help you read this?" I hesitated.

Spenser didn't say anything, just smiled.

Three weeks later, I faced the empty platform drenched with sun where the campers were to perform. A girl in a long gown peeked out behind a set, then scurried backstage. Parents, their voices at a low hum, segregated near the folding chairs shaded by trees. A counselor with a hat and black t-shirt picked up a microphone and wound the cord around his arm. When the performance started, I was confused as to the time and place of the setting, because although some of the campers wore long robes, most of the others were in their ordinary summer shorts. Spenser stood in a large group upstage, and scanned the audience to reassure himself that I was still there.

Backstage when I played Princess Rosalie in the fourth grade, I'd peeped out through the curtains into the crowd, looking for her, the very special one, my mother. Once I found her, the show could go on. Her presence, her face, her smile, filled the auditorium with a warm glow. Now I was there for Spenser.

I strained to piece together the plot and hear the lines. The lead, Molly from Brendan's violin class, perhaps was a princess from Transylvania, and everyone had arrived at this haunted castle inhabited by monsters. On cue, Spenser came running in from up left, screamed, and dropped down dead.

For the final song and dance extravaganza, all the kids lined up on stage as the boom box blared the rock song accompaniment. In the second row, with the sun gleaming off his blond hair, Spenser bopped in time to the music, engaging every limb of his body in exaggerated and energetic movement, totally immersed in the dance.

Here was another small epiphany, another glimmer that Spenser was going to make it. Any director would have cast that kid after watching an audition with that much enthusiasm, that much sheer will power, that range of expressive emotion.

Spenser's camp counselor, Star, had her own rehearsals that summer. In August, she was Peter Pan in Theatre on the Levee's summer musical. Spenser worshipped Star, Caroline Selby.

In the air-conditioned theatre on a hot August night, Tom, Brendan, Spenser and I awaited seeing her in the show. Ice cubes tinkled when the waitress poured water. The soft tablecloth brushed my bare knees. On stage, the heavy curtain rippled over a thin blaze of light. We listened to the drone of other voices filling the theatre, and silverware clinking against porcelain plates. Tom and I had been married two months.

After the waitress brought the salads, I was studying the program when Spenser shouted in anger. His face was red.

"I didn't know you wanted a salad," Tom said, holding the plate of greens aloft.

I knew the script, but Tom didn't. Spenser was indignant because he should be treated like a distinguished patron of the theatre, sampling the entire menu like everyone else. Tom scraped some of his own lettuce onto Spenser's plate.

The curtain finally rose. Star flew into the nursery wearing the customary Peter Pan green tunic and cap. She flapped her arms as she crowed, and lifted in her harness, flew across the stage.

A boy behind us gasped when Captain Hook pulled out his musket. Spenser, spellbound, soaked up every moment of the production. He clapped along with the audience when Tinker Bell's light started fading, letting her know that we do believe in fairies.

For his last Halloween, Spenser dressed up as Peter Pan. In the photograph of the Halloween parade at Chippewa, Spenser is costumed in an emerald green tunic. He carries something in his hand. The wind blows his hair across his forehead. The camera freezes him just as he lifts his right foot off the ground. I remember those shoes. The girl preceding him wears a white wedding dress and veil, swept by the wind to her left.

J.M. Barrie, the playwright who wrote *Peter Pan*, did not always lead a charmed life. When he was six, his older brother died in an ice-skating accident and the biographies indicate that his mother may never have been emotionally present for young James after this death. Instead, she would lie in bed for days, grieving her lost child. As an adult, Barrie befriended the Llewellyn boys after meeting them in Kensington Park, and from their mutual adventures he spun the stories of pirates and Peter Pan. In popular estimation, the play is classified as light children's fare, with swashbuckling pirates and journeys to a mythical neverland full of adventure.

A closer examination of the text reveals that it is laced with loss, and nearly an obsession with death that is viewed as a triumphant liberation. When Peter Pan is trapped on the Mermaids' Lagoon, the drum beating within him states, "To die will be an awfully big adventure." What an enigmatic statement.

Spenser is captured in a timeless photograph framed with musical instruments, taken before the ordeal of his death. The serenity of his smile is untarnished by the mutable hours, weeks and seasons. My little Peter Pan, who never grew up, went to Neverland, and learned to fly.

Some of the children from the Playhouse in the Park summer theatre camp were in the production. Belle Johansen, with the stage lights shining on her fair face, sat crouched as one of the little Indians. I squirmed with guilt. When were the auditions? There might have been a part for Spenser.

After the curtain call, only the feet of the actors remained visible in the bright rim of light near the stage floor. The audience stood up and formed single-file lines leading to the exits. Tom thumbed through his wallet, wondering how much we should leave for a tip.

"Spenser, after the performance, it's customary to go to the green room to congratulate the actors. The room isn't really green, that's just what they call it," I said to him.

We traversed down one long corridor, then another. When we arrived in the green room, a large area with frumpy couches, it was deserted except for one little girl with long brown hair, who still wore her costume.

"Spenser, Spenser, it's you!" she said. "Did you like the show? What did you think?"

She shone with awe and wonder. I have been in shows, so I know how it feels to change from my costume into jeans, and venture out into the green room, hoping to find my friends among the crowd. Then they find me, this permutation of Margaret but really not Margaret, who with stage makeup is still partly in character, still in a liminal state. If they compliment my performance, their facial expressions indicate whether they are sincere, whether anything magical happened in the dark expanse beyond the footlights, whether any lives had been changed.

However, I've also been in the audience. I know what it is to clutch a coat in the green room, hearing other ecstatic shrieks not intended for me.

"Now Spenser, congratulate her." I gave his shoulder a little shove.

The little girl with the brown hair ran back into the costume rooms, calling out, "Spenser is here. Hey you guys, Spenser is here!" Several other children appeared right away.

"Spenser, you came to see our show. Give me five. Did you like it?"

"Spenser, hey man, how's it going?"

More children came out, as if on cue. They beheld him with wonder, treated him like a little god. Spenser smiled back. As this scene unfolded, I struggled to get my bearings. I mapped out the ordinary objects in the room: rug, table, couch, to determine if I could trust my senses as even more children marveled at Spenser. Nobody ever made such a fuss over me.

Spenser fell in love that summer, not only with the theatre camp, but also with another camper named Belle Johansen. Belle, like Spenser, wanted to sing, dance and act more than almost anything else.

Spenser bolted away from me one afternoon when I came to pick him up from the camp. He chased a small grey compact car and bellowed like an animal. The driver slammed on the brakes, proceeded slowly and then stopped abruptly again. Spenser ran after the car.

Belle Johansen and her parents were in the car.

During the next school year, Belle played in an orchestra concert with Brendan. She filed into the darkened school auditorium with the other musicians who carried stringed instruments and bows. Dressed in a pink blouse and a long skirt, her ankles wobbled on short heels. She was slightly off balance, but not more so than the other pubescent girls who were taking baby steps in women's shoes. The tomboys among them probably longed for the comfort of tennis shoes, for the sheer joy of rolling down hills and climbing trees when their bodies were beanpoles, when they didn't have to worry about protecting tender breasts and emerging curves.

Now these girls jutted out their chins as they tottered into this strange new world of wearing makeup and fingernail polish, of suddenly becoming women. Beyond the precipice of dressing for the orchestra concert awaited menstrual blood, falling in love, becoming orgasmic, delivering a baby and perhaps even burying that child in the silent, dark earth. But now their view was obscured by the tinsel of lip gloss and fluttering eyelashes caked with mascara.

Spenser instantly spotted Belle Johansen. His complexion turned beet red and he hid his face behind his program. Having a crush on someone is never easy, especially for novices who lack experience with such raw, powerful emotions. Spenser, concealing himself with a flimsy piece of paper, must have felt magnified, his scarlet cheeks so horribly on fire. Throughout the entire concert, Spenser's program was never more than a few inches from his face.

Once at home clustered around the dining room table, Spenser asked, "Why was Belle Johansen wearing that pink blouse?"

"She wore it for the orchestra concert. She had to dress up."

"But why was Belle Johansen wearing that pink blouse?" Spenser demanded to know the answer. I had no idea why he was insistent, because there was nothing unusual about the blouse.

"It looked perfectly fine on her," I answered.

Over the din of clearing and rinsing the dishes, Spenser again chimed in, "Why was Belle Johansen wearing that pink blouse?"

Even as I tucked him in and only the night-light illuminated the room, the question haunted him.

"Why was Belle Johansen wearing that pink blouse?" he asked again from his bed. Never before had Spenser become so perplexed over an ordinary object. Nor did he ever seem to object to the color pink or any particular blouse. But with the note of betrayal in his question, the pink shade of the blouse and the carmine hue of his complexion at the concert started to blend together and make sense. Perhaps he noticed that Belle never wore an attractive pink blouse at the summer camp, so it signified her growing older and becoming more attractive. Perhaps Spenser feared that the adolescent blood pulsing through her veins would take her far away from him, to a place where he could not yet follow.

Belle and her parents came to the funeral. She was in middle school, and would go on to attend a high school with magnificent theatre facilities so she could pursue acting. As she approached the casket, her eyes were downcast.

"I am really so very sorry that Spenser died," she said to me, as her parents stood by. I did not tell her that Spenser's face was beet red when he saw her at the orchestra concert.

Spenser's body lay in the casket a few yards away from her, underneath purple liatris and red roses. His head rested on a white pillow, and his eyebrows formed high arches over the lashes of his shut eyes. The sunlight streamed through the small red diamonds of the stained glass windows. I hope that he knew that she was there.

CHAPTER 27

Pain in the Side

Life was so easy that first summer that Tom and I were married. A feeling of contentment swept the whole house clean. During the summer evenings, we would linger outside, watching the last pinkish blush bleed from the horizon. We'd then leash the dog and take off north for a walk on our dirt road in the dark because we could not get enough of the luxurious nights. The whippoorwills and barred owls sung from the trees, and as we wended our way under the verdant arching branches, crickets and toads trilled in a thick chorus.

"It hurts," Spenser said. He pointed to his thorax region. His pale face, shrouded by darkness, expressed no intense pain. Neither did his voice. Instead, his countenance was the same as always, one of bemused contentment.

"What hurts? Your side?"

"It hurts," he said. He trotted along, without stopping or bending over, with no apparent agony on his serene face.

As a steep hill lessened the gravity underneath our feet, our walking broke into a jog. The spring peepers trilling in the meandering stream, the bats flying in jagged and irregular angles over our heads, beckoned us to plunge down into that hollow.

"It's probably just a stitch in your side. Bend over, stretch," I told him. "That used to happen to me when I rode horses."

On other summer nights, with the locusts screeching, Spenser might say softly, but only occasionally, "It hurts." He again would point to his chest, with a slight smile. It never hurt when we were in the house. It never hurt when we were eating dinner. It never hurt when he got up in the morning. Only sometimes at night, amidst the thick, sweet scent of Russian olive trees, did it hurt.

According to the autopsy report, Spenser died from T-cell lymphoblastic lymphoma, stage IV, arising from the mediastinum. The report states that "the significant gross findings included a large white, fungating mediastinal tumor (1,350gm) which encased the heart, aorta and great vessels, and extended posterior and inferior to involve periaortic, and mesenteric lymph nodes as well as both kidneys and adrenals." Further, the bone marrow was "completely replaced by tumor cells with no megakaryocytes and no evidence of normal hematopoiesis," and besides being present in the heart, left lung, spinal cord, both kidneys and adrenals, the tumor cells were also present in "sections of gastroesophageal and gastroduodenal junctions." The resident pathologist concluded the summary by stating, "It is likely with a tumor of this size the patient would have been symptomatic."

I swear to you, other than his terrible appearance the weekend before he died when his chest bulged out from the tumor, we had no warning, other than this soft, simple statement of "it hurts" that he randomly said, only sometimes, during walks on summer nights.

"Why didn't we take him to the doctor when he first told us it hurts?" I now will ask Tom as we hike on the dirt road. During a full moon the countryside is so bright that we don't need flashlights.

"I remember thinking at the time that maybe we should have," Tom answers. The dog trots in front of us, dragging her leash.

"But we did, we did take him to the doctor, the Tuesday before he died. They diagnosed a sinus infection," I say. By the time we emerge from the tunnel of trees, the vista opens up into wide fields. This is usually where we hear the chuck-will's-widow.

So, sometimes when the branches are laced with dainty ice and we're bundled up, or other times when the rolling hills blaze with red, orange and yellow, we keep having this same conversation. Why didn't we take him to the doctor?

"But we did, we did end up taking him to the doctor."

"The Tuesday before he died, and the diagnosis was a sinus infection." We keep circling back to this deserted, rusty place, where questions and intentions lie strewn around like abandoned junk cars, their chrome glinting in the sun.

A few months after Spenser's death, I sat on the plaid couch in the basement, talking to Spenser's pediatrician on the telephone.

"They all think we're crazy," I began, my elbow leaning on the arm rest. "I guess I should have known that he was sick. But really, he had no symptoms. He had been tired for a month, and that's really all there was."

I was not telling the whole truth. There were those times walking the dog, under the overarching woods at dusk, that Spenser smiled, pointed to his chest, and said, "It hurts. Here."

Now I listened to the pediatrician's calculated phrases. "There's really no way that anybody could have known." He deliberated even longer, and in that space I speculated that he was teetering between compassion and potential lawsuits.

"The only way the cancer would have been detected would have been a chest x-ray," he continued, "and it just isn't practical to do a chest x-ray every time a mom comes in complaining that her kid has been tired."

Imagine all the calls pediatricians field at all hours of the day and night from hysterical mothers ranting about a cough or a scratch. Being their doctor would require superhuman patience and tact. I don't blame them for not detecting Spenser's condition earlier.

Another issue is whether it was my fault that Spenser died of lymphoma, a form of cancer. The child certainly didn't drink or smoke, and I'm not aware that he was exposed to dangerous substances, but we know that industrial agriculture, through its use of pesticides, herbicides and synthetic fertilizers, is pumping poisons into our food, soil, air and water, gasoline-powered engines are emitting toxic fumes, and we are exposed to carcinogens through the manufacture and daily use of many consumer goods. I now know, but did not when Spenser was alive, that consuming meat and dairy increases the probabilities of specific cancers. In isolation, each one of these carcinogens passes FDA standards, but when they are all combined, we are imbibing one heck of a dangerous brew.

But who is going to stand up to Monsanto, Exxon or Dow Chemical? We light luminarias in memory of the dead, but we are only paying them lip service. The harsh reality is that in our culture, we value short term economic gain and maintaining our "standard of living" more highly than preventing the suffering caused by cancer.

So even though we participate in Relay for Life, and I ran in a marathon sponsored by The Leukemia & Lymphoma Society—they are squandering their resources by believing that science and technology will deliver a magic bullet cure. Many, many more lives could be saved if they attacked the causes at their roots.

In the middle of another reminiscence, one of many after he died, Tom and I strolled down the hill, stepping on the coarse, shifting gravel beneath our feet. Our arms were twined around each other's waists, and we tottered or leaned as one unit.

"He was ten, but what would have happened when he was a teenager?" I asked. Now as we emerge from the arching branches, the fields light up under the full moon. "He had crushes on girls. He loved Belle Johansen. They all would have thought of him only as a friend."

"Yeah, that's another way women have of saying they don't want a relationship."

"Who would have married him? Well, maybe another disabled person, but what would his quality of life have been? Where would he have worked?"

A train whistle moaned in the distance. It was about midnight, so we turned around.

"Maybe his death was a blessing. Maybe he is better off dead." I didn't know if I really meant it. Tom set his mouth in a straight line.

"No, it was a horrible tragedy. A very sad thing. He should be here with us. No, he is not better off dead."

"But that psychic said that he had a ten-year contract, that when he came in he knew he was going out quickly," I said. As we ascended the steep hill, my breathing became labored. "A road show. She called it a road show, with high energy and great humor and a great sense of calm. That he had no regrets about anything in his life, because he did it all."

The late spring blossoms of the Russian olives wafted a sweet menthol fragrance. The road was dappled with moonlight, and all kinds of night creatures throttled in full force: rattling, droning, hissing and shrieking in an exuberant crescendo.

CHAPTER 28

Belle

I stood outside a modern split-level house, its bright trim contrasting with the white carpet of snow on the lawn that encircled it. The morning sunlight, despite the dark trees with their jagged limbs stripped bare, whispered the same promise, that everything is possible, that there is always another beginning, that everything lost yesterday will resurface today.

A girl opened the door. He loved her so much. The same lily complexion, the same sandy blonde hair, the same facial features, but what happened to the child? Belle, now in college, had grown up.

We ascended a half-flight of stairs into the kitchen where I pulled up a chair at a wooden dining room table stacked with newspapers and magazines.

"Poncho." Belle scolded a large dog, dark and spotted, whose soft muzzle grazed my wrist with wet little puffs of breath. She clasped a Coke can up against her navy blue T-shirt. We chatted about how she had just returned from seeing the puppet show, *Avenue Q*, in New York. On this January afternoon, in the kitchen of this quiet house, I wanted to explore the role that theater now played in her life, if she still loved it as much as she once did. As much as Spenser did.

"That summer when you were in *Peter Pan* with Caroline Selby, we came to see the performance. Spenser so totally loved that show." Summoning the memory seemed to break the ice.

"Even though I was a cast as an Indian, I wanted to be a Lost Boy, but I wouldn't cut my hair because I was going into seventh grade. I didn't want to be made fun of."

"What do you remember about being at Playhouse in the Park with him?"

"I remember," she said, while looking off and grasping the Coke can, "that I was surprised at how well Spenser could sing during an audition."

"What part was he doing?" I asked.

"Funny." She made a quick gesture with her hand. "I remember he was wearing something funny. A wig or something. He had a part and he did it well. Eventually everyone loved him, thought he was so cool, realized he was such a nice guy."

"What was your first impression of Spenser?" I asked.

"At first I was afraid of him because he kept chasing me. Who is this kid running after me? Then I realized," she took a short breath, "'Oh dear, he had a crush on me.' Then I got to know him. He was so sweet. Then we would hang out together."

"Do you remember when he came to see you in the seventh grade orchestra concert?"

Spenser, his face red as a beet. Spenser, with the program held up in front of his face He stayed that way for the entire concert, after he saw Belle, Belle Johansen in that pink blouse.

"I remember seeing Spenser at that orchestra concert and he was so afraid, so nervous. I was trying to say 'Hi,' and I think we probably did talk, but at first he was so shy. Then I was in a play in seventh grade and he went to that." She paused. "It was in April. I remember saying, 'Okay, I'll see you at camp,' and then that never happened. I gave him a big hug," she said as I scribbled her words in my notebook.

Belle's words slowed down, came to a stop as she became embarrassed. We know what happened ten days later. He died.

We both may have been thinking that if we kept replaying that incident, maybe we could cut and splice it, edit it somehow, to produce a different ending. But we can't because we're the puppets, clumsily dragged across the stage, our painted faces locked in idiotic grins. Somebody else, the mastermind, is pulling the strings.

An ordinary conversation, ten days before he died, and nobody had a clue. The play at the middle school featured some memorable, stunning performances. Some of these kids would go on, do more remarkable things in theatre, develop their talents in college. Spenser fell off by the wayside, never did any of these things.

I decided to drop the bomb.

"As Spenser got older, do you think any girl would have dated him?"

"I don't know. He was different."

"If Spenser were your age, would you have dated him?"

She squeezed the Coke can a little tighter.

"If I just met him, I don't know. I think I would see if our personalities went well together. I would have to have an attraction to him, have to see if anything was there. He definitely would be a good friend. Romantically, I'm not sure."

I know it wasn't fair to ask. They would have been mismatched. You can't ask any typically developing girl to pair up with someone who is developmentally delayed and looks slightly strange, even if he is a nice guy. Maybe Spenser could have paired up with a girl with similar abilities, but he was attracted to the actresses, the leading ladies, and even had a particular penchant for the blondes.

"Belle, what do you think is the underlying message in *Peter Pan*? Why does it have such a lasting appeal?" I asked.

"We all go through not wanting to grow up, being afraid to grow up. But the message is that it's okay to grow up, we have to, or we will be frozen in the fantasy land like Peter," she said.

"Given a choice, do you wish you could be a younger kid again, or the age you are now?"

She hesitated. "All in all, the age I am now. I'm more independent. Twenty. That will be a new decade, a very 'up' decade."

Brendan, also twenty at the time of this interview, was in college, a semester in London. I wonder why I don't contact him as much as I should when he's at school. After all, it's not his fault that he reminds me of his brother.

The interview over, I made notes about the kitchen setting. The pink counters. The refrigerator with colorful family pictures. Some decorative plates. Spenser's timeline stopped, but Belle, the young woman with the same grey eyes and sandy blonde hair that she had as a child, is at a portal with blazing light, as she steps before her footlights to greet a radiant future. She will be just fine.

She escorted me down the half staircase, and I went out into the winter sun.

CHAPTER 29

The Nutcracker

Christmas is magic, a time of hushed anticipation, when we store our wishes in a secret box warmed by the embers of our hearts, and when you're a child, it seems like Christmas will never get here.

"Christmas is Tuesday," Spenser stated, right before his last Christmas. He sat on Stan's maroon couch, his jacket falling off his shoulders.

"No, Spenser, Christmas isn't until next Monday," Stan stated. Outside the picture window, the headlights of cars shone on the snow-packed street. We were all tired and hungry. It was time to get home.

"No, Christmas is Tuesday," Spenser shouted, bouncing up and down on the cushion.

Stan laughed. Spenser apparently imagined that he could hasten the date of Christmas, if only he believed hard enough and declared it so.

Back at home, we could smell the pine aroma of the cedar tree that we had dragged down the snowy hill and across the frozen creek. Its colored lights illuminated ornaments from Christmases past: the Santa Claus riding a bear from our trip to Minnesota, the plastic snowman that hung on our tree when I believed in Santa Claus. On Christmas morning, when the sunlight shone through the needles of the tree, all the wrapped gifts decked in bows would appear.

The following weekend, we huddled in the darkened theatre during a ballet performance of *The Nutcracker Suite*. Perched on the edge of his seat, Spenser watched Clara dancing on pointe as she twirled around with her adored nutcracker held at arm's length.

Finally, the solemn gong of the clock struck the hour of midnight. An invisible wire pulled the top of the Christmas tree, so that in its vertical ascent the tree loomed larger and larger, until it towered over everything else. Once at its height, the tree erupted with dazzling lights.

"Cool." Spenser's clearly audible voice, the only sound coming from the audience, rippled like a wave down through the rows of those in front of us. As the wave swept back up the elevated rows, it carried the laughter of everyone who had heard Spenser.

On Christmas Eve, after the church candle lighting service, Tom and I wrapped presents into the early hours of Christmas morning. After we tiptoed downstairs and arranged them under the tree, we fell into bed.

"Do you hear something rumbling around downstairs?" Tom remembered asking me. I slept through his comment.

In the morning, when I dragged myself down to the kitchen, Spenser stood among rumpled wrapping paper, clutching his Woody doll. He had managed to open every gift bearing his name tag, every one, in the dark of the middle of the night, but left the rest unopened.

"Spenser, what did you do? It won't be a surprise for you anymore."

He pushed the button in Woody's back, and the toy responded in a metallic voice. The brown cowboy boots and limp blue-jeaned legs of the doll dangled beneath Spenser's arm.

In the afternoon, after the gifts were opened and all the bows and torn paper which covered the floor were stashed away, Brendan and I unzipped our violins from their cases. Tom tuned his mandolin. The assembled family guests sat in a ring on the couches, waiting for an impromptu Christmas concert.

Spenser sprang up and down on the couch next to my mother, making crying noises.

"Spenser, please be quiet. We're getting ready to play."

Spenser mumbled something about "conductor," so Uncle Tim carried a stepstool in from the kitchen. Next we found him a wooden spoon. Spenser held his hands aloft, then signaled us to start playing, moving his hands in rhythm to the music. Pulling my bow across the string I rolled my eyes and chuckled at my son, the actor.

We buried his Max Steel toy with him, but not the Woody doll, which sits with a plastic smile next to Spenser's picture on the fireplace mantel.

CHAPTER 30

The Conference

WITH THE BACKDROP of the shouts of children and sound of dribbling basketballs in the adjacent gym, a group of teachers, administrators and Stan and I congregated around the long table in the conference room in early February for Spenser's annual IEP (Individualized Education Program) meeting.

I flipped through the eleven page report, arrested by the paragraph regarding intelligence: "On the Wechsler Intelligence Scale for Children, Spenser scored a verbal scale of 66, a performance scale of 64, and a full scale of 62." I'd been living with this mentally deficient child for years, who was shattering my misconceptions regarding developmental delay, such as late one night, when Spenser chose a long *Star Wars* story with many pages of fairly sophisticated text for his bedtime story.

"I'm tired, Spenser, can we read it some other time?"

"I'll read it to you," Spenser said. I relaxed, allowing him to concoct the story. He opened the paperback book in his lap. I sat up straighter, because although I was expecting him to improvise a story, he stated every single word correctly, with no mispronunciations or hesitations. I subsequently related this incident to his special education teacher.

"Oh yes, Spenser always memorizes the whole story," she said, nodding her head in total sincerity. Having read somewhere that there is a positive correlation between memory and intelligence, I blinked, wondering which one of us was crazy.

I rack my brains, but I can't remember that Spenser ever asked a stupid question. Nor did he make comments that could be characterized as "dumb." You would think that you would constantly have to explain things to a developmentally delayed child, but instead, he always seemed to get it. Jean even described him as "very intelligent." No, argued my internal monitor, he was mildly developmentally delayed. These tests proved it.

Yet, although his overall physical appearance might not brand him, if you engaged him more closely in conversation you would know that his mental functioning was slightly amiss due to his choppy, nasal speech and his general affect. Also, he walled us out when he assumed that deadpan expression—which sent chills through me when he was a baby—that vacant unseeing gaze into a no man's land which nobody seemed to inhabit, as though he were already a corpse. Although it never seemed appropriate when he was a young child, I eventually would have asked him how he felt about having Sotos syndrome, being disabled, whether he perceived himself as being different. We could discuss it when he got older.

I never got the chance.

On a Big Chief tablet, neatly lined, I discovered sentences in Spenser's handwriting several years after his death. His letters were neat, precise, executed with care: "Give me my toys. I have my mom with me. Come with me. I am done with my lunch. Someday I will be there." The enigmatic message startled me, " Someday I will be there." This abstract statement, vague, yet declared with conviction, stood out from the other concrete observations. Someday he will be where?

"Brendan, Brendan, look at these sentences. Do you think he meant anything special by this one, 'Someday I will be there?'" I sat in front of the computer, upstairs, with winter birds at the feeders outside the window. Brendan, now twenty-one, shifted his weight to his wrists as he leaned over the file.

He read the sentences. In a week he would leave for London, Brendan, the kid who lived. He paused, equivocated. "I don't, maybe he . . ., I don't know, Mom."

The IEP conference was lasting over an hour. We shifted in our chairs. The teachers needed to get back to their classrooms. I kept reading the report, glancing up during the discussion about Spenser's social/emotional functioning. "At recess Spenser doesn't usually choose to play in a structured game, but likes to play make-believe characters, or games of chase."

The consensus of the educational professionals was that Spenser should not be pretending that he was a monster because now that he was nine, it was not age appropriate. He also shouldn't be chasing other kids around on the playground during this game.

"But it's kind of hard to get him to stop," Bob Simons, Spenser's second grade teacher stated, "when the person doing the chasing is the big boss, the principal of the school." His was a casual, offhand statement that did not provoke any rebuttal, while I wondered why the principal would spend so much of his time playing with my child.

Years later when I interviewed him on a dark, winter afternoon, Bob Simons turned away from me after I entered his classroom. He wandered past pictures of a polygon. A red bowl pinned to the wall asked, "Who's Hungry for Multiplication?" Boyishly good-looking, Mr. Simons sported a neatly-trimmed beard and mustache.

"Spenser really enjoyed the role playing we did, like when we acted out vocabulary words such as 'excitement' or 'disappointment.' He was always good at that. He liked to joke and kid around a lot."

He twirled a white pen between his fingers. "He had an ornery side to him."

He stared off into the distance. I sat and took notes. Because Mr. Simons was moving so slowly, and there were such long pauses between his responses, I wondered if I was making him melancholy. Because as Spenser's mother I assumed that nobody's grief could surpass mine, I marveled that others lamented his passing.

"He didn't like to be noticed as different with his abilities. I do remember that he was good at storytelling and sharing experiences." Bob Simons avoided eye contact with me as he ambled around the room. In the lengthening evening, I could sense the outside darkness descending over the building, settling in like an inevitable fog.

"He loved art and illustrating. He would make monster sounds. He liked to kind of hide and startle you once in a while. At recess he would be with a group who were chasing each other."

I recorded Mr. Simons's memories as they unraveled. As I supplied the prompts through my questions, he conversed as if he were being filmed.

"I don't remember a lot. I know there were a few quirks with his behavior, but no major problems. He was a pleaser. I had a special place in my heart for him. As far as kids making fun of him, if it happened, I don't remember it. Since he was there from kindergarten on up, you know, his head size was different, but I just don't remember anything like that. Not that kids can't be cruel, they can be."

He gazed past a February calendar with red hearts that counted the days.

"Writing was really hard for him due to his coordination. But then his brother Brendan wasn't the neatest writer either." I bristled at his observation that Brendan was less than perfect. "Spenser had a very big smile, was bigger than the rest of the kids, fairly tall, and he lumbered when he walked with his shoulders forward. He had a tall forehead. I don't how to describe his eyes, they had a different look, generally. It was easy for him to blush—his whole face. He fought colds really bad, had chapped lips, they were really hard on him. He had big feet, didn't he? Yes, a good shoe size. As time went on, there was less difference between him and his peers."

"Had he grown up, what do you think Spenser would be doing ?" I asked.

"Had he lived, he would still be happy go lucky. A job? Something limited, but he was somebody you could count on—honest, trustworthy, food preparation maybe. There would be a few jobs out there for him. He'd work for you, absolutely." He met my gaze.

His cell phone rang. He told the caller he was about ready to leave.

"He would have done something he enjoyed, like a hobby. I just know I really enjoyed kidding with him, being around him."

He put his arms through the sleeves of the grey, heavy jacket, and hoisted it up over his shoulders, bracing himself for the steel wind of the winter evening. I followed him out, down the glistening hallway that a janitor was buffing with a humming machine.

CHAPTER 31

Star

D URING SPENSER'S LAST WINTER, when the leaves exposed the raw, bony branches of the trees and the cold winds lashed the deserted playground equipment, Tom and I took Spenser to see a production of *The Secret Garden* in Heyworth Auditorium, which has a huge proscenium stage and chandeliers suspended from a very high ceiling. We had come to see Caroline Selby, nicknamed Star, Spenser's summer camp counselor, because she was stage managing the production.

Whenever the curtain rose and light flooded the myriad seats in an auditorium, Spenser never fidgeted. Whatever happened on any stage hypnotized him. Even at an outdoor production of *Macbeth* the previous summer, the arcane Shakespearian language had proved no barrier for him in divining the prophecies of the haunting weird sisters, with their cloaked figures gyrating in the twilight breeze.

After the actors had taken their last bow, we proceeded to the green room. Spenser had not seen Caroline Selby since the previous summer. He planned to surprise her, so he grinned in anticipation.

In a room with high, narrow panels of stained glass, we waited for the actors to arrive. People talked quietly. Spenser took a Styrofoam cup filled with fruit punch, and grabbed an oatmeal cookie studded with nuts and raisins.

I didn't see anyone I knew. Spenser waited with his coat on, open and unzipped. He rested his arm on a heavy oak table, carved with graffiti.

"Is Star coming?" he asked.

"I'm sure she will," I assured him.

Tom and I had seen Star performing a few months earlier in her high school madrigal concert, but Spenser had not been with us. We wanted to greet Caroline after their performance, but waited too long. We watched as she gathered up the folds of her long skirt under her coat, sprinted across the parking lot with choppy steps in her high heels, got into her car and zoomed away.

I glanced at my watch, and flipped through the program filled with biographies and advertisements.

Still Star did not come. Only a few actors had appeared. We had been there a half hour, forty-five minutes. It was really getting late.

"Is Caroline Selby here tonight?" I asked a girl of about high school age.

"Oh, no, she's not here. She's out of town this weekend, visiting prospective colleges."

We had waited for nothing. Zipping up our coats, we started down the long hallway.

"Well that's too bad, Spenser. Maybe you'll see her some other time."

Spenser sat in the back seat of the car in the dark, very still. He started to sob. Even though he was at the age when he tried not to cry anymore, the tears ran down his cheeks.

I turned around from the front seat to see his pale face screwed up in the darkness.

"Spenser, sometimes people disappoint us, even if they don't mean to. She had no idea that you were coming to see her."

Once we got to Stan's house, Spenser's bottled up anger exploded. He screamed about how Caroline had not been there, shoved open the back car door, and plunged out onto the lawn. In the headlights, I could see him darting back and forth in front of Stan's outside yard light, whirling around in the dead zoysia grass. I listened to the dull clang as he kicked that light pole again and again.

After Spenser died, I left a message on Caroline's machine, but she did not attend the funeral. I later learned from another drama teacher that Caroline had a debate tournament the same weekend.

"That debate coach would have killed Caroline if she went to the funeral. I know that debate coach. She has one hell of a reputation and gets excellent results, but she's as strict and unyielding as a ramrod. No, Caroline would have had hell to pay. A funeral wouldn't have been any excuse." I fingered the folds of my dress, uncertain whether this explanation would have been any consolation for Spenser.

During another winter following Spenser's death, in a drawer I found a small notebook with a pear on the cover. Spenser had been dead for nine years, but I recognized his writing by the spacing between his letters and his distinctive calligraphy. He had written at the top of the page, "Caroline Selby," and underneath it, "Mr. and Mrs. Selby. Also, in the middle of the page, "The Selby family."

Notwithstanding their age difference, Caroline never would have married him. Neither would Belle. I cringe to imagine Spenser on the telephone, his heart drumming in his chest, calling for a date for the senior prom. Perhaps, if we could have adjusted his expectations, he could have found happiness with a girl with disabilities. But perhaps such a girl would have fallen so short of a leading lady he never would have been interested. Young children, despite their disabilities, are cute, and professionals offering special services to them project optimism, but I draw a blank pondering whether the world would have been kind to Spenser as an adult. If not, I would have been listening in the shadows, eavesdropping, dreading the sobs, while my heart shattered along with his.

Chapter 32

The Dancer

A month before Spenser died, the weather acted like it usually does in Kansas at the end of March, with sputtering winds, a few late snows and the skies cast in steel grey. On such a day, we transplanted iris roots into the heavy wet soil of our hillside. Tom and I dragged them in heavy sacks and fetched trowels. There were hundreds to be planted, donated by friends who were moving.

Silhouetted against the grey sky, Brendan dug holes as he braced himself against the gusty winds. Spenser sat on the bare ground at the top of the hill. He cast his eyes on the trowel, but made no motion to pick it up.

"Spenser, can't you help?" I scooped aside some dirt, and laid the rhizome in it, its hairy roots trailing from its bottom.

He was not refusing out of laziness or obstinacy. He seemed forlorn, crying out to me without using any words, but I didn't have time that afternoon for his moods. I didn't force him to plant because living in the country really wasn't Spenser's thing. He never took an interest in the chickens, the onion tops pushing their green blades through the earth, the red aromatic tomatoes bowing down the vines.

No, he was a city kid. His syncopation was the traffic whirring by on busy streets, the neon lights blinking on crowded boulevards, the art, music, and dance that popped up through the cracks in the urban sidewalks.

Earlier in the month, when the boys and I joined Tom after his business meeting in Washington, D.C., we rode on the subway train.

Suddenly for no apparent reason, as if rehearsed, Spenser stood up in his purple jacket and started dancing, jerking his body to a rhythm only he could hear, in the center of the aisle.

"Spenser, sit down," I hissed, but the woman wearing a knitted cap regarded him with kindness, and the man across the aisle didn't seem to be offended either.

Watching his staccato movements, I imagined that there would be other city nights for Spenser, spotlights illuminating black stages with blinding shafts of light, and underneath the radiance would be Spenser—dancing, singing or acting in some future unknown place. Spenser, somehow, would be in the midst of all of it.

Jabbing my trowel again into the earth, I could see that getting Spenser to help with these irises was hopeless. He seemed tired, and his heart just wasn't in it.

Within about a month, the grey cold weather lifted. The daffodils pushed up through the mulch with green spikes, and the redbud trees sported little purple flowers.

The tulips were next. Bright yellow and red ones dappled the ground at the park at the school carnival in mid-April, where children chased each other with water balloons.

I anticipated Brendan and Spenser would run ahead and play before I ever reached the ticket window. By the time I reached the shelter house, Brendan had taken off, but this Saturday Spenser stayed by my side.

At my post by early afternoon, I readied the treats for the kids who managed to hook the plastic toy fish in the wading pool. I scanned the playground. Brendan was probably on the playground equipment, but Spenser stayed behind, perched next to me on a straw bale.

"Don't you want to do anything? Don't you at least want to get your face painted?"

Spenser sat still, and didn't seem to be thinking or feeling anything, other than the anguish he communicated through his eyes.

He was having an off day, but he was hard to read. He would rarely communicate what was bothering him, so I had long since stopped asking. There was no telling what he was thinking, especially when his long, distant stares took him someplace else.

Easter Sunday passed in a rush of cooking omelets for a houseful of people, so I was relieved when Spenser didn't protest that there was no time to hunt for plastic eggs.

A week later, I climbed the stairs to get to the telephone clanging on the wall.

"Hi, Margaret? It's Jeanelle Bronson." She was Spenser's third grade teacher. "I just wanted to let you know that Spenser has seemed tired lately, just not himself."

"I know, I've noticed it too, but I've had him in after-school care because I'm trying to get more work done at the office. Before he came straight home on the bus. I get the feeling he doesn't like it," I explained.

"That could be it, but I would have him checked out," she said.

I pulled out the telephone book, flipped through the pages, and made an appointment.

Spenser wore his purple pullover to the doctor's office. The nurse practitioner listened to his heart and lungs. Her stethoscope roved over his chest and momentarily stopped. She peered into his ears with an otoscope, squinting behind the narrow beam of light. She commented on his runny nose, his swollen lymph nodes the size of acorns, and Spenser's weary, distant gaze.

"Does he have frequent colds?" she asked.

"Yes, he has a perpetual cold," I said.

She wrote out a prescription, tore it from her pad, and handed it over.

"It's just a sinus infection," she said.

This was the Tuesday before he died.

CHAPTER 33

The Sympathy Card

S HE WAS A KIND WOMAN, patient and long-suffering, who lived by the Scriptures. Her children have related that every morning she would waken them with, "This is the day the Lord has made," and squirming under covers, they would answer, "Let us rejoice and be glad in it."

The sympathy card said that she had something she wanted to share with me, privately.

She smiled on the following Sunday morning, her usual greeting. The skin crinkled around her eyes behind her glasses. On a couch in the narthex, upholstered in brocade, she delivered her message in a determined, even tone.

"A few weeks before Spenser died, I watched him during the time with the children."

Spenser, with the other children clustered around him, would have sat on the steps which lead to the altar during the children's sermon.

"He had a halo around his head. I have never seen anyone with that before, or since."

"A halo?"

Her earnest smile did not falter. "I also have lost a child, a boy," she confessed.

"What happened to him?"

"He fell out of a tree."

She offered no other details, but remained seated in the narthex, a patient, saintly presence.

Sometimes they die. She was able to relate this incident, forty years after her child's death, with the objectivity of a news reporter, because the pain eventually subsides. The pain, which in the aftermath is incapacitating. But even this pain fades with time and must eventually be set aside, like fine china wrapped in tissue paper after the Thanksgiving meal, for there is work to be done. We who have lost children have a great deal to do to honor their memories.

Chapter 34

The Elephant Man

In late April, I drove into Stan's driveway on a Sunday afternoon. The two boys trotted toward the car.

"I don't know what's going on with him. He's been sick, looked thin like that all weekend," Stan said. He headed back to his front door.

Spenser's face was long and drawn. He advanced toward me with a body that was crooked and twisted, skeletal. He wasn't the same boy. Spenser resembled the "Elephant Man," John Merrick, now immortalized in an eponymous play and film, whose deformities caused by neurofibromatosis resulted in his extremely large, misshapen head and twisted posture.

Once home in our own driveway, I glanced over my right shoulder at Spenser, who leaned his head against the car door, with the seat belt slung across his shoulder.

"Spenser," Brendan said, "you have to start eating. If you don't, you're going to die." He punched the last word of his sentence, "die," which caused Spenser to burst into tears. He didn't want to die. Not that Sunday afternoon.

The night deepened, and about ten o'clock I turned on the bath water. As Spenser cautiously lowered his thin body into the water, I relived all the terrors that I confronted when he was a baby. This was not my child. He was emaciated. His body twisted slightly to the side, as though he had a wicked curve in his spine, and his sternum was protruding forward out of his chest.

I called the emergency room.

"No, I don't think we'll need an ambulance. He is breathing without any difficulty," I said. "I can get him down there right away."

I yanked open his drawer, and pulled out some clothes for Spenser, his maroon t-shirt with the fierce tyrannosaurus rex baring all his sharp white pointed teeth. The lettering "extinct" was splashed in neon orange. Next I rolled open my wooden closet panel and wondered what I could sleep in all night. Having experienced several hospital stays when Spenser was a baby, I was familiar with the cold sensation of vinyl-upholstered waiting room chairs that stick to the skin at three in the morning. I didn't know that when I drove Spenser away from this house where he had lived all his life, I wouldn't ever be bringing him back.

I was scared, because this journey to the hospital seemed to have a deeper, more penetrating significance. We drove along in the bouncy white Jeep, the headlights carving out our path. Words of an unbidden chant filled my mind. "Yet in this darkest night, you kindle the fire that never dies away, never dies away." As the car surged through the dark night, the melody swelled and receded as it did during Friday evening Taize services, when we lit candles and solemnly proceeded to the altar in a small chapel.

I left on the interior light so I could watch Spenser, while my mind conjured up a sharp image that contrasted with the dull black asphalt of the road. I visualized Mr. Don Hodges, Spenser's elementary school principal, who pushed Spenser on the swings during recess, and imagined how heartbroken he would be at Spenser's funeral. Mr. Hodges, of all people, yet there was his face in portraiture, wearing a coat and tie, stricken with a grief that no one would ever fathom.

"No," I screamed, "I'm just imagining things. I'm being irrational. That's all it is."

At the emergency room, Spenser and I passed through a corridor which was under construction. A security guard pointed us toward a harried-looking man who probably dealt not only with gunshot wounds, but also a steady stream of patients night after night with inconsequential complaints.

"What are you here for?"

I pulled up Spenser's shirt to reveal his grossly protruding chest.

"This just isn't right," I said.

"I'm sure it's nothing, ma'am. Probably nothing to worry about. Just sit down, sit down over there," he directed in a loud voice that was pitched for the deaf.

Spenser and I waited for a long time before we were called back to a room, where we sat on the examination table, kicking our feet against it. I leafed through a *Ladies Home Journal*, stealing away to gardens, luscious recipes and new spring clothes, while Spenser leaned against me. Through the curtain we could hear the doctor conversing with parents of a toddler who howled in response to being stitched up. We shifted our weight on the crinkly paper covering the examining cot, sighed and waited. But it was pleasant, just whiling away the time with Spenser. He was almost always a good boy, and never complained. The hospital would take care of him, but I called Stan and Tom on my cell phone, just in case.

"Momma, will my teacher Mrs. Bronson come to see me in the play this summer at the Playhouse in the Park?"

"Of course she probably will, if you ask her," I answered, sneaking a glance at the next article.

A nurse entered the room, knelt down and ran her hands down the calves of Spenser's legs.

"Hmmm," she murmured, brushing a brown strand of hair away from her face, "these spots on his leg are called petechiae." She pursed her lips.

I didn't hear all of her words because I was concentrating on all those little red spots. There were a lot of them. The toddler on the other side of the curtain was quiet now and the overhead fluorescent lights beamed as brightly as ever, but a shadow had crept into the room.

"We'd better draw some blood. A technician will be here in a minute," said the nurse.

The technician came in right away. Her straight very dark hair was parted on one side. She held up her carton of instruments and advanced toward Spenser.

"We're going to draw some blood. It won't hurt, it won't hurt at all, and it will only take a minute."

Spenser froze as she closed in on him, with her voice rising. "We have to draw this blood, and it won't hurt, it won't hurt at all."

"No!" Spenser shouted defiantly, his voice cracking, as the technician in her white lab coat came closer. So this was not going to be easy.

"Spenser, come over here."

"No!" he yelled, dodging behind me. He'd had so many pricks: in the neonatal unit, when he had croup as a two-year old, and even the previous September when he was hospitalized for an unexpected staph infection.

"No, no, no!" he sobbed, jumping up and down in front of me, his upstretched arms rubbing against my breasts.

His face contorted with tears. "Spenser, you have to," I said.

The last phrase he ever heard from me was really as simple as that.

By the time Tom arrived, at least four medical technicians were holding down Spenser, one for each arm and leg. They climbed onto the examining table, using their arms and knees to hold down his extremities. He no longer struggled after his eyelids snapped shut. In contrast to the previous chaos, the room was suddenly quiet. I faded out for a moment.

"Michelle."

A tableaux of four women framing Spenser came back into focus. The one who had spoken looked up from her straddled posture. Spenser's lips were blue.

Tom threw his arms around me as Spenser's gurney was rushed into the next room.

When we were able to see him a few minutes later, he was still alive. He was breathing through a ventilator, his eyes were tightly shut, and he seemed to be further away from us than he had been in the examining room.

The doctor, having seen the x-rays, stood like a stone, his white coat glistening in the hallway of the emergency room. The nurse at her station reached for the charts and spoke with resignation into the phone receiver. Tumors. Occluding his lungs. All over his body.

"We're going to fly him by Lifestar to the University of Kansas Medical Center. We don't have the facilities to adequately deal with tumors that are this advanced, and they have specialized pediatric facilities," the doctor stated. Upon hearing this news, I didn't panic, scream or lose my composure at all. Perhaps I had automatically reverted to denial.

Outside, the helicopter waiting to transport Spenser sliced the black spring sky with its whirling blades. I shivered with the night air blowing around me, wondering whether I could handle speeding through the sky in that glass box. After I strapped myself in, I waved to Tom whose arm moved back and forth like a pendulum. The pilot handed me some headphones with which I could communicate with the technicians in the back. I pushed the button to hear them say Spenser's blood pressure had dropped but now it was stabilized.

As I was floating through the sky, marveling at the pinpricks of light below, I did not comprehend the gravity of the situation. Because he was wrapped in the embrace of medical technology, I believed everything was going to be fine. In our glass catacomb, Spenser and I sailed over the houses, the trees, and the plowed fields. We were "walking through the air" just like James in *The Snowman*, to the haunting title melody that captures both the beauty and sorrow of Spenser's life. Maybe we even flew over our own house, because it was in the helicopter's path. In years since, when we have looked up from our deck on hot July nights at the sound of that noisy chopper churning through the sky, we remember Spenser's journey, and say a prayer for the occupant.

The helicopter landed on the launching pad at KU Medical Center and the technicians, young men dressed in dark clothes, transferred Spenser to a gurney, encircled his body with straps, and rolled him into the building. Down corridors and through double doors, I was ushered to my vinyl chair in the waiting room, where I would spend the night.

I walked down the hall to where Spenser, unconscious in his hospital bed, was laid out in a curtained space of intense white lights and gleaming silver technology in the pediatric intensive care unit. He seemed so very far away. I had passed other curtained rooms in which other children slept, perhaps in comas, perhaps in the velvet grasp of natural sleep. I observed Spenser, framed in the stillness. There was really nothing I could do, so I returned to the dark seclusion of the hospital waiting room. I dozed in and out of consciousness. My skin peeled off the sticky vinyl chair when I shifted. Around the corner, at the gleaming nurse's station, a young woman peered down at charts, the only sign of life. It was three in the morning.

A young male resident assigned to night duty appeared before me in a white coat and stethoscope. He told me that Spenser's status was grave, but I wasn't alarmed, because I trusted that he would be all right now that he was in the hospital, where they could perform the medical miracles necessary to save him.

The next morning, the black telephone on the table rang. The small room, with a few other chairs and no interesting magazines on the table was empty, except for me.

"Should I come over there?" Tom asked. I sunk into the baritone of his voice. "I really couldn't sleep last night. I kept waking up, thinking about you and Spenser."

I held the receiver against my ear, straining for Tom on the other end. I had missed being curled up next to his warm body, with my head on his outstretched arm, that supported my head like a pillow.

"It's nine-fifteen, so I've only been here an hour. It doesn't feel right being at the office. I'm coming over there."

The phone rang again. My sister, the calm, patient, mediating middle child. She would do anything for my brother and me when we were little.

"So how's Spenser doing? I told the principal that my sister and nephew were in the hospital so she called a substitute. I have to wait until she gets here."

With the night dispensed and light flowing in through the windows, by mid-morning the hospital was up and moving. Mothers of sick children, especially very sick children, know the chill of hard linoleum floors as they kneel down to pray, clutching cold steel hospital bed guardrails in the middle of the night. In the morning, it gets better. Outside the waiting room, people passed each other in the halls, single file and in pairs, pushing creaking machinery, pressing dinging elevator buttons.

But the daylight had not roused Spenser. As I approached him, he lay very still in his hospital bed between white sheets, inhabiting that far off space. His respirator supplied him with oxygen through a plastic tube coming out of his mouth. His heartbeat was monitored by a green line that snaked across the screen.

Every night at home in his room, stealing into the dark I would kneel beside Spenser's bed and whisper a prayer when he was about to fall asleep. I now crouched over and said these words:

"When I go to bed at night,
Someone tucks the covers tight.
And just before I sleep I say,
Thank you, God, for this nice day."

The respirator continued its swishing drone. Spenser did not smile, nor open his eyes, but I sensed that—just for a moment—Spenser's spirit edged towards me. I deemed that the competition for his soul was now a toss-up, and that he was deeply engaged in conversations with angels, whose whispering, encouraging voices were convincing him to come to the other side.

CHAPTER 35

Third Grade Teacher

I started writing this memoir about Spenser about two years after he died, quite by accident. I was editing a manuscript for a writer who was receiving feedback from prospective agents and editors that his prose was lifeless. I agreed, but was having trouble conveying to him that he needed to bring the reader into the scene with vivid, descriptive details which conveyed emotion. Finally, I banged out on the computer, "Do it like this." Then I typed out the scene about taking Spenser to the emergency room, and how he turned blue, and how one of the nurses looked up at another and broke the silence with the word, "Michelle."

After rereading the scene for typos, I shoved my chair away from the keyboard and said, "Oh, my God." So I eventually told Janelle Bronson, Spenser's third grade teacher, that I was writing a book about him when I contacted her, as I did with everyone else I interviewed.

Janelle Bronson appeared in her doorway, wearing a yellow sweater, jeans skirt and brown boots. There's something of a carefree girl in the spring of her step and the bounce of her short bobbed hair that links her to her students.

In the room, brightly-colored alphabet letters skipped around the perimeter of the walls. I sat on the same green and white plaid couch where Spenser was photographed at the beginning of his final school year. He had a school directory in his lap, wore a shirt with large, bold stripes and smiled straight at the camera.

"Is it okay if I sit here in this rocking chair?" she asked me.

"Of course." I took out my pen and paper pad. "What do you remember about Spenser's physical appearance?"

She fingered the big wooden beads on her necklace.

"I remember his hands and feet. Like an adolescent, he was gangly. I remember his stride. When he was younger his gait was different, it was not as smooth."

The school was quiet except for a custodian dragging equipment. Janelle looked at a place on the wall just over my shoulder.

"At recess," she continued, "it was the imagination thing, and there were always a lot of noises that went with it. When he was younger, he was always confused about the world around him, bewildered because people weren't acting the way he was reading them. By the time I got him and he was mine, he seemed to gain some confidence. By October or November he worked his way into a group of boys who played specific roles in pretend games. As he was better able to talk and respond, they did also."

"How do you think he felt about being different?"

Janelle rested her chin on her hand. She shook her head slightly.

"I don't know. What do you think?"

"I don't know either. If he were older, it would have been fascinating to have those conversations. We just never got to them before he died."

Her face brightened. "He was beginning to come into his own. I skipped the rough parts, when he was learning, 'Oh, so this is school.' I benefitted from the efforts of all the teachers before me. I got the easy part. I got the gravy."

"Did anyone ever make fun of him?"

"I'm sure they did, but not the people growing up with him. It was generally the new kids who were trying to fit in. Once or twice I did hear, 'Well, how come he's like that?' or 'That's a weird way to run.' I explained, 'Everybody has stuff they're working on.' Kids who said something usually had their own set of problems, and that's why they were trying to divert attention away from themselves. He never said anything to me about it."

Sometimes when he came home after school, Spenser bore a serious, dejected expression, as though he were reliving a painful experience. But he wouldn't talk about it, and went directly to his room to play with his action figures. Because I was tired from work, and busy going through the book bags and the mail, I was glad that he was self-contained. I probably should have taken more time to investigate the stories behind those dejected expressions.

"Did Spenser have a crush on anybody?"

"Amanda Walters, maybe? I don't know if this had any meaning, but he would put things in her locker."

I paused and studied my notepad.

"Do you remember what you were doing when you first learned of his death?"

"I was on recess duty. On the soccer field. It was afternoon." She chose her words carefully, as though in a trance. "I saw Don walking down the steps and I knew from the look on his face that something awful had happened. He was pale. The way he was walking was different; it was slow. It felt almost like I was underwater."

She continued reliving the memory.

"When he told me Spenser had died and asked 'Do you want me to take your kids?' I said, 'No, they're mine.' That was the three to three-fifteen recess."

Three-fifteen. At the hospital, that's about the time I was ushered in to see the body. Outside the room, the chaplain dialed the telephone, spreading the news of his death.

"I managed to hold it together until the last child was out the door. Then I locked the door and called the parents. I wanted each one of them to be told by Mom and Dad, not me. I didn't want them to hear it on the bus."

I kept writing. "So when the kids came to school the next morning?"

"It was very quiet for a long time. Finally one of them said, 'Is this really true? Did you ask his Mom?'" She laughed a little.

She got up to get a box of Kleenex. "Somebody said to me, 'You need to take out his desk.'"

The desks in the room were arranged in formations, with the chairs piled on top of them. Fluorescent lime tennis balls covered the feet to pad the scraping noises.

She clutched the Kleenex. "I said no, he cannot just disappear. We kept it for about a week and took turns sitting in it. We kept all of his stuff, his pictures displayed, his name on the bus notes, his name on the locker. It was important for him to be there. I still use his glue. Sure, I have to refill it, but my bottle is Spenser's glue bottle."

She picked up a bottle of white Elmer's glue with the orange screw-on cap. I could see the letters in my handwriting in black magic marker: "Spenser."

"Don has a picture of Spenser in his office. He went to his office after Spenser died and stayed there."

I gasped. Janelle continued, her eyes directed at me.

"He plays with other kids. Of course, he's the principal." She slightly shook her head. "I don't know if I can even explain how different it was with Don and Spenser. Don plays in all kinds of situations, but he and Spenser had their own roles and lines."

She searched for an example, and stopped for a moment. "If somebody were to walk in from the outside, they would think that Spenser was related to Don. You love all your kids at school. If you're worth your salt, you invest in every one. But some crawl deeper in there, burrow deep into your heart, and you never know who it's going to be."

Janelle ushered me down the hallway, through a shining tunnel of bright fluorescent lights overhead and a gleaming, polished floor below, past the classroom pictures lined up in the halls, toward Don Hodges's office. She plucked one key from the jangling bunch on her round key ring and the door to the principal's office swung open.

On a long table were his family pictures, a young woman in a bridal dress, a young man in a military uniform. In front of these, he had mounted a picture of Spenser in an upright frame, a picture from the funeral service program—small, black, white, and gloomy. I resolved to get him a better picture.

Janelle locked the door. I was still reverberating from the sight of the small picture as we returned to her room.

"I was so happy when I got to the point where I could grin when I thought about Spenser, because that kid made me smile. These same memories, I will not have them for each of my students. I do not have these memories just because he died," she said, opening the door to her classroom. It was completely dark outside. I only had a few more questions.

"What do you think Spenser would have been doing at twenty-five?"

"Doing a job with some kind of detail. Figures, drawing, putting things in columns. He liked organization. That year he was coming into his own. You could see him exclaim, 'Oh, I've got it.' All these particles of information stuffed into his brain, they all started coming together. He was an organizer who could decide where things went. Art, graphic arts. In computer labs, KidPix, he could manipulate pictures and colors. I can see him in his own apartment. I don't know if he would be with someone else or not."

I had no more questions, so I pulled on my jacket, flinging my scarf across my shoulder.

Janelle hesitated. "I hope he knows how much he mattered to me. If I would have done more for him, he would have been too embarrassed. But we both did our best and that is the best you can do."

Her pace quickened as she headed back to her desk, closed a notebook with a thud, and locked a drawer.

CHAPTER 36

Phooey to Any Disability

L ATER THAT SPRING, I walked through whipping winds to the entrance of Chippewa Elementary School in order to interview the
principal, Mr. Don Hodges. I passed the tulips we planted for Spenser,
their silky petals strewn on the ground, exposing thin, naked stalks
atop fading vegetation. The Kansas wind, always blowing, banged the
clasps attached to the long rope against the metal flagpole. Inside the
glass double doors, Don Hodges waited in his office. A large, gentle
bear of a man, he befriended every child in the school.

Mr. Hodges came out to greet me and stood framed against his
office door. He was dressed in a red and white pin-striped shirt, and
had steel grey eyes and jolly ruddy cheeks, that peer out from his Santa
Claus suit at the Christmas assemblies. His dark hair, becoming tinged
with grey at the temples, was parted on the side. He gazed directly at
me, but I skirted his glance. With our broad smiles and customary
pleasantries, he and I were playing characters whose role was to get
through this interview without becoming overly emotional.

"Come right in and have a seat." Family pictures lined a ledge, the
bride in a white gown, the young solider in a military uniform. In front
of these was a plain black-and-white picture of Spenser.

"I brought you other pictures," I said, removing a variety of school
photographs from a large white envelope. "Which ones would you
like?"

Mr. Hodges studied the pictures, his thumb and forefinger pushing them apart. Spenser at eight with a goofy smile against a green background, and Spenser as a younger child wearing his Dalmatian puppies t-shirt. His school picture when he was nine, which stands in a glass picture case inside the main entrance of the school.

"No, these are yours," Mr. Hodges said modestly.

I grabbed the scissors. "Which ones?"

He smiled. "Well, I guess maybe that one and perhaps this one here." I trimmed away the white margins with the blunt-edged scissors. It gave me something to do. We had to get through this performance.

I put away the photographs. "Do you know what you're going to do next year?" I asked in regard to his impending retirement.

"No, no definite plans," Mr. Hodges laughed, as charming and guarded as ever.

I opened my spiral notebook and jotted down Mr. Hodges's name at the top. I adjusted the cap of the pen.

"What do you remember about your first impression of Spenser?" I began.

"His smile, his warmth, and his friendliness. It would catch anybody's eye."

"What memories come to mind about him?" I kept writing without looking up.

"I just see him having fun, smiling, easygoing. I also saw him as initially being very conscious about following the rules, staying in line, not talking. Sometimes he would say to me, 'They shouldn't be doing that.' He would spot them and tell me."

"Why do you think Spenser would tell on others?"

"He was just a good person, brought up right. He understood rules and consequences."

I don't know if I can take any credit for what Spenser did right, or whether we have that much influence over our children at all. They each seem to come with their own little personalities, and are set on a predestined course that they stumble toward despite our bumbling mistakes. Spenser was generally happy, and usually smiling, despite the fights between his father and me, the divorce, and my occasional emotional distance as a single mother. He seemed to forgive everybody.

On second thought, he acted as though people were fine the way they were, that there was nothing to forgive in the first place.

"Do you think he was aware of being different?"

"If he was, he did not outwardly say that. I think and hope all our kids were wonderful with Spenser. I never heard him say that anyone had teased him. After he came back from Disney World he said, 'Did the kids miss me when I was gone?' I told him, 'Oh, Spenser, we definitely missed you.'"

I know that sometimes kids teased him because that's what Brendan told me. Of course they wouldn't tease him in front of the principal. He never complained, never told on them, must have been acting. "How is it that you started playing with him on the playground?"

"I played with him because he was fun to be around. I would come out the back doors," he said as he crouched down, "and I would be looking around for him. Then I would notice him looking around for me. We were both looking for each other."

"What kinds of games did you play together?" Even though I should have been copying down details about the room that I might not remember later, I just kept writing. As long as I narrowly concentrated on transcribing his words, I could keep my emotions at bay.

"Various kinds of makeup-type games. One was a chase game. Other times we would be behind the wheel," he said, positioning his hands as if driving. "I might say, 'You're going to wreck! Watch out!' Spur of the moment things. He'd swing a little bit. I'd push him. Then he'd try to push me, but I was too big."

"Do you remember that year at enrollment when Spenser came to your table, and without any other greetings, you and he said to each other, 'Aye, aye, sir, reporting for duty' and saluted each other?" This pantomime took me by surprise on that August day at the beginning of the year. When Spenser approached Mr. Hodges he snapped into character, saying, "Sergeant Reid here, at your command," and Mr. Hodges replied in a loud voice, "Yes sir, reporting for duty." Then Mr. Hodges slouched over in his chair and turned his head from side to side to see if anyone else had witnessed the conversation.

"I think that we did salute. That was a military-type thing. Other times we were detectives. He was supposed to be an agent, have a number, we just made it up as we went along."

"What were Spenser's strengths?"

"The trueness to his word. If Spenser was your friend, he was a real friend and a friend for life." Outside the metal clasps clapped against the flagpole.

"What do you think we learned from Spenser?" The interview was almost over. A few more questions, and I could leave, take off the mask.

"Maybe two things. You can positively affect other people with your smile, warmth and friendliness. He also stands for 'phooey' to any disability or handicap. He impacted our lives more than we impacted him. We worked at teaching him academics, but he taught us about life every day."

"What was his main contribution?" I stared at my notebook, and kept scrawling the shorthand. I could decipher it later.

"That everybody is, I believe everybody was his friend. Kids today don't always remain friends for very long. Somebody who is your friend at lunch is not your friend by recess. Spenser was flat-out your friend, never wishy-washy."

I didn't remind him that we played "You've Got A Friend in Me" from *Toy Story* at the end of his funeral, or that Spenser had dressed up like Woody for a number in the school talent show, or that Woody now sits on the fireplace mantel with a plastic smile on his face, leaning up against Spenser's picture.

The interview was over, and I had not cried in front of Mr. Hodges, even though there were moments when I memorized the contours of the pen, or lines across my notes.

Once outside, the sunshine made the brightness of every color so much more vivid. The trees and flowers, planted by the Cub Scout troop in Spenser's memory, swayed in the breeze to the rhythm of the clanking flagpole. The redbud tree was smothered in lavender, the roses were previewing pink, and the bobbing crab tree put on its bravest face.

CHAPTER 37

The Angel Pin

By mid-morning the pediatric intensive care unit was populated with all the day people. One of them was the pediatric oncologist assigned to Spenser, a large woman who exuded confidence and optimism.

My sister stood beside me as I sat in a chair by Spenser's bedside. The oncologist had reviewed Spenser's chart, and conferred with the night staff.

"Cancer is divided into four stages. By the final stage, Stage IV, metastasis has occurred, and in this case, the malignancy has spread to his lungs, liver, kidneys and many other internal organs." She held clinical notes clipped to a metal chart. "I'm ordering radiation and chemotherapy. Radiation will be the first line of offense in shrinking those tumors." A white coat covered her dress.

"Have you ever had a patient with a cancer this advanced who survived?" I asked.

"I did have a teenager, once, who was in a similar condition and fought his way out of it," she replied.

Logic dictates that when faced with Spenser's precarious situation, I should have been hysterical at this juncture, but I wasn't. Instead, in the eye of the storm, I become focused on the task at hand, navigating with hardly any emotional interference, because I know there will be ample opportunities for breaking down once the crisis has passed.

Radiation was to start immediately. Along with Tom and my sister, I followed alongside Spenser's gurney as he was wheeled through the throngs of people crowding the hallways of KU Med Center. We passed escalators, soaring ceilings, acrylic impressionist paintings on walls illumined by small lights. Steel grey elevator doors opened and closed, and the rollers of Spenser's IV tower would jump and lurch over the uneven surfaces. Spenser was still unconscious, deeply unconscious. It was about time that he woke up.

As Spenser's gurney rolled past a random man in the hallway, his eyes bulged out in horror at the sight of Spenser, and he jumped back, as though frightened by a snake.

Next we clustered together in the radiation waiting room. Magazines were splashed across tables that broke the lines of the chairs. The waiting room was deserted except for an older woman in a wheelchair and a couple sitting against the far wall. Soon this couple journeyed toward the exit door, the man slouched over, shuffling along, with the woman trailing behind him.

The woman, wearing a blonde wig, looked like an aging beauty queen, with red lipstick, black mascara, a fashionable dress, and heels. She smiled and began a conversation with me.

"So, do you have someone who is undergoing treatment?" she asked.

"My child. A boy, ten years old."

"I have a little angel I want to give you, so we can always hold hope in our hearts for those we treasure. I hope everything goes well for you and him today," she said.

I glanced at the keepsake, a small, metallic angel. I unzipped my bag and put it in my coin purse. It's still there. The woman's husband, handsome but hunched over, ambled out of the waiting room. I intuited that he was not going to survive.

The radiologist explained that Spenser's situation was very grave. The black x-ray he posted against a backdrop of light had white amorphous masses that obscured the rib cage.

"So, according to this chart, the patient was brought in yesterday? He had no previous symptoms?" he asked in a clipped foreign accent.

"He had been tired for about a month. That was all the warning we had, until the chest x-ray last night in the emergency room." The radiologist's black eyes pierced me.

"The best thing we can do, to make any progress, is to target these areas with radiation. The tumor must be diminished in size. Yes, that's right, we have started. The first session was today," he stated.

Spenser had been tired, just tired. He suffered from frequent respiratory infections since he was a baby. He drooled until he was about five or six, so the collars of his pullovers were always wet. The glands in his neck were usually swollen to the size of acorns, but the radiologist would not have known any of this.

The radiologist shifted his weight, and clasped his elbows with folded arms across his chest. He delivered his monologue without pauses or inflections, conversing as though he were talking to people whose sensibilities were as opaque as the darkened x-ray screen. He did not seem to understand how we could not have known about Spenser's condition. In any case, he explained, it was going to be an uphill battle, with intense radiation and chemotherapy.

Spenser's gurney was wheeled back into the room. I regarded my child, eyes firmly sealed, feathery eyelashes slanting downward toward his pale cheekbones. His aspect was becoming grey, even ashen, and still unconscious, he seemed to be spiraling further away. My job anchored me to the world of phone calls and conferences in a downtown office. As I stood before the radiologist, I knew that notwithstanding my fascination with my career, I would discard it in an instant to replace it with a future of nursing this child, if only he would live, if only we could have him for another day.

A noisy hubbub of people populated the cafeteria. My sister introduced me to Pam, a laboratory technician friend of hers, and we conversed with laughter, as though I did not have a child who was dying, who would be dead in several hours.

"So you have a patient here?" asked Pam, holding her fork in mid-air. "You know this is a wonderful facility, state of the art, a teaching hospital that is on the cutting edge of the latest technology and research. This is the best place that he could be."

First thing after lunch, a cardiologist explained to me that he would be draining fluid away from Spenser's pericardial sac with a long needle.

Earnest, and bespectacled with sparse light brown hair, he spoke with the optimism of a coach before a game. Another medical procedure. I returned to my station in the waiting room to make more phone calls from the gold vinyl chair.

About ten minutes later, the pediatric oncologist appeared in the doorway. Her countenance bore an eerie, supernatural aura that peeled me naked.

"Spenser has gone into cardiac arrest. They're doing everything they can to resuscitate him," she said in calm, scripted language.

He is dead, he is dead, he is dead. I closed my eyes and tunneled down into the deepest part of myself. My sister later told me that I screamed.

"You screamed, girl, you screamed," she told me years later over the phone. I sat on the stool with my elbows on the breakfast bar.

"Who was with me?" I looked down at the white-tiled floor.

"Tom, Tom was sitting on your right. When he heard the news he started crying, and put his head on your shoulder," she answered.

"Well, then, where did you go?"

"Then I went out near the nurse's station with the chaplain. I could kind of hear and see what was going on. It was just like *ER*, girl, on television. Medical people were running into the room from all over, and they were yelling things at each other, like 'Try this.' They were really working hard, trying to save his life."

"They wouldn't let me go in there. I do remember that the doctor suggested that I stay out, that it would be too horrible. Maybe I should have gone down there anyway," I said. The yellow recipe box sat on the counter.

"What could you have done? You'd only have been in the way. Can we talk about something else? Have you called Mom lately?" I noticed my reflection in the glass windows of the cornflower blue hutch. I couldn't have watched it. Not then, the defibrillator machine, the electric shocks, the violent jolting of his dead corpse, the medical personnel grappling for his soul, but losing it. Maybe now. Maybe after sitting with his dead body, seeing him in the casket, watching it being lowered into the concrete vault, kneeling on the grave as the dirt was shoveled over it I could do it, but not then.

As I sobbed in the waiting room, the phone rang.

"Hello, Paul Parnell here. I just heard that Spenser was in KU Med Center and was calling to see how he was doing." His voice had a cheerful veneer.

"He's not doing well. They just told me he went into cardiac arrest." I was trying to be polite to my minister, but my words came heaving out in jagged sobs. I couldn't compose myself but tried to be coherent. "He had cancer, a very advanced stage. We didn't know. We took him to the emergency room just last night. Now he's dead."

The oncologist appeared in the doorway again.

"They've been trying to resuscitate him now for ten minutes. No success yet, but they're still trying." I studied her composure, her frame with the white lab coat filling the doorway. I didn't understand the rationale behind these progress reports, that she did not know he was dead.

She returned in twenty minutes. Then thirty minutes. Then at 2:56 p.m. on April 30, they pronounced him dead.

Legs and white coats, cut off at the waist, that had been running and pushing machines past the doorway paraded across, going the other direction. Heavy footsteps. Dejected sighs. Loss, defeat. Sad thing, to lose a child. I didn't know who they were, so couldn't thank them for trying to save Spenser's life. If only I could have told the cardiologist, "It wasn't your fault." I could imagine his leaving the hospital for the day, driving home in rush- hour traffic, replaying Spenser's final moments in his mind, wondering if he could have done anything differently. No, it's not your fault. Spenser knew that his time was up. You just happened to be there when it happened.

Another nurse appeared in the doorway. "You can go in now and see his body."

I turned my head straight to my minister, who had driven over and now sat with me. His intense dark eyes met mine with a wide, open expression, as though we were on stage, and he was waiting for me to say my next line. We marched together, past the curtains and glass cubicles, each step taking us closer to the room.

Spenser lay in a pristine white hospital bed, with the top half slightly inclined. The soft blue turquoise of the walls matched the blue flocking in his white hospital gown. The white sheets, folded over, covered him up to the chest. His arms were tucked under the sheets. The nurse had removed the ventilator, and the strip of tape that held it to his nose and mouth. His straight blonde bangs were combed over his forehead, his eyelids were locked and his mouth was shut. He could not have been mistaken for being asleep.

No, because there was an unnatural stillness, a sense that the soul was no longer in the room. His pale frozen countenance, that would never draw the next breath, declared that he was dead.

My initial repugnance over viewing the dead body was replaced by a probing, clinical kind of curiosity. I pried open his right eyelid with my fingers and viewed the familiar swirl of colors in his iris, the gold mixed with green, with a few flecks. The animated glow which formerly radiated from his eyes had been replaced by a dull, vacant stare, like that of a frog with fixed opaque eyeballs that never blink. His eyes were blanks.

"What did I do when I first saw Spenser, when you, Rev. Parnell and I got to see his body?" I would later ask my sister.

"You stood at his bed, crying, and simply said, 'Spenser, I will always love you.'"

Predictable, perhaps. Nothing really surprising. But it's been years since the death, and now I'm digging out from under the rubble of the shock to record all the still snapshots from memory, to catalogue them in some sort of order, so I can dissect the visual elements in each frame, before they are all buried.

I grabbed Spenser's hand, and clasped onto his arm. The body was still warm. I thought about gathering him onto my lap before rigor mortis set in, but he had gotten too heavy. He was taller than I had realized. Some of the blonde hair, so platinum when he was a toddler, was turning brown. At ten years old was he still my baby, or was he becoming a teen? But then again, death had paralyzed his growth spurt so he wouldn't be getting any older. I didn't know what to make of all this, because I had spent his childhood years reading parenting books about daring to discipline and working with teachers. Now, even though he was no longer living and there would be no more teacher conferences, I realized that I would continue into an uncertain future but remain his parent. My role as his mother was not obliterated by his death. Of course the relationship had changed, and I would spend the rest of my life defining and exploring the new bond until I died.

A friend of Tom, who also worked in the hospital, joined us. He sat, looked down at the body, said nothing. It was the last Monday in

April. Rev. Parnell brought up the subject of the funeral, that it should be in a few days.

"No, I want to wait until Saturday, so people don't have to take time off work," I stated.

"I don't think people will be concerned about getting off work for something like this."

My friend Sharon had no vacation time, no sick leave, a stack of unpaid bills, and collection agencies calling. "No, I want to wait until Saturday."

A young male hospital employee entered the room, dressed in green surgical scrubs, a gown and padded blue shoes. The lilt of his voice suggested concern, and his attention was focused on me, but I could not understand what he was talking about. He kept talking, wanted something, would not go away.

"So you're asking me to consent to an autopsy? Is that all you wanted? Yes, I have no problem with that." I don't know that I answered his question. Maybe he was talking about organ donation. During the autopsy, the pathologists sheared off Spenser's skull, so that when they sewed it back on for the funeral, there would be an ugly red scar circling his head.

About an hour passed. There was nothing much to say. But still I was with him, did not want to leave his side. His body was starting to stiffen up. I was not frightened or revolted by this dead body, lying there swollen and still, because it had been a part of mine. Since having Brendan and Spenser, tears, sweat, blood, poop, and vomit didn't bother me anymore.

Stan and Brendan had just arrived. A murmur of voices indicated some confusion about who would inform them that Spenser had died, so I ventured out into the hall. I faced Stan as he came closer, unsuspecting, still dressed in his suit and tie from work. Brendan beside him, dressed in his school clothes of khaki shorts and a navy blue polo shirt walked straight ahead, his tranquil gaze warming somewhat at the sight of his mom. They were framed by the tiled linoleum floor and the glass curtains and cubicles as they came closer and closer.

"Spenser is dead," I simply stated.

In the waiting room, Stan started keening, a strange, high sustained sound, and Brendan sat sobbing on my lap. Because he was thirteen years old, he was kind of heavy, and I could feel his hip sockets pressing against my legs. I wrapped my arms around his waist and rested my head on his back.

Tough kid, Brendan. Composed and quiet, when he gazed at his brother's dead body. First the divorce. Then this death. It was certainly not what I had ever wanted for him.

Brendan would stay home from school the next day. He would lie under his North Woods quilt with the cabins and black bears, and even though he could hear the voices of condolence callers, he would not come out to greet them. The following morning, Brendan got up early, got dressed, gathered his books into his book bag, and caught the school bus. He said he didn't want to miss any more classes or homework. After school he would bring home cards, handwritten inscriptions on folded white pages from other middle school boys, advising him to be a man and to be tough.

The afternoon wore on as I kept watch over Spenser. Five o'clock, six o' clock, it had been several hours since his actual death. Tom's friend stayed until the end, keeping a silent and doleful vigil.

Finally there was nothing more. I said one last goodbye to his body, then Tom, Brendan and I turned our backs to him and drifted past the waiting room into the hall. We wound through narrow hallways with signs leading to radiology or cardiology, caught an elevator and found ourselves in the airy, high-ceiling space of the main entrance, where many people buzzed around, followed their daily routines, changed shifts.

We went through a revolving glass door and out into the late April afternoon. Some cars passed on the road, and green grass grew on the banks under the viaduct. As we headed toward the parking lot, the warm air and natural sunlight embraced us, drawing us into the intoxication of spring. To think, outside Spenser's hospital room, it had been like this all day. If dry leaves would have greeted us instead of the green blades, his death would have been more difficult to bear.

We drove home, saying nothing, watching the bright light fade from the horizon. We heated up leftovers and sat down in the green wooden chairs at the kitchen table, facing the wall. Three of us now, instead of four.

CHAPTER 38

The Immediate Aftermath

As the news of his death spread, sympathy cards began arriving in the mailbox across from the orchard on top of the hill. The phone also began ringing, and reassuring voices I had not heard in years expressed their sorrow. I relayed the story to each empathizing voice at the other end of the line, siphoning off a little more of the pain with each telling.

I moved with deliberation through the next few days, completing tasks such as sorting out pictures for the funeral display. When the weight of grief slowed me down, I rested, reading books about the afterlife. Because grief had been such a constant companion before I remarried, I had become acclimated to it, so I stayed alert, finely tuned for any communication from Spenser, so recently passed over to the other side.

Because it was the first of May, everything in the garden was popping out. While I was seeding and digging, not really concentrating on anything, Spenser seemed to be there, but in a different dimension. It was a buzzing, a hovering, a sense that the air was electrically charged with precise particles. Especially in the north garden with the fairy rose bushes, I had to admit something was totally different.

Perhaps departed souls are right here with us, but in this other dimension, if only we could hear or see them. I experienced a similar feeling a month or so later. At a Boy Scout picnic, a man in an off-shore boat fell into the lake and drowned near our shelter house. It was tragic, of course, and everyone felt sad and helpless, but I was feeling something more, this same droning sensation I had never experienced before Spenser's death. Later still, driving through the site of a car accident where there had been a fatality, I again experienced this high voltage intensity charged with heightened dread, probably because these were untimely deaths. In contrast, when in the garden with Spenser, the awareness was not moribund, but still very insistent. After a few months, I lost the ability to perceive this buzzing, charged dimension.

On the telephone, Stan told me that Brendan may have felt guilty about Spenser's death.

"Why?" I asked him.

"At my house, the day before Spenser died, Brendan was upset with Spenser and said that he wished he were dead, and lo and behold, the next day he's dead," Stan stated.

I pushed open the door to Brendan's bedroom where he was lying under his coverlet. The room was dark, but cool and quiet.

"Brendan, what's going on?" He shifted in his bed at the sound of my voice. "Brendan, I just talked to Stan. You know that there's no link between telling Spenser you wish he were dead and his death, don't you?" I could see his head on the pillow from the light from the doorway.

"The reason I said I wished he were dead is due to jealousy," he blurted out.

Brendan graduated from high school with a 4.0 average. Spenser was euphemistically characterized as "developmentally delayed."

"What? Why would you be jealous of Spenser?"

Brendan adjusted the covers under his chin.

"Because he was better than I was."

Years later, Brendan would spend a semester abroad, graduate from a prestigious college and attend law school. Spenser received special education services.

"Why do you say he was better than you?"

"He put me to shame, because he always tried things and didn't care how dumb and retarded he looked, and everybody loved him."

"But you have gifts too, Brendan. Plus, Spenser's not here anymore and you are. We just have to make the best of it." I closed the door.

At the funeral home before the weekend service, Spenser's body lay in state in a darkened room with one spotlight shining on him. The guest book had already been signed by a few visitors. Flowers were arriving: huge sprays of gladioli and springtime bouquets of yellow daisies and pink carnations.

Stan, Tom and I sat in an adjoining room with the funeral director, leafing through examples of funeral service brochures in huge notebooks. The funeral director, a middle-aged man with a receding hairline, gestured to even more printed programs, strewn about on the table.

"Why are we sitting here in silence? I'm supposed to be choosing one of these?" I said. It occurred to me that wedding and funeral preparations are very similar.

I decided on a program with lavender larkspur, light purple phlox and long-stemmed Queen Anne's lace. The horizon was cast in a purplish haze, but illuminated with random fuzzy lights. In its mystery it alluded to that hinterland where Spenser may have gone, that space beyond the veil.

We chose a particular cemetery because of its proximity to Gates Park, where Spenser participated in Playhouse in the Park. Ducks and geese flapped their wings as they settled on the cemetery pond. On happier days, the boys and I had fed them bread crumbs after frequent trips to the zoo. I would later abhor some of the rules of this cemetery: that caskets have to be buried in concrete vaults so as not to indent the precious lawn, that no flowers can be planted by the graves, and that all loving mementos placed on the graves, even if they are plastic and can withstand the weather, are trashed twice a year for "cemetery cleanup," but there really isn't much of an opportunity to comparison shop when you've got the decomposing body of a child.

"This area is known as the Four Gospels section," said the agent as she drove us through the cemetery. The tall statues of the saints stretched out their hands from the four corners of their square, but in the barren section, only dead grass doused with synthetic chemicals and herbicides started to green up.

We circled around to an area with white sycamore trees in front of a pond. Noisy red-winged blackbirds fluttered among the thick vegetation. This was the place.

"The poet, the high school girl, who published the children's book is buried over here," the cemetery agent stated.

As I considered laying Spenser next to this girl, I felt as though I were being pulled in another direction, as though I were a vaudeville player being pulled off the stage with a crook. I sidestepped like a circus horse, front foot behind back foot, left over right, as though hooked by the waist.

Then I came to a stop at a grave marker inscribed "James Hart."

"He was that policeman who was killed in the helicopter crash. His fellow officer who also died is buried over there."

The wind picked up, and cool gusts rattled the branches of the sycamore tree. A male blackbird with bright red and yellow epaulets perched on top of a rush and exclaimed, "Ooh-wheeeeee!"

"I think we've made our choice," I told her.

I never knew James Hart, but Sharon had told me about her helpful young colleague with dark hair and striking masculine features. Serving as a police officer and being killed in the line of duty would have made James Hart a real-life action figure.

Spenser had decided where he wanted to be buried. Someday in the future, our bodies will lie next to his. Before this day, I had never thought about where I was going to be buried.

With the gravesite selected, I concentrated on the funeral. As I headed out on the interstate, I knew that *Leo the Late Bloomer* by Robert Kraus would be an appropriate reading. Leo is a little tiger who couldn't do anything right, much to the consternation of his father. But eventually Leo bloomed by reading, writing, and drawing: "He also spoke. And it wasn't just a word. It was a whole sentence. And that sentence was. . . I made it!'"

Who would read this story at the funeral? Me.

On the Saturday morning of his funeral, the sunlight filtered by the stained glass windows cast soft patterns on the carpeting where Spenser lay in his white casket.

I hovered near him. His porcelain features were still, except for a laceration circling his skull just under the silky hair. He was still very beautiful, but very dead. I searched for the mole under his right ear, but the bloating of his corpse eclipsed it. He was cold to the touch, having been refrigerated until the funeral, and emitted a faint, acrid odor. Because he had died on a Monday, the funeral director had chafed over the suggestion of a Saturday funeral.

"Decomposition can start to be a factor in that period of time," he had advised.

Embedded in the white satin lining, Spenser was flanked by his favorite action figure, Max Steel, and a nutcracker. The dolls lay beside him now, colorful and steadfast.

People were bustling about in the narthex, but hardly anyone came over to view the body. I remained with Spenser, striving to keep our connection intact.

"It's really time that we started the service," said the funeral director, leaning in front of me. His gold watch ticked away the seconds. As he lowered the lid of the coffin, a shadow fell across Spenser's face. I would never see his body again in this world.

Inside the sanctuary, the organist played "The Ash Grove." Occasional stifled coughs punctuated the trill of the sprightly treble notes, but mostly the congregation was silent.

"I am the resurrection and the life. Whosoever believeth in me shall not perish, but have eternal life," the minister's voice rang out.

After a hymn, it was my turn to read *Leo the Late Bloomer*. I ascended the red-carpeted steps to the pulpit with sure steps.

"Forgive me if I start crying," I announced before I started reading, but I was determined to deliver the text. All I had to do was to say the lines, just say the lines. Having reached the conclusion, when Leo the Late Bloomer attains success, I addressed the last line of the story to the lid of the white coffin.

"Spenser, you made it," I said to him.

Once back in my seat, Janelle Bronson, Spenser's third grade teacher, approached the pulpit. She wore a dark dressy jacket and pulled the microphone down closer to her face.

"I was Spenser's teacher at Chippewa," she began. Her light brown hair, in a page boy, fell softly around her face. Her voice wavered, but she continued.

"A while ago we had a new student. She watched Spenser pretty closely." I turned my head to hear her soft voice.

"At first she kept her distance, but pretty soon they were sitting together, and once were in deep conversation on the couch." The congregation shifted forward, edging closer to hear her faint words.

"Then she told me, 'I finally figured out why Spenser's different.'"

"Oh," I said, "Why is that?" Ms. Bronson paused. "'He's different because he's nice to everyone,' she told me."

Along with gasps and laughter, shrieks erupted from the congregation, almost before she could finish her last line.

The service was almost over. We had been sitting there a long time. It was time to go back out into the world, but not before listening to a recorded version of the song, "You've Got a Friend in Me" from the movie *Toy Story*.

"You've got a friend in me," the vocalist sang in a jazzy, syncopated beat. "You've got a friend in me." The morning had stretched toward noon, yet those gathered commemorated this jaunty, odd, somewhat misshapen child, until after the last benediction, when the funeral directors swung the casket sideways and wheeled it down the left aisle. The minister followed, with determined strides that parted his robe as the fringe on his vestments swung back and forth.

After the graveside ceremony, the tent was taken down and almost everybody went home. I knelt by the grave. The ground was partially filled in with dark, loamy dirt.

"We just have to get one more load of dirt, but it will take a while," said the mustached gravedigger.

"I'll wait," I said. I leaned forward and placed my right hand on top of the mounded soil, as though its rhythmic pulse could penetrate the frigid earth and warm my child's lifeless heart.

CHAPTER 39

The Police Officer

Spenser had been dead for about a month. I sat at my desk in the office, reading a case file at about ten to twelve. The place was deserted.

I slumped back in my chair, my legs straight out in front of me, while scribbling a note with my right hand. Then I shoved the file away, and bent over to put on my walking shoes.

With a push on the bar of the glass door, I thrust myself into the wind corridor that whistled around the building. Walking in the shadow of the monolithic edifice, I spied a flower bed, glowing in neon brightness, far away on the northeast corner of the government building grounds. The flaming scarlets and magentas blazed as though on fire.

Grey, faceless people passed by me as I strode toward them, never taking my eyes off the ethereal swirl of hypnotizing colors. Were these common bedding flowers of a different color, or a new species previously unknown in Kansas?

I crossed the street to the northeast corner and stopped with a jolt. The names of slain Kansas police officers glistened on a plaque mounted on a massive jagged rock. The seductive flowers had enticed me to this spot. Knowing that I might be confronted with the name of James Hart, I wanted to flee, but surely, with so many inscribed names, I wouldn't be able to find it.

James Hart. There was his name, front and center. My breaths grew shallow as I hovered like a bird, the second before it flies away.

This was no coincidence, and there was no exit. I collapsed onto the stone bench, surrounded by the churning colors of the flowers.

I closed my eyes, bowed my head, and listened. I heard slight static, as though Spenser were making a long distance phone call, and James Hart, older and longer in the afterlife, was guiding the connection.

"Momma, momma, momma, momma," Spenser's voice entreated me, sounding exactly like when he was alive. I had already forgotten how he would chant my name a number of times in order to get my attention.

"What is it, Spenser?" I answered for the thousandth time. I closed my eyes more tightly, staring into a pitch black universe.

"Momma, I'm happy here."

It was his little voice, absolutely, but only the sound, no visual image. I eased into this deep and dark space.

"Momma, momma, momma, momma," Spenser repeated again.

"What is it, Spenser?" I tunneled further down, waited, and trusted.

"Momma, I love you."

He had nothing more to say, but the pulsating blackness remained. Another image intruded, a dark young man, powerful, omnipotent, some other entity. Energy emanated from him, as though he were eclipsing a celestial body, but I could discern only an outline of this avatar, sitting in a lotus position.

"I just want to be done now, to go with Spenser," I whimpered.

"No," the avatar commanded. "It isn't your time yet. There are other children who need you."

There are other children who need you. A reason to go on, wondering who they might be, whether they could inhabit and brighten Spenser's empty room.

I opened my eyes, left the sanctuary of flowers and turned toward the office. By communicating, "Momma, I'm happy here," and "Momma, I love you," Spenser had said it all.

Spenser never spoke directly to me again, but on subsequent occasions, he may have been in the house. Sometimes he hid things, other times he found them for me.

Other boys did come to the house, real boys, Lane and Tristan, whom we adopted two years later when they were three and five years old. They careened through the rooms with boisterous abandon, except at night, when they slept like stones in Spenser's old bedroom.

"Do Lane and Tristan get up at night, play, and make all kinds of noise?" Tom's brother asked at the breakfast table during one of his visits.

"No, I've never known them to get up, except to go to the bathroom. Then you hear doors slam, but nothing else," I answered, leaning against the counter.

"Well, I heard all kinds of loud noises, like they were dropping things on the floor," he said to me, stirring the milk in his cereal. The guest bedroom, where he had slept the night before, is directly underneath the boys' bedroom.

"It was probably Spenser," I said to him. His eyes formed blank pools in his head.

Spenser is still in this house, with our family.

CHAPTER 40

Another Christmas

On most ordinary days I can walk past the glass case in the entrance hall of Chippewa containing Spenser's picture. He smiles from the golden frame, frozen at nine years old, watching everything that goes on in the school. But when I enter the gymnasium for the school Christmas assembly, I'm enveloped by Spenser's presence. The classes file onto the risers to sing Christmas carols, the teachers serenade the students, and Santa Claus arrives. He wouldn't miss it for the world.

In Lane's third grade classroom, the children's desks faced a table with wrapped toys and a Christmas tree. Chocolate chip cookies, cheese, crackers and fruit punch were lined up on the window sill on either side of me.

Lane sat staring at me from his desk, his eyes fixed on me with serious concentration. I had no idea what he was looking at, or why his face bore such a stern expression. In the midst of a Christmas party, Lane would usually be running all over and putting his hands on other children. Leaning up against the heat register, I grieved for Spenser.

A girl unwrapped her gift, a toy with connecting magnetic rods. Those little rods would end up all over the floor, disconnected, scattered, lost.

I stopped in Tristan's room before the busses were called. We almost made it out the door before a set of grandparents stepped forward with a huge bag filled with individual treat bags. More candy, more wrappers, more little plastic Santa Claus heads that only make a sound ten times before they are broken.

Lane and Tristan ran around on the sidewalk before getting into the car, despite a chilly wind. Once in the car, they turned on the inside car lights, played with the locks, and would not get their seat belts on. More bags rustled, more candy came out. Wrappers would be on the floor mats, wedged into the seats, and stashed in little pieces in the side door compartments.

At home in the driveway, Tristan wouldn't go into the house because he was fixated on his pinewood derby kit. He broke the seal so the pieces would be scattered and lost, rendering the car worthless.

I screamed at him to get into the house. He fell to the car floor, yelling, "I won't come into the house." I grabbed for an arm, but he was heavy, and laid out on the car floor. As I unlocked the front door I castigated myself for being a horrible mother, who should have taken the time to handle the scene differently.

The bright overhead dining room light revealed that the house was a mess. There were papers piled on the dining room table, and book bags flung on the couch, crammed with treat bags and little plastic toys that would all have to be sorted. I didn't have the energy to carry the laundry basket to the basement. I would have to clean up all this clutter before Christmas. I was so tired.

In their room, junk was all over the floor. Before I put them to bed, I made a half-hearted effort to sort through the debris, barely making a noticeable difference.

Once in bed, illuminated by a soft night light, Lane and Tristan were quiet, tucked under their quilts. I draped my arms over the guardrail of the bunk bed, and leaned my head against my arms.

"I'm sorry, boys. I haven't been very patient today. I guess I'm sad about Spenser, and it can get overwhelming."

Lane sprang up from his pillow, his head and shoulders outlined in profile against the dim night-light.

"But Spenser was beside you all day today," he said.

"What are you talking about?" I peered more deeply into the darkness, into his wide round eyes.

"In the room, today in the room. When I looked at you, he was right there next to you."

In my snapshot memory of Lane, I pictured that concentrated expression he drilled into me as I leaned up against the heat register.

"If you saw Spenser, why didn't you tell me this before?"

He looked down and fidgeted with his bedclothes, turning the fabric softly in his hands. Lane was, after all, only about nine years old. "I was afraid you would say I was making it up."

"Okay, well then, as for Spenser, what did he look like?"

"Dull."

"Dull?" I watched him more closely, but he seemed to be telling the truth. "What are you calling dull?" This was not a word he would ordinarily use.

"Like you could see through him. Like he was not really there. Like blurry, if you hold your finger up, and make your eyes go back and forth like this." Lane held his index finger straight up before his face, and made quick, darting motions with his eyes.

"Lane, are you lying to me about all of this? Are you making all of this up?"

"No." He hesitated, as though I might punish him. Still he exhibited the rapt expression, the willingness to talk, even though I did not know where the dialogue was leading.

"What was Spenser saying? What was he doing?"

"He was whispering to you."

"What was he saying?"

"I couldn't hear him." His shoulders rose in a little exasperated shrug.

Tristan was softly breathing in the lower bunk. They both smelled sweet and clean after their baths.

"Then why weren't you afraid? Wouldn't seeing Spenser have scared you?"

"It wasn't the first time I saw him."

"When did you see him before?"

"He wanted to go out to play. To play games with us. It was November."

"Just this last November?" I asked. Through the hazy darkness, I saw Lane smile, the smile of a pleasant memory.

"So where was he?"

"Coming down the stairs to go outside. Then he vanished."

"Was he dull and blurry when you saw him that time?"

"Yeah."

"Lane, are you making all this up? Are you telling me this just because you think I want to hear it?"

"No."

I hugged him. It was late. His arms folded around my neck, and he gave me a wet kiss on my cheek. Of course he would say he was not making it up. As to whether he was, there was no earthly way of knowing. But was it Wordsworth, who besides talking about trailing clouds of glory, believed that young children were more in tune with the other world because they are so recently departed from it?

Then there was another time during the past November, a few days after Thanksgiving when Lane volunteered to get the pumpkin pie from the basement refrigerator.

When he came back upstairs, he slumped down in his chair, and fiddled with his silverware, looking puzzled and confused. There was no mistaking that something had happened.

"What's the matter, Lane?"

"When I was downstairs," he began, "and got the pie from the refrigerator, a hand knocked on the glass panel door. I heard the noise and when I looked up it waved. Then it vanished." Lane imitated the wave, a quick, friendly impulsive shake of the hand.

Now he's afraid to go into the basement alone, especially after dark. Further, I know that wave. It's exactly something that Spenser would do.

Half a year later, a summer late afternoon, mercifully devoid of the direct sun, drew me outside of the house. I intended to thin the radishes and carrots, but the weeds in the zinnias waylaid me. I pulled quickly, right hand over left, as the roots dislodged easily from the black, moist soil.

The tires crunched on the gravel as Tom rolled into the driveway, bringing Lane and Tristan home from day camp. As the afternoon shadows lengthened, I grasped a big weed with both hands and tugged.

Lane and Tristan kicked a soccer ball in the side yard underneath the red maples. Their disembodied voices dotted the sweep of the wind, which muffled their words.

Their voices floated closer. I peered through the leaves of the river birch tree, squinting to focus. Two blonde boys traversed the screen framed by the shimmering leaves, single file. Lane was first, the taller one, darting through my range of vision. The second boy wore a cap, with panels of alternating red, blue and yellow, and under the cap, platinum blonde hair. His head was shaped like Spenser's, and as he lumbered along, shifting his weight from side to side, Spenser's gait, I could not attest that his feet touched the ground.

Tristan did not have a jaunty cap of red, blue and yellow, unless he got it from summer camp.

"Tom! Tom!" My voice broke as I screeched through my vocal chords.

He didn't hear me.

"Tom! Where did Tristan get that cap?"

I was still surrounded by the scrim of drooping river birch branches.

"Tristan isn't wearing any cap," he answered.

CHAPTER 41

Lily Dale

S everal years after Spenser's death, I grabbed a library book off the shelves while browsing for something to read, which was *Lily Dale* by Christine Wicker, a journalist who traveled to this Spiritualist community in New York where mediums converse with the dead. Just south of Buffalo, this tiny community dotted with gingerbread Victorian houses thrives during welcoming weather, when throngs make pilgrimages to the mediums who set up shop, in hopes of receiving messages from their dearest departed.

One night in early summer Tom laid in bed, propping up a map with his elbows on the quilted bedspread, planning our vacation. Having grown up in Buffalo, he wanted to take the boys to see Niagara Falls.

"While we're in that part of the state, could we also visit Lily Dale?" I asked.

"Where is it? Oh, right here, just off this Highway 60." Then he smiled at me, as though it were all ridiculous, except to a mother who would do anything for a message from her child.

We were going. I made an appointment in advance with one of the mediums. Whether other people would think me crazy was of no concern. I hoped for a sign, a communication, a reassurance from the voice once familiar and now silent.

Cedar and fir trees hovered over the road as we drove toward Lily Dale. At the entrance, a graceful arc with the white metal letters "Lily Dale Assembly, The City of Light" beckoned us to a place not so much that time had forgotten, but where time didn't matter.

We could view a small lake from the front porch of a large white wooden clapboard building, the historic Maplewood Hotel. The porch was lined with rocking chairs, where strangers chatted, becoming friends. On the grounds were a museum in a small brown house, a library, a bookstore, an assembly hall, a church and rows of streets lined with small cottages. Some of the nineteenth century houses were pristine, with prim gardens, picket fences and Victorian trim, but a few others, grey, dark and seemingly abandoned, were falling apart. Because everything was within walking distance it felt like a summer camp.

Lane and Tristan slammed the car door, and shouted in their little boy voices. Our room in the Maplewood Hotel was plainly adorned, with modest beds set against walls with aged wallpaper on a bare wooden floor. There was no television, telephone, carpeting, or air-conditioning, only a small adjoining bath with a porcelain sink and a plain wooden door that opened onto an empty hall. I wondered whether there were spirits in these rooms.

In the late afternoon, Tom and I hurried down the trail through woods that led to a clearing called Inspiration Stump. While we were treading on pine needles and crackling sticks, we were fueled with adrenalin, both because we were late and also because we were some-what afraid. It did not seem natural to be rushing headlong into expe-riencing communication with the dead.

Spectators sat in the amphitheater. Wearing hats and sunglasses, they cast wary glances at the gathering clouds, which spat occasional raindrops. The first medium who was introduced cast her eyes rest-lessly over the crowd. I could feel myself shrinking from her gaze yet hoping she would call on me.

"May I come to you?" She pointed to a group of women seated before us, of different ages, yet with uniform dark hair. One was a heavy middle-aged woman sprawled in a loose-fitting tie-dyed shift.

Her outstretched arms encircled her daughters, one on each side, who were younger and more stylishly dressed.

"I'm seeing an older woman, perhaps a grandmother, a great-aunt, with a long dress of the style of the old country," the medium began. She was a short middle-aged woman wearing khaki shorts and a black shell and sandals, who would have been indistinguishable in any crowd.

The maternal woman momentarily paused, but then nodded.

"I'm getting an 'M' name, possibly Mary, possibly Marie or Martha. I sense she is on the paternal side," the medium spoke with steady insistence.

The young women on either side of the woman drew closer, twittering, whispering in the large woman's ear.

"I'm seeing a kitchen. She's in front of a woodstove, with many pots boiling, possibly pasta. Italy. I'm sensing she is either from Italy or cooking Italian food." The medium hurried on, her words and thoughts tumbling out, as though she were closing a sale.

The women, seemingly having reached consensus on the spirit's identity, sat still and listened.

"She was of an advanced age when she passed over into spirit. She still watches over all of you, especially a son, a John or perhaps a James. She wants him to monitor his health, and not allow himself to get so stressed. She brings you peace. She departs in peace. Thank you for allowing me to serve spirit."

The crowd clapped, and even though several other mediums performed, I was not singled out that afternoon.

The next morning I stood and applied my makeup in the mirror over the porcelain sink. I was wearing a pink sleeveless top, with a few softly gathered frills, and a broomstick skirt that reached nearly to my sandals. I pulled my eyelid taut and applied the eyeliner with an even, dark stroke. I wasn't afraid. I felt instead communion, a connection to the peaceful souls in that village resting in the sunlit forest. Before this day there had been times when I could sense Spenser's spirit. I just couldn't hear anything he was saying.

I strolled down the street toward the house of the medium under whispering trees. Third Street was not hard to find. The morning sunlight, with just a slight touch of warmth, was soothing. I moved forward in a cocoon, of seeing and not seeing, because underneath my serene surface, I dwelt with grief in a leaden, crepuscular world where nothing much is felt, other than a dull, monotonous ache.

I found the house number. A cheery garden crammed with summer flowers surrounded a simple sign hanging on a white post.

I hesitated because I heard voices inside. After two women passed by, I ventured into the hallway.

Mimi, the medium, called out that she would be right with me. I stood waiting among boxes of books and phonograph records stacked to the side, and clothes piled into baskets.

Mimi invited me to sit opposite her in her reading room. Hundreds of books lined the walls. Mimi wore a soft blue oversized shirt over white slacks. Her platinum hair framed her smooth complexion with soft wisps and curls. I wanted to be mothered by this older sister, to repose endlessly in shared confidences in the cool of this room that shut out the rest of the world.

"First of all," she began, "it will save considerable time and playing twenty questions if you can direct me to the reason you are here."

"I lost my son Spenser when he was ten years old," I answered.

She reached forward and flicked on a tape recorder.

"As we open the door to communication in unity with the Holy Spirit, we give thanks for we know the words spoken for Margaret are filled with your love, truth, wisdom and understanding."

I opened my eyes again after this prayer. I waited for what she would say next. She dove into her narration without stopping for a single beat.

"The first image I had was a little boy with like a little cap on a bicycle just having a good old time. Now there's also something about the way he's showing himself to me that makes me wonder if that's a picture he wants to send or if that was really part of his life. Was your son ill before he passed?"

I nodded.

"I suspected that that's what it was and if you would do me a favor? Would you just sit up a little and I'll tell you why. When you sit with your chin in your chest you're in what we call 'in cave' which is in feelings and it's hard for me to get to your heart if you're so locked in your feelings."

I straightened up in my chair. She meant business.

"There was a way that he showed up on the bicycle with the cap that said to me 'This was not how my life was when I passed.' All right? That would say he was not able to do things that a normal ten-year-old child would be able to do. He is coming to tell you that he is now a normal ten-year-old boy. Okay?"

As I started to cry, she gestured to the Kleenexes. "These are here, and not to worry because the record for tissue use was twenty-two in a half hour and I know you're not going to get there."

"He comes around with laughter and ease. The word 'ease' is very important because my suspicion is that nothing of his life was easy. Was he ill almost from birth?"

"Sotos syndrome," I answered sullenly, acknowledging the demon for what it was.

"What was that?"

"Sotos syndrome."

"I don't know that one."

"One in ten thousand births. He was mildly to moderately developmentally delayed." I began the litany.

"Well, this kid is not slow for a moment. Okay?"

"Right, right."

What was I saying? According to academic testing he was mildly, and more accurately, moderately developmentally delayed. Yet there was a brightness, a spark that shone through as clearly as with any gifted child.

"He's talking about being able to breathe easy, all right? That would tell me that perhaps pneumonia or a lung condition was somehow involved at the end of his life."

Metastatic cancer, completely filling his lungs, the tumor so large that it pushed out his sternum and distorted his chest.

"He's saying that he can breathe easy. The baseball cap tells me that he's engaging in normal boy things. All right, and then again the breathing easy keeps coming up. He talks about how he never felt different and he says that's because you made sure that he never felt different, which made it so possible for him to live a whole life in ten years."

I did treat him like a typically-developing child. Spenser simply did things his way, and nobody laughed. There's nothing funny about absolute sincerity.

"Yet in being a bit of a loner there was a great social nature about him. He loved being the life of the party. He shows himself with a red Bozo clown nose and a top hat and a cane, and I suspect he would have loved magic tricks."

"Actor," I stated.

"Actor? Yeah, but magic tricks for some reason. He's been in spirit for quite a while, hasn't he?

"Four years."

"Is that all? It feels like he's been in spirit for an eternity. That tells me that when he came in he knew he was going out quickly. So coming into this lifetime was just," she made a quick sound through pursed lips, "a road show. A road show with high energy and great humor and a great, great sense of calm and needing for you to know that he has no regrets about anything in his life. He did it all, and that's because you made him do it all."

I shifted in the chair and rearranged my skirt.

"And he said, 'I came to show people that you can live life and not be afraid, because I was never afraid.'"

Mimi paused, momentarily suspended in a conversation that I could not hear. "He kind of looked around and said, 'Well, maybe thunderstorms if they were too long when I was a little kid. When I was a little kid,' all right?"

Sometimes when the thunder and lightning crashed in the night sky and rain pelted the windows, Spenser would appear beside my bed in the quiet of the darkened room.

"He wants you to not be sad."

What? What about grief therapy support groups whose mantra is that no one ever gets over the death of a child?

"I mean, he really wants you to not be sad, because there is no failure in anything that happened here. No failure. He came in with it. He went out with it, it was his deal. He also signed up for it, all right? In the grand scheme of we have a job to do and when we're done, we're out. You graduate and you're done."

He signed up for ten years, only ten years. I knew that after he died, sensed it strongly. The September before his death, he had a mysterious staph infection and was hospitalized for a few days. Even though he recovered, I yelled at him when he was asleep in the hospital bed, "Spenser, quit trying to die on us!"

"He signed up for it, and he did it joyfully, and willingly, and the only times that he complained were when he became so incredibly uncomfortable, but, even though people perceived that he might be in pain, it wasn't pain, because he didn't have a capacity to feel pain."

Metastatic cancer. Stage four. All over his body. No complaints. Sitting in the waiting room, kicking his feet against the examining table, thinking about the summer. All through April, slightly tired, but functioning normally. Going to school. Planting irises on the side of the hill. Almost dead.

"That's true. A very high threshold for pain." I confirmed this to her in that room stacked with books.

"That was the blessing, the inability to feel pain. You call it a 'threshold.' He's laughing at that. Big word. 'You call it a threshold?' He says, 'God didn't give me the senses to feel pain like others feel pain. It was so that I could do my job and not suffer.' All right?"

I stared at Mimi, engaged in this conversation with Spenser that I couldn't hear.

"Even though his body should have been wracked with pain, he didn't feel it because God had protected him. It wasn't there. When he looked at his contract before he came in and was talking with his angel and packing his school backpack of all the things he needed to bring to earth school, the angel said, 'Let me give you something that will keep you from feeling pain,' and that's what made him brave."

She paused and remained silent.

"Is your mom still alive?"

"Yes."

"She was really a huge part of his life."

No, she wasn't.

"The thing of it is, he says, 'She has to cry,' because as long as she doesn't cry, then he stays here."

I made a strange sound because this startled me.

Mimi got tangled up in some of her own words, and stopped.

"Boy, that's new. Every now and then I get a new piece of information from somebody in spirit that I don't know. He is so linked with his grandmother that until she cries, it leaves him here too much because she's holding on to him so tightly. Do you understand?"

"Huh," I marveled. "I didn't know that."

"I didn't either. He said it, I pass it on. She is in more pain than he was, and she will be in more physical pain than he was if she doesn't let go of him. I dare you to explain that one to her. I don't know what words you're going to use."

Whenever I visited my mother, she fastened her eyes on the knitting needles in front of her, and wrapped the yarn around one needle, then pulled the other needle through, rhythmically, for many stitches.

"Tears are a full heart's safety valve," Mimi explained, "and her heart's blowing up. Does she have congestive heart failure?"

No. She wasn't overweight, her father was a string bean who lived into his early nineties and there's absolutely no history of heart failure in the family. I couldn't expect Mimi to be right about everything.

"She's got to let the tears out. I go back to tears are a full heart's safety valve, and then when we have emotional fluid in our heart it creates physical fluid in our heart. I'm not a doctor, I don't diagnose, I don't prescribe, but it sure does look to me like your mom is right on the edge of having some real serious heart problems."

About a year after this reading, my mother nearly died of a heart attack. She lay motionless in the emergency room, beyond us, seemingly past death, past being a cadaver, her countenance a ghastly image. The only sound in the room was the rhythmic whoosh of the manual breathing apparatus strapped onto her mouth. The emergency room personnel told us to say our goodbyes.

"And I don't see her passing, I don't see anything of that, all right? But I do see that she's setting herself up for some health problems."

Despite all odds, within a week my mother gained consciousness and was fine.

"The other thing is, she has to look at your son as being a gift . . . oh, okay."

Another one of those pauses. Like hearing someone talk on the telephone, I could only hear Mimi's end of the conversation.

"He was like a beautiful bouquet of flowers, and as this beautiful bouquet of flowers arrives, you love it, and you enjoy it, but there is always the knowing that there's a point where everything will have to be tossed out, put away, the vase washed, and put back on the shelf. If you hang on to the old flowers, then you surround yourself in darkness. Does that make sense?"

Of course I could relate to flowers. I can't plant enough of them.

"You know it's really interesting because as your son stands around, he's kind of got his hand on his hip, and he's poking around and being a little nosey, and trying to learn some new words he needed to learn, he's just having the best time. And he wants you to have the best time, too."

"Is he with actors, doing any theatre?" I asked.

"Not really, but right here he's center stage all by himself. Whatever else is going on in his world, he's not showing it. There's a tremendous sense of peace, there's anticipation of being able to come back again at some point."

We talked about adopting Lane and Tristan, my profession, what Tom does for a living.

"Spenser says he's just sitting on the deck behind the back seat in the car because he can lay down and get his back up against the window because he can watch everything from there. He couldn't always watch everything from where he was. And he's having a great time. He comes and goes. Sometimes he's around, and sometimes he's not, and things get moved. And you know when he's there, so he says, 'I don't have to tell her when I'm there.'"

Months earlier, I couldn't find a fall wreath that should have been stashed in boxes way back in the storage room. When I opened the front door the next day to find it lying in the middle of the foyer, I jumped back a foot. Later I interrogated everybody in the house, and their blank gazes confirmed that they hadn't touched it.

"But he also wants to let you know that he's there. He says that you guys have got to find your happy place, because the new kids on the block need to know what it's like to grow up in a happy place, not in a place that's sad because of what isn't there. He's real stern about this because he says, 'Mom, you just don't laugh enough.'"

I made little murmuring sounds. I grieved for my child and she talked to me about happiness. Although I could picture Spenser's happy, silent smile, I didn't want to change my orientation. Not then. Grief is quiet and peaceful; living is noisy, complicated, and tiring.

"You need to laugh more. You need to be silly. He's being a perfect kid. 'Play games and run around.'"

"Does he have anything to say to Brendan, his older brother?"

"He wants to make sure that he doesn't feel that he has to live his life for Spenser. He has to live his life for himself, and he may think about him and remember him, but he should not make his decisions with the sense that he has to fulfill two lives."

"Right, but he's real closed off. He wouldn't tell us any of this."

Brendan stayed behind his bedroom door when visitors paid mourning calls. The day after Spenser died, he laid on his bed all day. The next day, he got up early in the morning, grabbed his backpack, and went to school.

"You have a whole family that's closed off."

"But not the two little kids, Lane and Tristan," I protest.

"Because they didn't grow up in this. These two little kids have walked into a family that's full of sadness and full of loss. It's important for them to know that they were not brought into the family as replacements for him, and they need to know that every day. But nobody talks about Spenser from any perspective except wrapped in sadness. Over and over, and he's using your mom as a metaphor, that you've got to loosen up here so that he can get on, because as long as he is the center stage of your family, he will be the center stage only in a small way, and he came to live life in a big way, and the bulk of his life is after he passes. You're holding him as a ten-year-old and he needs to move on. I don't know how you guys are going to do it, but you've got to let go of this."

In this small front room where she holds the readings, with the hall full of boxes and laundry baskets filled with clothes, she was encouraging me to let go of Spenser. With my hands resting on my lap on top of my skirt, I wanted to wallow in grief. The few tears had not washed away all my eye liner. I decided to consider it.

"I think we've made really good progress."

"There's such darkness," she answers. "You may have made good progress, but there's such sadness and trepidation. You've gotten past the 'Did we do everything we could have done?' He says, 'You've got to put the giggles back in.'"

Giggles. I never use that word. Neither did Spenser.

"And more of them. And more giggles. As for Brendan," Mimi looked down and paused, "part of what he's feeling, he's like your mother, is the sadness for the loss of his brother. All right? Margaret, I would suspect that there was so much attention put on Spenser and he didn't get his share of it, that there was a piece, where he said, "I just wish he'd die and get over it.' And then there's the guilt that goes along with that. Just have a conversation with him and say, 'I don't know what you're feeling, and it would be perfectly normal to wish any of these things, but you didn't have anything to do with his passing.' And take that monkey off his back. He's a good kid."

Oh, Brendan. You're a wonderful kid.

"And he's smart and he's bright and he's lost his funny."

"Totally," I agree.

"Yeah, because you all lost your funny when Spenser died. He was your funny. Yet now you have to find it on your own. I think within six months life will be very different in a good way. All right? Do you have questions?"

"One. 'Spenser, what would you have me do?'" I asked him through Mimi now. I ask this whenever I visit the grave, between the two sycamore trees in front of the pond thick with grasses for red-winged blackbirds. Whenever I look down at the bronze plaque, whether there is snow on the ground or green grass, I ask him, "Spenser, what would you have me do?"

"Laugh," Mimi honked like a goose. "Laugh. That's the only thing he wants you to do is laugh. Be happy. You have to remember what it felt like to be happy. Go back to the anticipation and the joy that you had before Spenser was born. That will in no way diminish your value of him. When you do that, you will go back to happy. Thank you. That was him, telling me, 'This is what you tell her about when happy was.' Go back there, and tell daddy to do it too."

I started to explain about all of that, but she had no more time.

"Okay? There you go."

I gathered myself up and walked out into the sunshine. The reading was not exactly what I'd expected. I was hoping for one more intimate conversation with Spenser. Be happy is logical, yet simplistic. Yet I could visualize Spenser, bopping around, playing boy games, the imp, the little sprite he always was. He always seemed to be on the verge of telling some secret hidden behind his wide smile, but we never asked, and he never told. Maybe it was to be happy and that all the excuses, the million excuses for not being happy are lame.

I turned the corner past a small white house with petunias planted in a tire and headed toward the park, wondering how many sobbing mothers Mimi encountered in her business as a medium.

Tom, seated on a park bench shaded by a densely-branched tree, smiled at my approach. Tom, darling Tom. Lane and Tristan kicked up wood chips as they careened from the slide to a swinging tire. Brendan played with them. Perhaps things could be better.

CHAPTER 42

The Shrines at the Theatre

Sometimes I wander around like a shade through the darkened, deserted halls of Theatre on the Levee, losing myself in the pictures of past theatrical performances. One particular day, I could hear the audience clapping during a live show, but up here on the second floor, the mounted photos capture productions whose sets have been struck years before.

I know many of the actors in the photographs, captured in their costumes under cool blue and pink spotlights. I learned their secrets between set changes, and partied with them after opening night. They are all older now; some of them are dead. Padding along with quiet steps, I stop before a picture of myself. The girl in the photo, her hands on her hips in tight black pants with a sultry smirk is me, thirty years ago.

The Japanese honor their ancestors, whose shrines are part of their daily lives. In our culture, we relegate death to hospitals and cemeteries, places apart, so we can forget, if not the love, the pain. Some people don't even believe in God, let alone an afterlife, because there is no way to explain it scientifically.

I drift past the portraits, and turn the corner looking for every hidden soul, to the very end of the hall. Somehow in this theatre, we need to honor Spenser. Peter Pan, of course. I can visualize Spenser in the garden outside the entrance to the theatre, cast in bronze with a tunic and jaunty feathered cap. In his stationary pose, he will seem to be dancing, twirling, his arm aloft, spewing fairy dust into the air.

There are other memorials for Spenser. Because they won't let us plant flowers at the cemetery, we've planted them at his elementary school so that the children, riding their bikes on the sidewalk or marching around the block during the Halloween parade, can ponder the inscribed words on a plaque, partially obscured by chrysanthemums, "You've Got a Friend in Me." As for the memory bricks commemorating the passage of the Oregon Trail through the town, I purchased one for Brendan and one for Spenser, the living and the dead. The pioneers parted the tall bluestem grass with their creaking wagons, which still waves in the wind and changes color throughout the seasons. The ancestors, crowded out by four-lane highways and blaring televisions, still murmur underneath the hum. The ancestors are still abroad, even after the roads are deserted and the businesses have closed up shop. The ancestors, sovereigns of the reverberating silence, will speak if we listen.

If you lose a child, your life changes. You also have choices. You can wither and retreat, becoming so diminished that you follow your child to the grave, or you can fashion a life that honors the child. I've devised numerous small memorials, such as the donations to charities, kind words for harried clerks, compassion that seems unwarranted. I judge all my efforts and expenditures against a new standard.

For example, one morning I substituted for the sixth grade classroom at Chippewa. The children clustered in groups before class, chattering excitedly among themselves. They pulled off knit stocking caps that created arcs of electrified hair. A few regarded me as a foreign presence in front of their familiar blackboard, but Spenser's friends knew me. I skimmed the teacher's lesson plan, neatly handwritten on a yellow legal pad: reading, social studies, science, math.

"I'll be in another part of the building with the assessment committee today," the regular teacher said before leaving. "You might watch that one. Just transferred in two days ago. He might give you trouble," she said, rolling her eyes.

The new boy with glasses named Shane was slightly husky, and did not belong to any of the cliques. He was wearing a yellow sweater and jeans, and talked to a boy next to him who did not respond. Shane wasn't causing any trouble. Instead, Derrick, the slight, elfish boy in the middle of the classroom, spoke out of turn. His giggles filled the spaces during the students' monotone recitation about Xerxes and the

Persian dynasties. When it was his turn to read, Derrick, wide-eyed, played to his audience, emphasizing his words for comic effect. He knew he was cute, and that he would always have friends on the playground. Shane was not amused by Derrick.

Recess did not go well for Shane. Nobody played with him, and when he picked up the dodge ball, Zachary yelled at him to give it back. Because he shoved Justin, a teacher threatened him with detention.

"I know, let's play a game," I suggested. "Shane, to get better acquainted, come up here and let people ask you questions,"

"I don't want to come up in front of the room," he said.

"C'mon, it'll be fun. Kind of like *Jeopardy*, or other television game shows." He sat glued to his seat. "I'll be up here with you. I'll help you."

Shane inched to the front of the room.

"What's your favorite subject in school?" I began.

"I don't like school," he said, peering down at the floor.

"Why not?" I asked, moving into his personal space.

"I get in trouble during recess. Nobody likes me. I'm always the new one without any friends." He slouched.

I tried to get inside this child's head, to read the eyes behind the glasses. He was a hard sell. I surveyed a sea of waving hands.

"Where are you from?" asked Derrick.

"Well, we moved here from Texas, but before that it was Kentucky. My mom says we might stay here for a while. She's trying to get away from my dad."

He lifted his chin, and pointed to a student.

"What's your favorite sport?"

"Baseball. Next?" His eyes darted quickly around. He called on someone else.

"How many brothers and sisters do you have?" asked Laura, her pink muffler draped around her neck.

"One younger brother. He's with my grandmother in Kentucky."

I looked at my nails after he returned to his seat.

"How many of you remember Spenser Gardner?" I asked. Over half the heads nodded in silent agreement.

"Did Mr. Hodges really play with him during recess?" More nods.

"Does he still come out and play with kids during recess?"

The nodding stopped. "No," said a boy off to the right side," now he has things to do in his office."

I took several breaths. The hair rose on my arms. I had a plan. If it backfired and they fired me, I didn't really need the money. Later I would wonder how such simple words created such an effect.

"What if Spenser were here, right here, right now this minute?" I asked.

The children froze, framed in a still shot, as though blinded by a flashbulb. In the next instant a few dived under their desks. One girl started running for the door. The rest remained rigid. Then Derrick giggled.

"Derrick, this is not funny, at all," responded Laura. Hers was the only voice punctuating the silence.

This was all over the top, but I continued to use it.

"Spenser believed in being a friend to everyone." My voice quavered. "If a kid was new to the school, Spenser played with him. You've all been strangers. Remember how it feels."

The suspended characters started moving again. Derrick slammed his book shut. Laura stood up and thrust her papers into a folder.

Shane came in smiling after the next recess. Some kids had played with him.

"I'm really glad we got to play with the new equipment today," he said.

His guard was down, a little further. He talked more expansively; and his gestures were more relaxed. He smiled.

He still had not caused me any trouble.

EPILOGUE

I survey the row of strawberry and rhubarb jam jars that gleam on the counter, cooling down from the boiling water bath.

I say out loud, again, "Spenser, I'm happy here."

I love growing vegetables and flowers, raising chickens and having animals, along with the kids. For me, it's the only way to live, with the Kansas wind gusting through the trees, carrying the song of the solitary meadowlark from the plains. The summer nights are packed with swarms of fireflies or towering thunderheads that roll in before it rains.

Spenser's portrait, framed in shining silver, smiles at me from the fireplace mantel. He lived here his entire life. I will never leave this house.

"Spenser," I confess to his portrait, "Maybe I was wrong. Perhaps I'm the impaired one for fearing that you had limits." I picture him dancing in the subway, twirling around with syncopated movements while everyone else sat on the perimeter. They were waiting for things to happen, but he was making things happen.

"To think I was worried. There was, would have been, always will be a part for you." I sigh and turn away from his photograph.

I refuse to deify him, or exalt him as a perfect soul just because he died. If he were here, shackled as he was by that disability, he would still be trying hard, doing things his way. I suppose there's grace in staying the course, even if we stumble. I don't know where he got his optimism, but he never lost it.

I give the lids a slight twist before I lower another set of filled jars into the canner.

I still occasionally have bad days, especially on anniversaries, when I don't feel like doing much, but the span that separates the occasional listless day from the active ones keeps stretching. For many people, losing a child is the worst thing that could ever happen, but for me, the divorce was more difficult than his death. I was surrounded by love and support when Spenser died, whereas I experienced the divorce alone.

The seasons have come around again to April. The trees flanking the hillside are adorned in a smattering of lime green buds. Each morning is more gorgeous than the one before.

Before Spenser's death, I could not relate to people describing the proverbial beautiful sunset. Now, perhaps because I am seeing the world through his eyes, every day is truly a gift. In response, we should all blossom into our limitless talents by creating more, learning more, serving more, loving more.

The excited voices of Lane and Tristan interrupt my thoughts. Peering through the kitchen window, I see that our Siamese cat has nabbed a bird.

"Grab Spider and get the bird. Maybe we can save it," I shout through the screen as I crank open the window.

I dash out into the yard. They deliver the bird to me, a male cardinal, with bright red feathers and a black mask. The bird shivers with tiny vibrations as I hold him. He lurches from my grasp and hops into a pile of leaves.

I gather up the bird again, cupping him in the warmth of my palms. His soft feathers bounce against my fingers as he struggles to be free. Recognizing that he is strong enough to fly, I raise my arm to the sky, and open my hand.

ACKNOWLEDGEMENTS

To begin with I would like to thank members of my dissertation committee: Maryemma Graham, Mary Klayder, Tom Lorenz, Laura Moriarty and Rud Turnbull who critiqued this manuscript when it was in the iteration of *My Son the Actor*. It never would have become a creative dissertation without your suggestion, Maryemma, and Laura, you went above and beyond with your precise editing, helpful suggestions and continual guidance.

Many thanks to my editor, John Paine, whose considerable skills transformed an experiment into a presentable manuscript.

I would also like to thank members of the Sin Eaters and Great Plains Writing Groups, who pored over endless chapters with patience and dedication, offering innumerable valuable suggestions and insights: Judy Graversen-Algaier, Angie Babbit, Betsy Boyce, Louie Galloway, Jean Grant, Sue Haley, Mary McCoy, Nicole Muchmore, Nancy Myers, Nancy Pistorius, Rebecca Powers, Lucy Price, Tammy Sabol, Robin St. James, Jeff Stark, Annie Stevens, Sue Suhler, Sara Taliaferro, Tessica Tallman, Craig Voorhees and Sherry Williams.

Thank you to the cover artist, Nina Niebuhr, whose artistry pictorializes the uncharted territory of grief.

A special thank you to Susan and Gary Chan and The Compassionate Friends, fellow travelers on the journey. Susan, you continue to open doors of support and encouragement.

This book would never have materialized without my publisher, Maureen Carroll, whose expertise and knowledge transformed *Searching For Spenser* from two-hundred-odd typewritten pages stashed in a manila folder into this book. If you would not have chosen it, it may never have left the bottom drawer of my file cabinet.

Finally, to all those whose names are changed in this book so as to protect your privacy, I will never be able to thank you enough for all you have done for Spenser.

ABOUT THE AUTHOR

Margaret Rayburn Kramar is an educator and author whose memoir, *Searching for Spenser*, explores how she was transformed through the death of her disabled child.

A graduate of Grinnell College, she received an MA in journalism from the University of Iowa. Subsequently employed as lifestyle editor for the Denison Newspapers, her work received awards from the Iowa Press Association Better Newspaper Contest and Herbert Bayard Swopes Memorial Awards. In 2012 she received a PhD in English from the University of Kansas and taught English composition, drama and American literature. Previous to the PhD, she was employed for twenty years as a civil rights investigator by the Kansas Human Rights Commission.

Her work has appeared in numerous anthologies and print and digital publications. A chapter from *Searching for Spenser* captured the first place award in the Kansas Authors Club Contest.

She and her family live on a small farm in northeast Kansas where they produce organically grown fruits, vegetables and free-range eggs.

Please contact the author at:
http://www.margaretkramar.com/

OTHER BOOKS YOU MIGHT ENJOY FROM
ANAMCARA PRESS

ISBN: 978-1-941237-08-3
$24.95

ISBN: 978-1-941237-14-4
$12.95

ISBN: 978-1-941237-16-8
$18.95

ISBN: 978-1-941237-13-7
$18.95

ISBN: 978-1-941237-05-2
$8.99

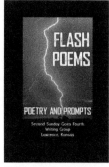

ISBN: 978-1-941237-17-5
$8.95

Available wherever books are sold or at:
anamcara-press.com

Thank you for being a reader! Anamcara Press publishes select works and brings writers & artists together in collaborations in order to serve community and the planet.
Your comments are always welcome!

Anamcara Press
anamcara-press.com